I0799801

POSTCARD HISTORY SERIES

St. Joseph

Missouri

A POSTCARD HISTORY

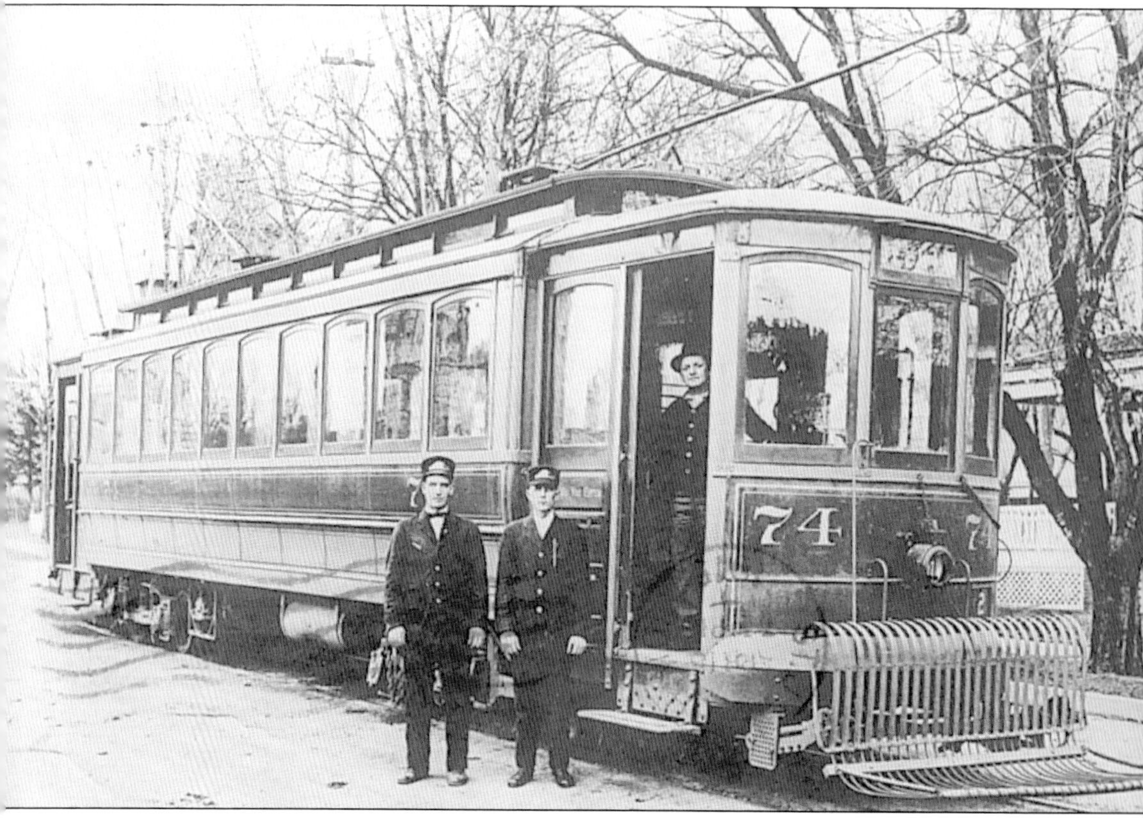

Streetcars fueled the first urban sprawl in St. Joseph, allowing residents to easily reach homes built to the north and east of the city. In 1890, the People's Street, Railway, Electric, Light & Power Co. bought and consolidated several streetcar companies. In 1891, one of the barns containing most of the city's streetcars burned. In 1893, the company was bought at auction and renamed the St. Joseph Traction & Lighting Company. By 1900, St. Joseph had 40 miles of double street-car tracks. The St. Joseph Traction & Lighting Company spent $500,000 between 1902 and 1904 to make sure the lines were well-maintained and the power plant was up to date.

Automobiles, buses, and coaches replaced the streetcars by 1932. Just six years later, the last streetcar made its final trip through the city.

POSTCARD HISTORY SERIES

St. Joseph

Missouri

A POSTCARD HISTORY

Robyn L. Davis and J. Marshall White

ARCADIA
PUBLISHING

ISBN 978-0-7385-0266-3

Published by Arcadia Publishing
Charleston, South Carolina

Printed in the United States of America

Library of Congress Catalog Card Number: 9966135

For all general information contact Arcadia Publishing at:
Telephone 843-853-2070
Fax 843-853-0044
E-mail sales@arcadiapublishing.com
For customer service and orders:
Toll-Free 1-888-313-2665

Visit us on the Internet at www.arcadiapublishing.com

*This book is dedicated to the men and women
who have worked diligently to preserve the history of St. Joseph.
May public support for their work continue to swell,
and may the generations after ours know the legacy left by these leaders.*

Contents

ACKNOWLEDGMENTS

The authors would like to thank Clyde Weeks, Cole Woodbury, Melanie White, and Greg Sekula for their generous help and support in the making of this book. In addition, the authors are grateful to Tessa Hellbusch at Arcadia Publishing for coaching them through the process.

INTRODUCTION

St. Joseph, Missouri, was well-known as one of the major portals to the West throughout the Eastern United States. By the end of the Victorian era, this was a prosperous city and a destination in its own right. Merchant princes developed catalog and warehouse businesses, light manufacturing, and the meat-packing industry. The legacy left by these entrepreneurs and those they employed can be found in the photographic postcards they produced. Today, these images are a durable photographic record of life in the city during the early 1900s. Through these images, we see that St. Joseph residents were proud of their city at the turn of the 20th century. They nicknamed it "The City Worthwhile," which was proclaimed on an electric sign one story high, on top of the tallest building downtown.

The sign is gone, but the records of the city's golden years remain, thanks to the many photographers here who captured the images on the postcards. Postcard collecting has enjoyed a recent revival, but it was even more popular for the first two decades of the 20th century.

This book concentrates on the first century of St. Joseph's history, from about 1820, when Joseph Robidoux began to settle this area, to the 1920s. The majority of the postcards are from the city's heyday, around 1900.

Today, this city in northwest Missouri is known still as a stopping point for weary travelers, some headed west and some simply visiting for the sake of seeing our city. Tourists visit the home where Jesse James was shot and killed, the stables where the Pony Express was launched, the home where Joseph Robidoux lived, and many other attractions. This book will be something for those visitors to take with them to remember us by, and will provide an opportunity for St. Joseph residents to glance into their past.

One

THE EARLY YEARS

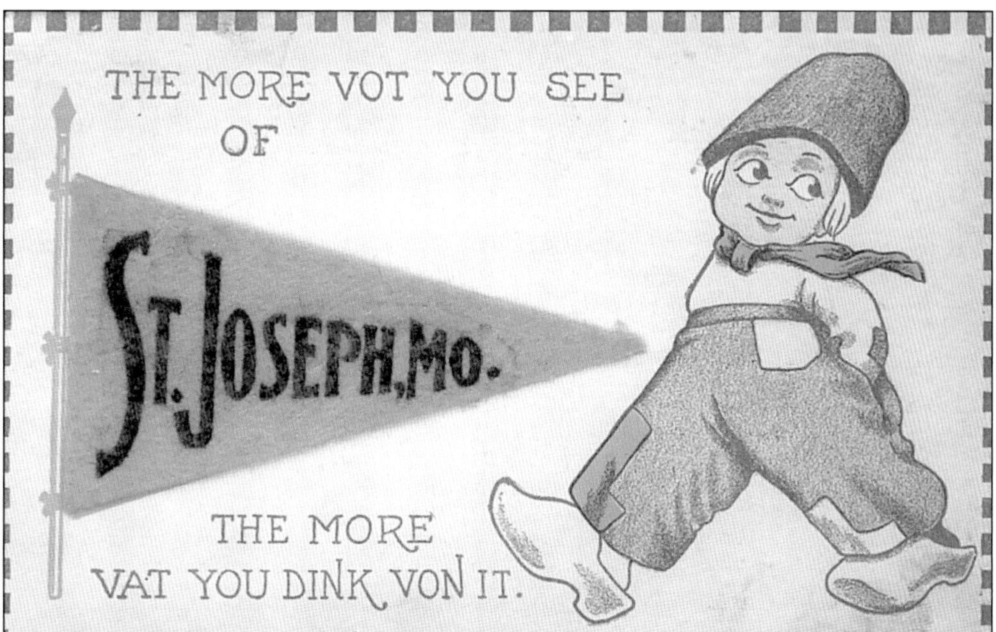

This card belonged to a series of humorous postcards incorporating a felt flag reading, "St. Joseph, Mo." The authors hope that you'll find this saying to be true: "The more that you see of St. Joseph, Mo., the more that you think on it."

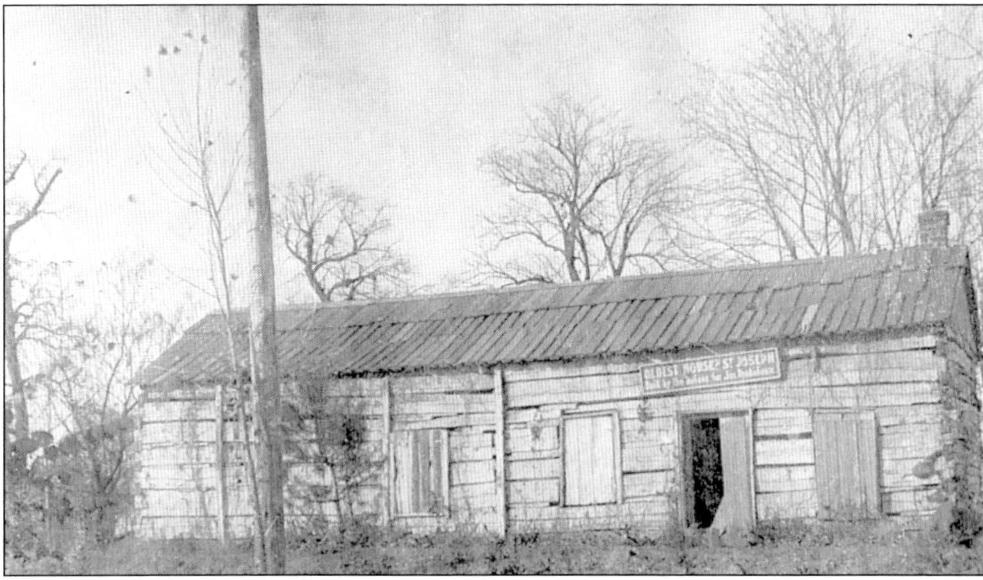

This modern card shows a photograph taken *c.* 1920 of the trading post built by Native Americans for Joseph Robidoux, the founder of St. Joseph. Robidoux was primarily a fur trader and entrepreneur who encouraged many other businessmen to move to Northwest Missouri. The city was named for his patron saint.

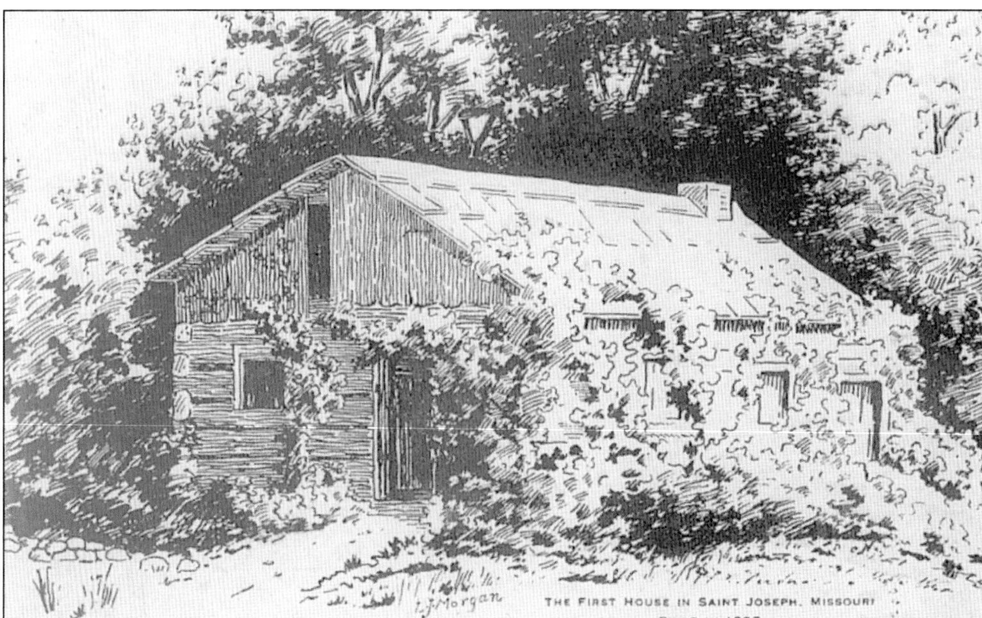

This is an artist's rendering of Joseph Robidoux's cabin on Blacksnake Creek, *c.* 1827. Though the postcard was made later, it shows what was probably the first structure in what is now called St. Joseph.

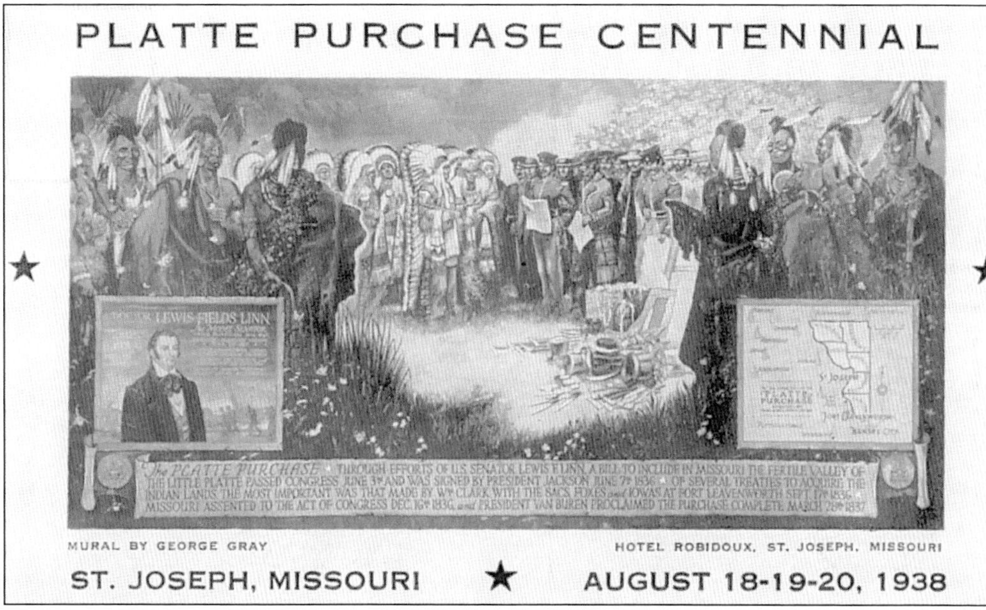

The Platte Purchase Centennial was held in 1938 to celebrate the 1837 addition of what would eventually become Buchanan, Andrew, Atchison, Holt, Nodaway, and Platte Counties. The painting depicting the treaty signing at Fort Leavenworth, Kansas, was painted by George Gray. It once hung in the (now demolished) Hotel Robidoux in St. Joseph.

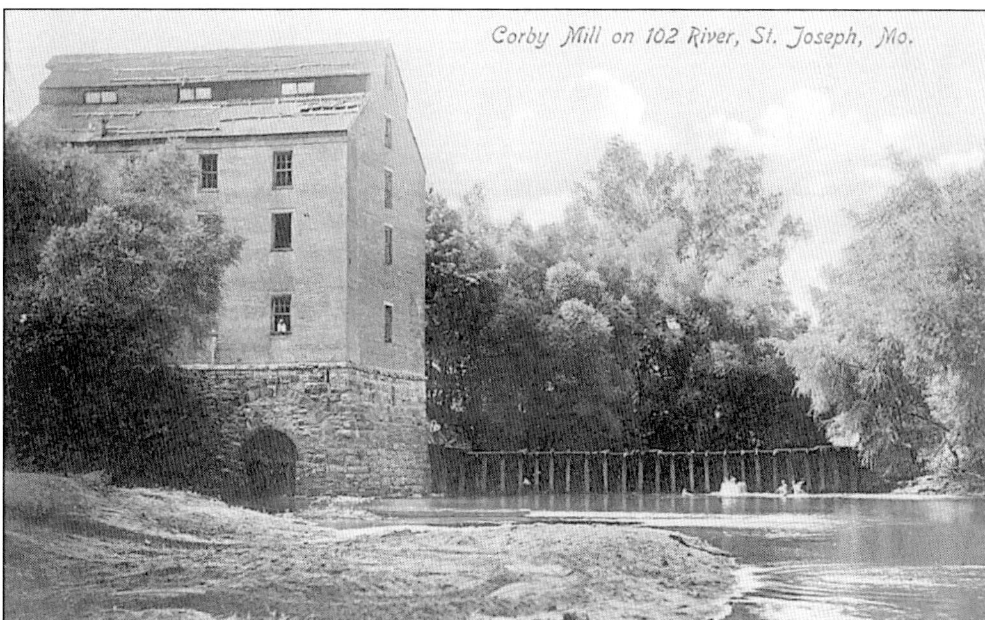

The Corby Mill on the 102 River was one of the first mills built in the area. The mill stood just east of the present-day Riverside Drive and Frederick Boulevard.

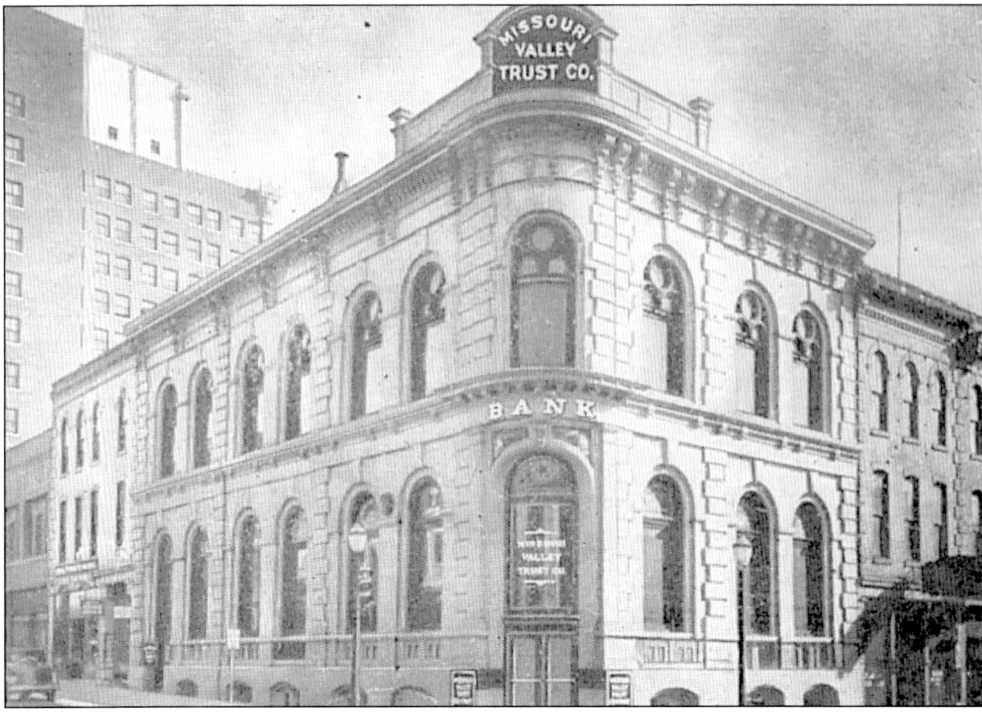

The Missouri Valley Trust Co. is still one of downtown's most notable buildings. It houses a museum on the first floor, showing the old bank. It was used as offices for the St. Joseph Area Chamber of Commerce within the past decade. The Missouri Valley Trust Co. was the oldest continually operated bank in Missouri. For a brief time in its history, the Missouri Supreme Court met in the building.

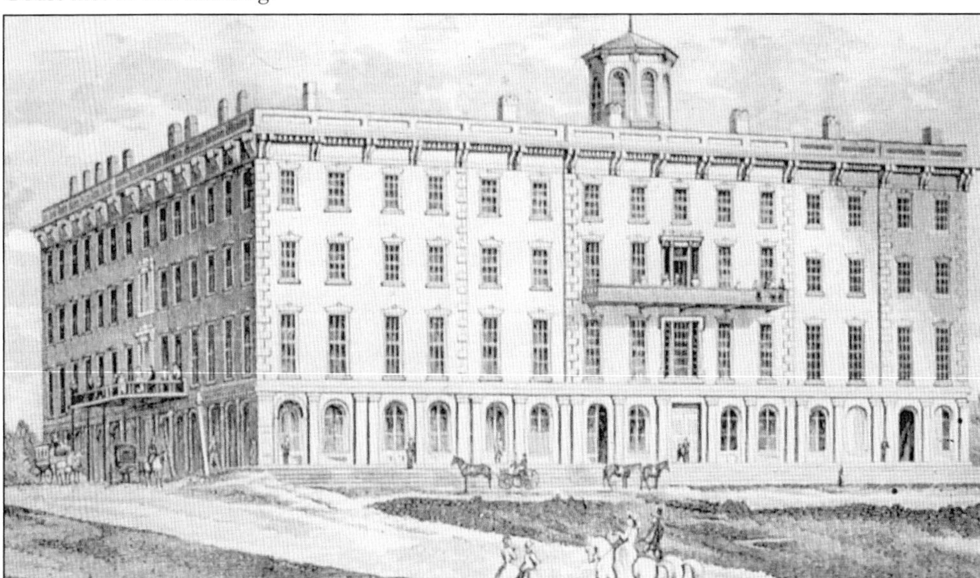

Known as the finest hotel west of the Mississippi when it was opened in 1858, the Patee House had several notable businesses with offices inside, including the Pony Express and the Hannibal and St. Joseph Railroad. The hotel is now a museum dedicated to St. Joseph history.

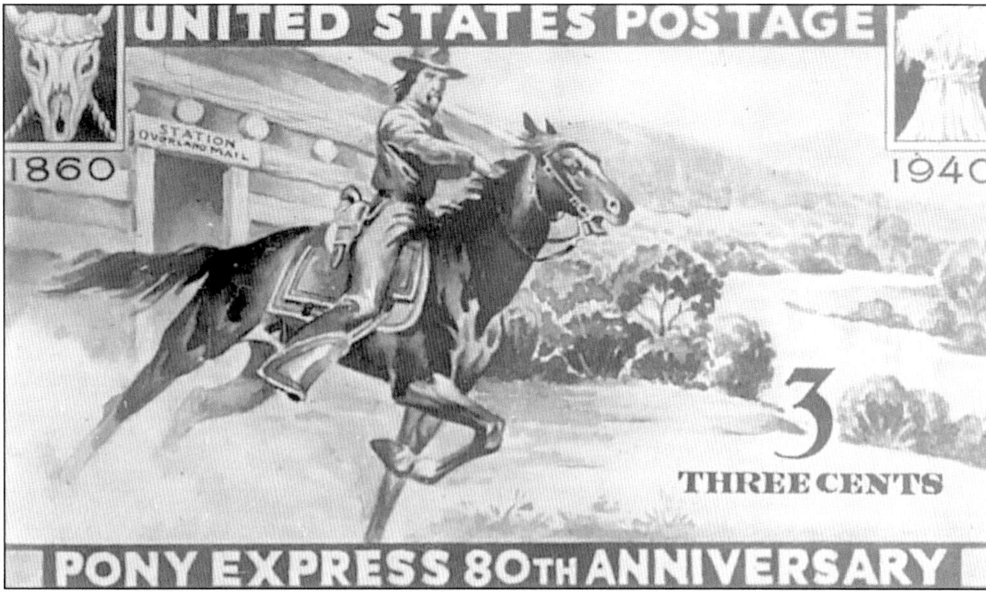

To commemorate the 80th anniversary of the Pony Express, the U.S. Postal Service issued a 3¢ stamp in 1940. The Pony Express followed a trail from St. Joseph to Sacramento, though only operating for 18 months. The invention of the telegraph made the service virtually obsolete. Now, a re-enactment of the Pony Express run is held annually.

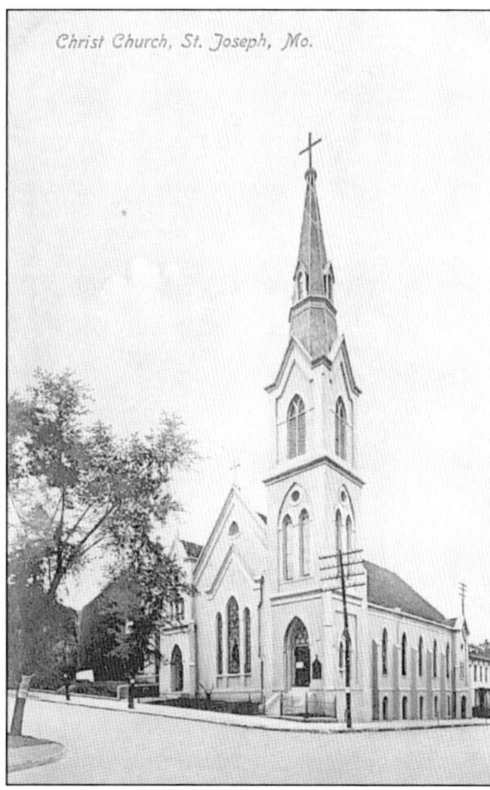

Christ Episcopal Church is the second-oldest church in St. Joseph. It was built *c.* 1877 and is the oldest building continuously used as a Protestant house of worship by one denomination.

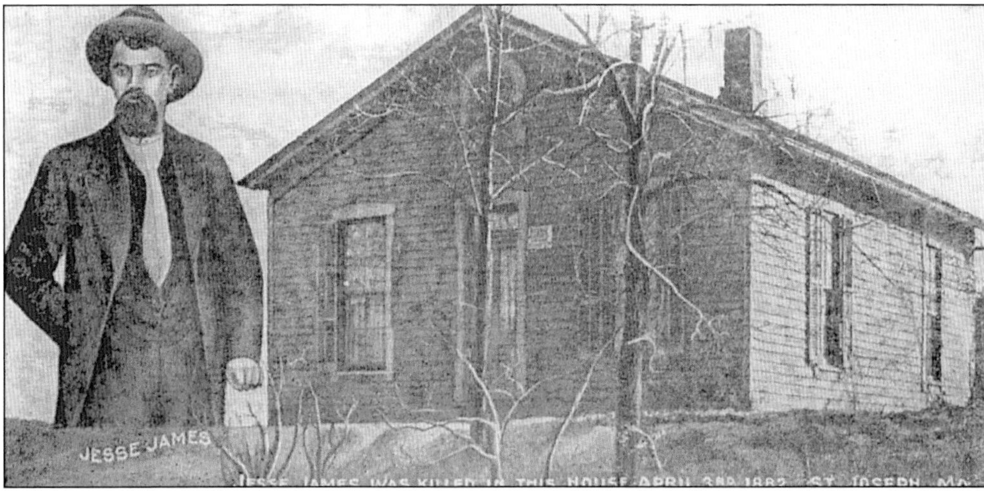

The house where Jesse James was shot and killed has been open for tours almost since the day he died. This 19th-century photograph shows a sign indicating a 10¢ admission charge for tours. The house is a vernacular structure that was built between 1855 and 1875 and has been moved twice. Today, it is located behind the Patee House museum and is still open for tours.

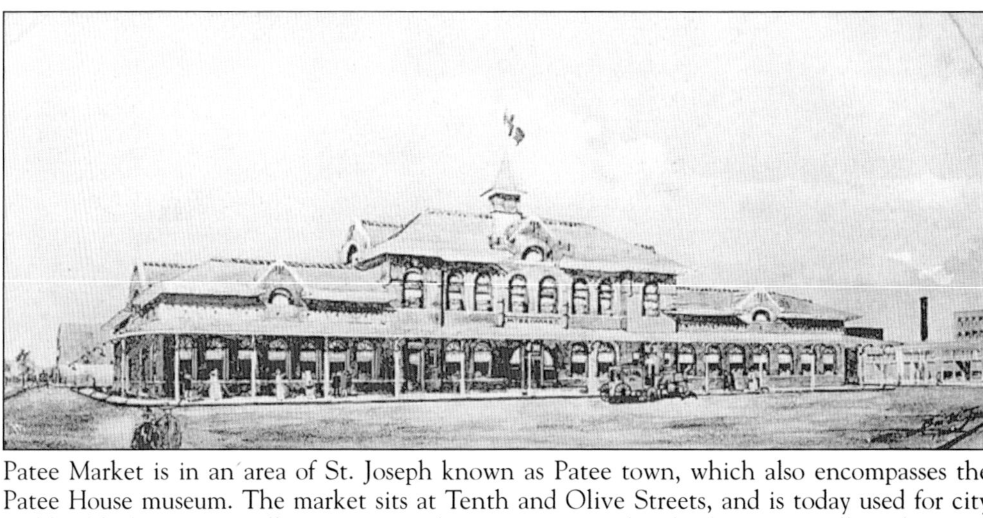

Patee Market is in an area of St. Joseph known as Patee town, which also encompasses the Patee House museum. The market sits at Tenth and Olive Streets, and is today used for city and health department offices. Its original use was as a market for farmers to sell produce and livestock. There are many differences between the building as it appears today and as it was depicted in this *c.* 1907 postcard.

The Humane Society erected this horse trough in front of Patee Market in 1905, according to the caption on the back of this card.

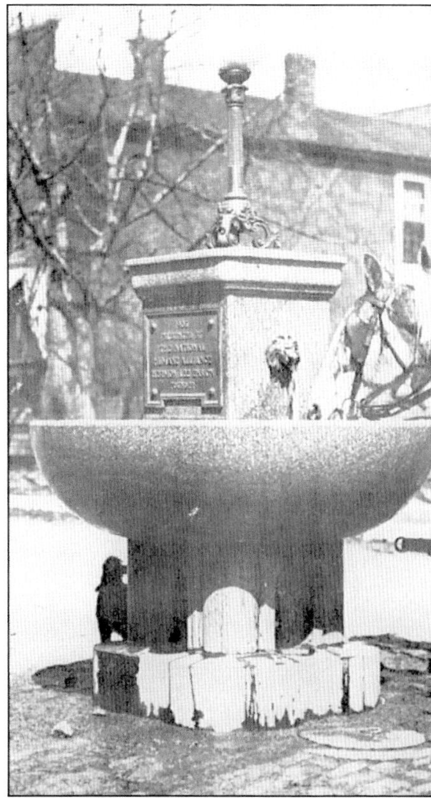

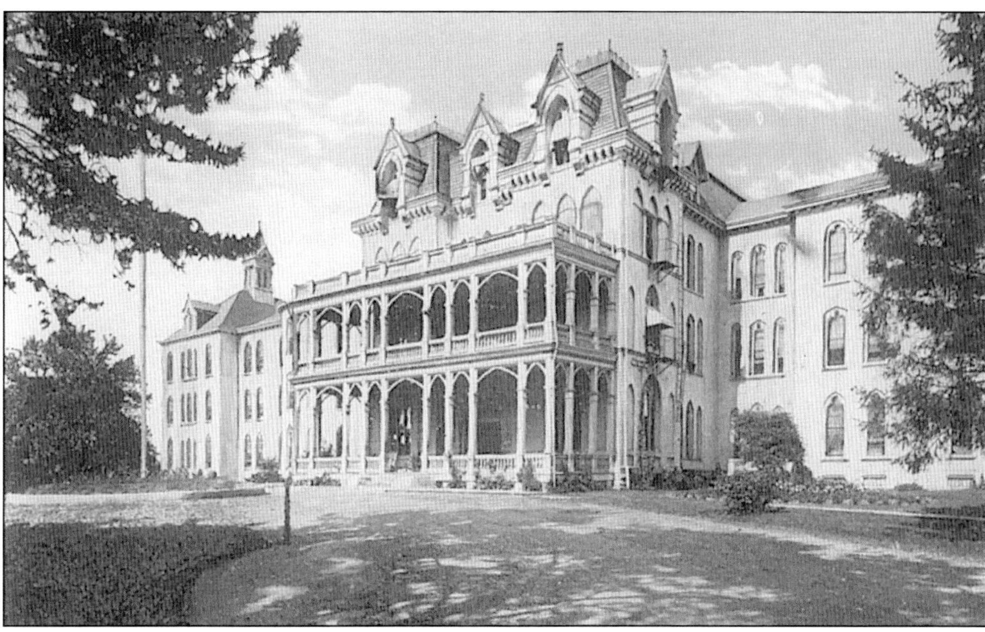

Extensive alterations to this Victorian beauty have made the administration building for the Missouri Insane Asylum No. 2 virtually unrecognizable. The building's interior has been altered to house prisoners and support services for a new state prison. The hospital's main building is still visible from Frederick Avenue, where it has been located for nearly 130 years.

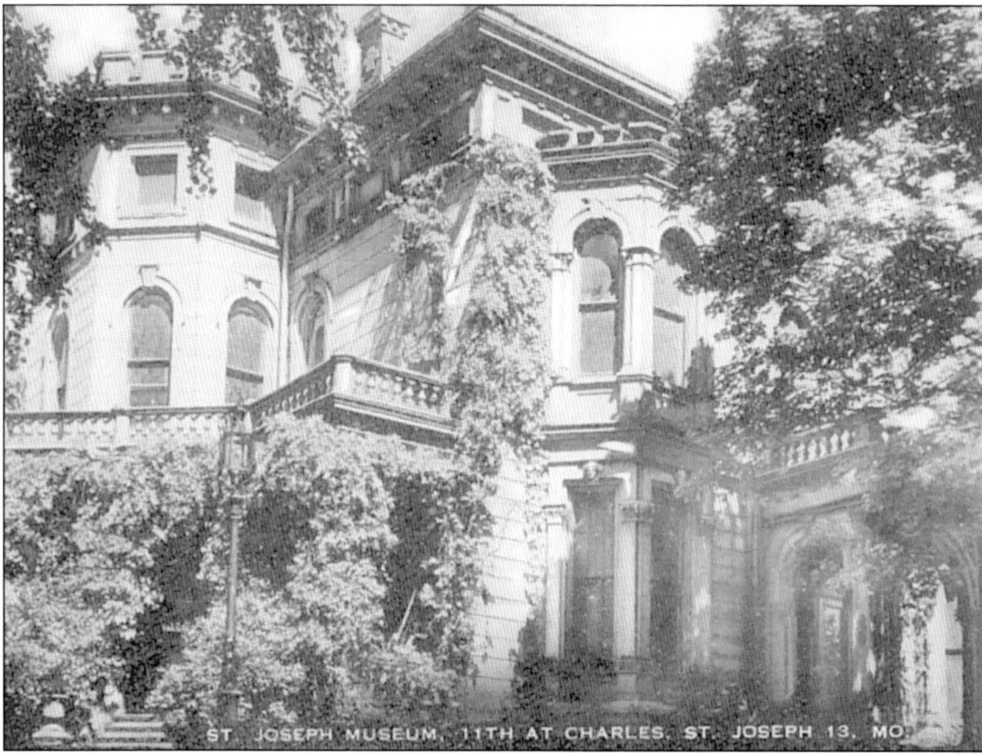

The St. Joseph Museum has occupied the Tootle-Wyeth mansion at Eleventh and Charles Streets for nearly 50 years. The museum, housed inside the Italianate-style home, has an impressive collection of Native-American artifacts and other items pertaining to the early settling of the area. The closer of the two views is actually a reversed photo that shows the south side of the home on the north side. The other postcard, which shows the house from farther away, is a turn-of-the-20th-century advertisement for electric lights, but it gives a nice view of the mansion.

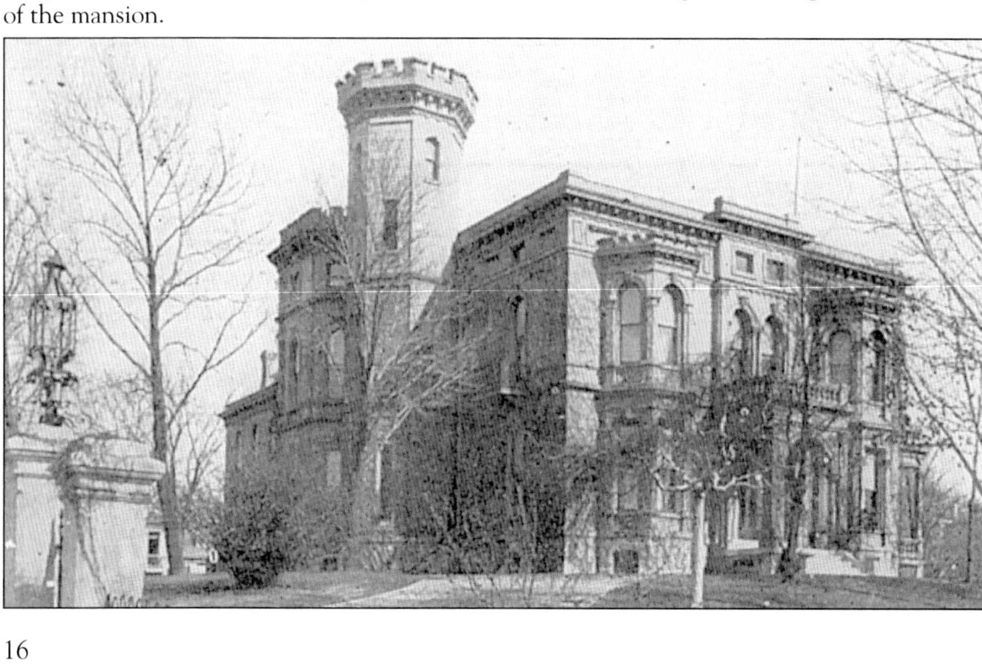

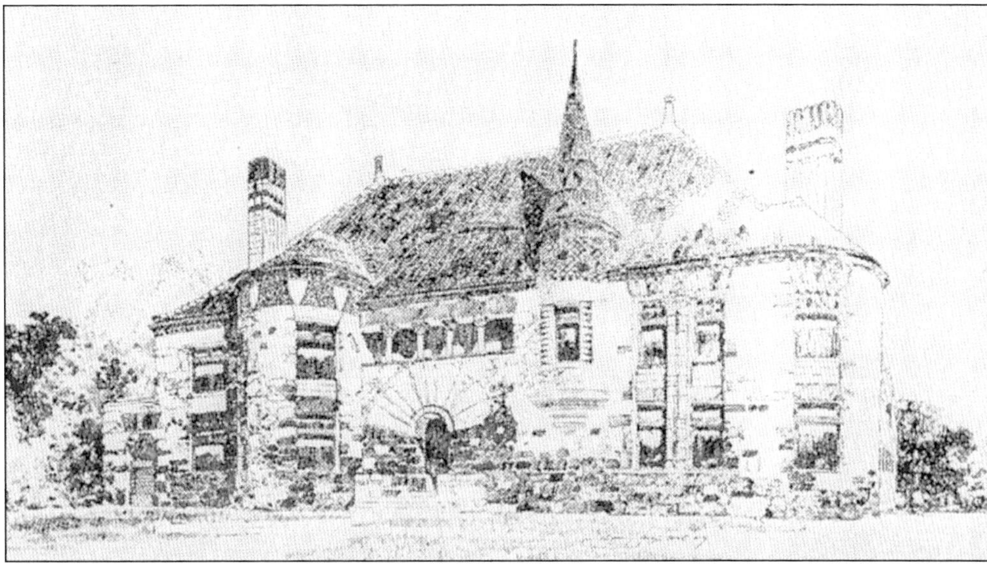

To many local residents, this is known as the wedding cake house. To lovers of architecture, it is one of the city's crown jewels. The Romanesque Revival mansion is located at the intersection of Nineteenth and Felix Streets. The house was owned at one time by the A.J. August family, who operated a clothing store in downtown St. Joseph. It became the home of the St. Joseph Museum when family members donated the property. It was designed by the architectural firm belonging to Edmond Eckel, a French-trained architect who worked in St. Joseph for 60 years. Noted draftsman Harvey Ellis likely assisted Eckel in the design. The home became a private residence again when the St. Joseph Museum moved to a new location.

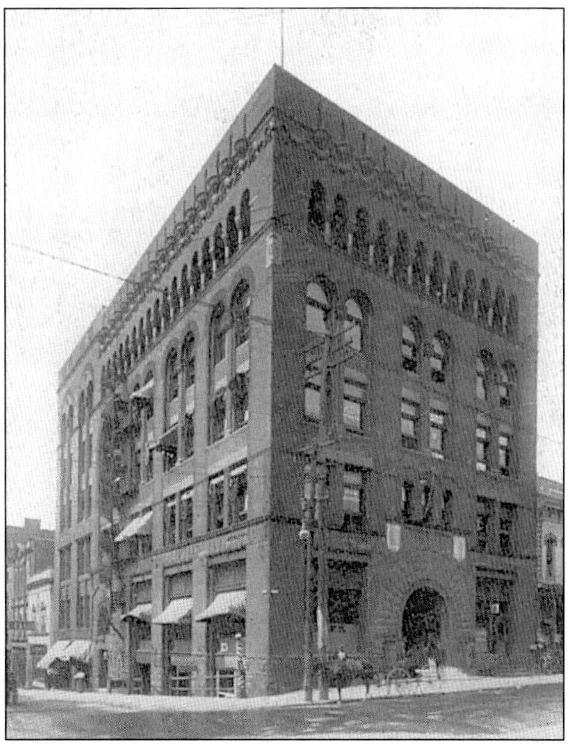

The German-American Bank Building was also designed by Edmond Eckel, who seemed partial to the Romanesque Revival style. It is still standing today, at the corner of Seventh and Felix Streets. The Pony Express Community Bank and the successor to Eckel's firm, Brunner and Brunner Architects and Engineers (the oldest continually operated architectural firm in St. Joseph), are also housed at this location. Harvey Ellis is believed to have been involved in the design of this building as well.

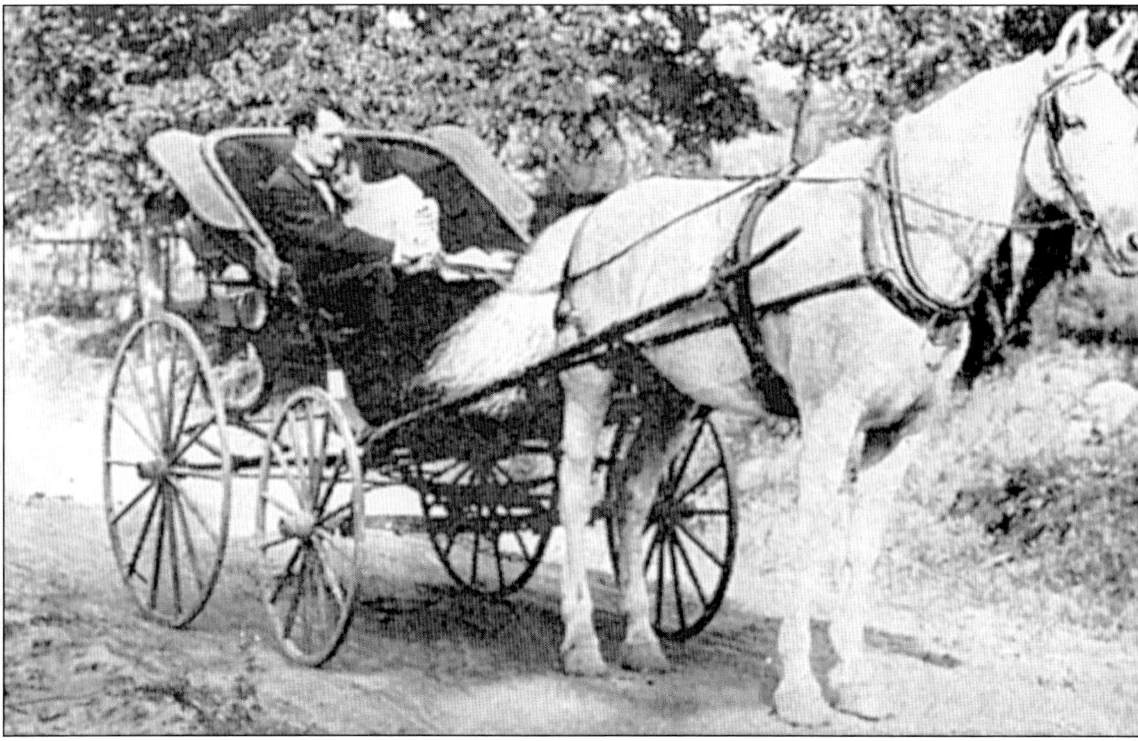

Eugene Field, the poet and newspaperman, was married to Julia Comstock at her father's home at 602 North Fifth Street. Field later wrote a poem citing the virtues of Lover's Lane, then known as Rochester Road. The city changed the name of the road in his honor. The bottom of the card tells of the former St. Joseph residents who were sitting on the committee to create a national memorial to Eugene Field. Today, there is a Gene Field Road and a Eugene Field Elementary School but no noteworthy memorial.

Two

VIEWS OF ST. JOSEPH

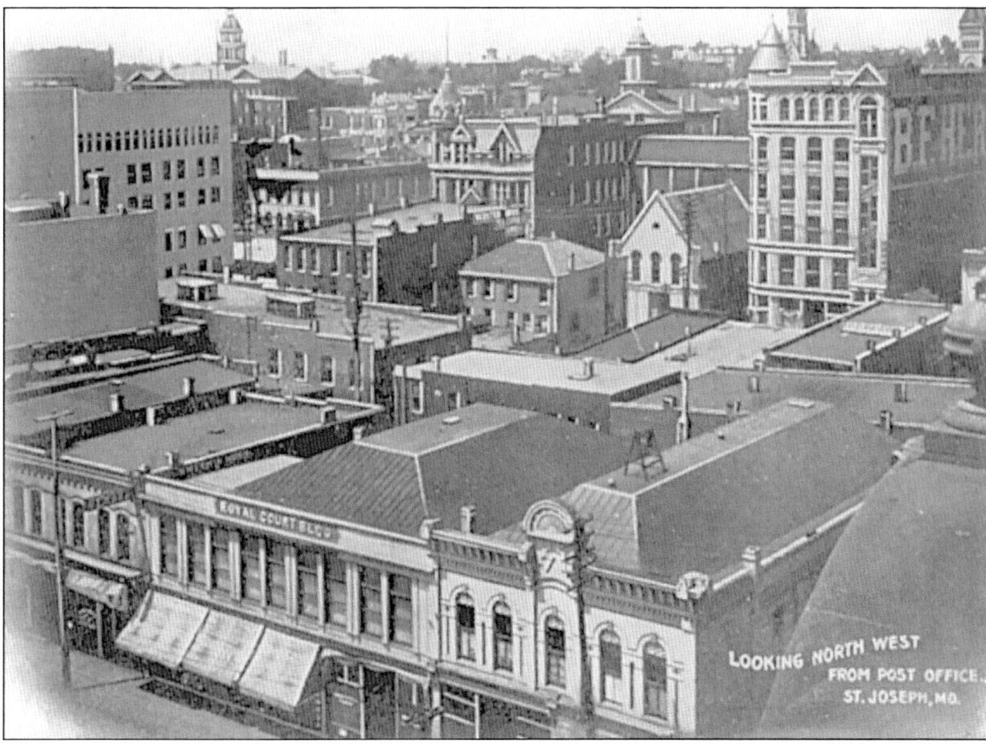

This view of the downtown business district, looking northwest from the post office at Eighth and Edmond Streets, shows a variety of buildings, some of which are still standing and others of which have been torn down. From the top left are the spires of the courthouse at Fifth and Jules Streets, the old First Baptist Church, Sixth and Francis Streets, the old Francis Street Methodist Church near Seventh and Francis Streets, Christ Episcopal Church at Seventh and Francis Streets, and the old First Presbyterian Church at Seventh and Jules Streets.

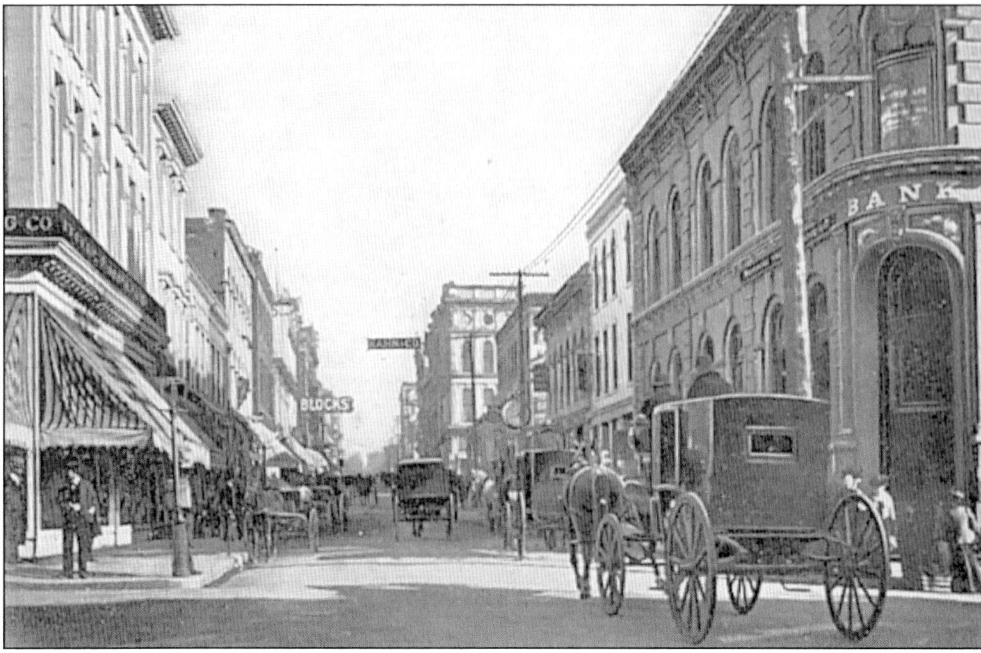

Felix Street in downtown St. Joseph was one of the busiest commercial streets at the turn of the 20th century, as evidenced by this rendering from *c.* 1906. The drawing depicts the intersection of Felix and Fourth Streets, looking east. The Missouri Valley Trust Building, shown here on the right, still stands today.

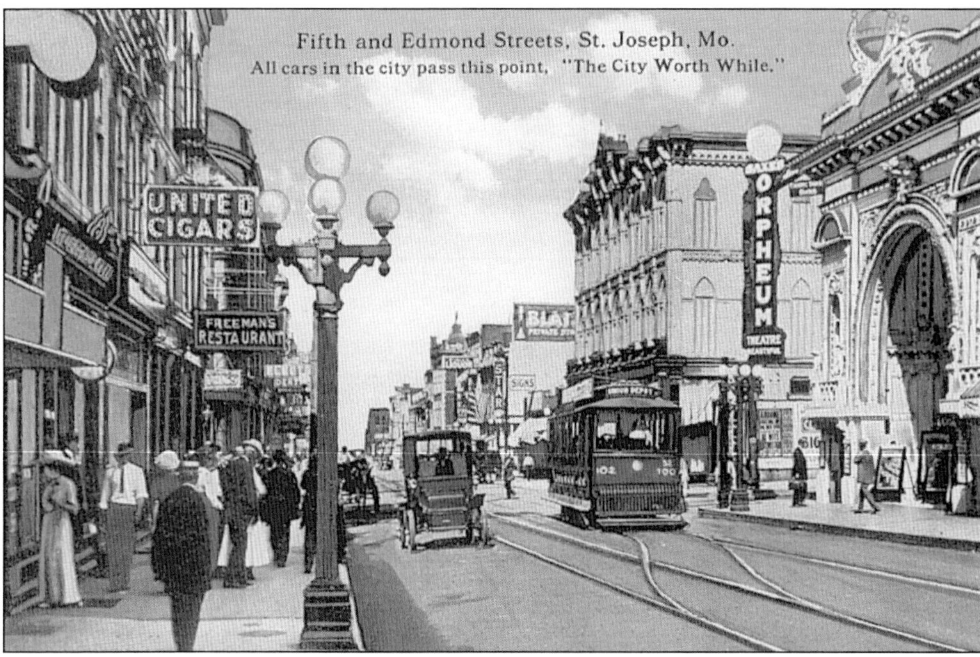

Just two blocks away, Edmond Street was bustling as well, with a streetcar taking visitors to the Orpheum Theater or shopping among the stores shown on the left side of the card. This card, obviously a later view than the one above since it features automobiles, mentions the city's slogan, "The City Worth While."

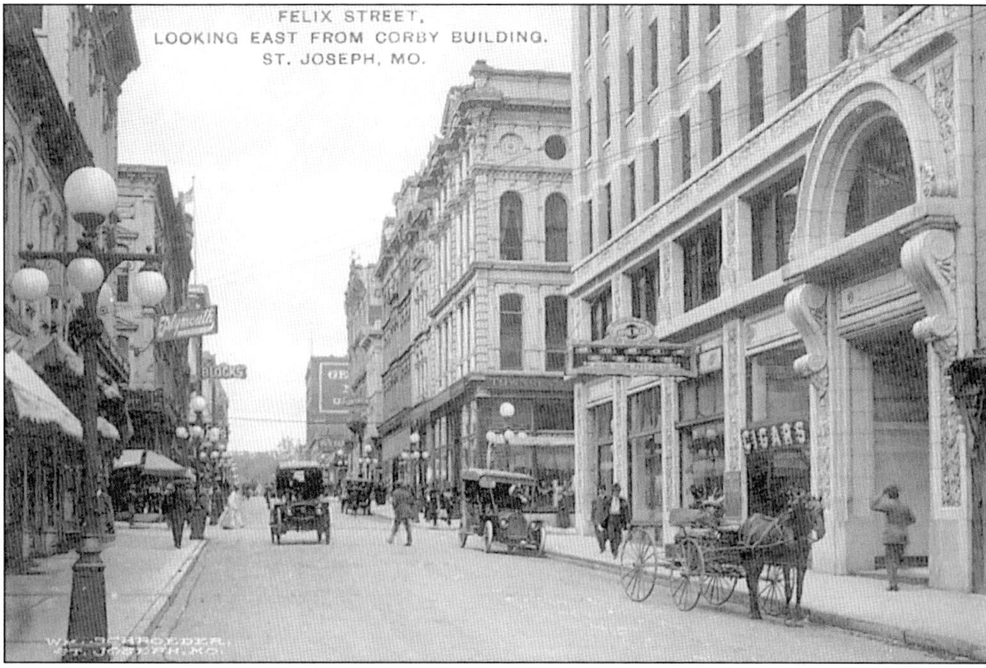

This postcard, with an interesting mix of both cars and horses on the street, shows Felix Street looking east from the Corby Building (right). The Townsend Dry Goods store is the next store on the right. The building still stands.

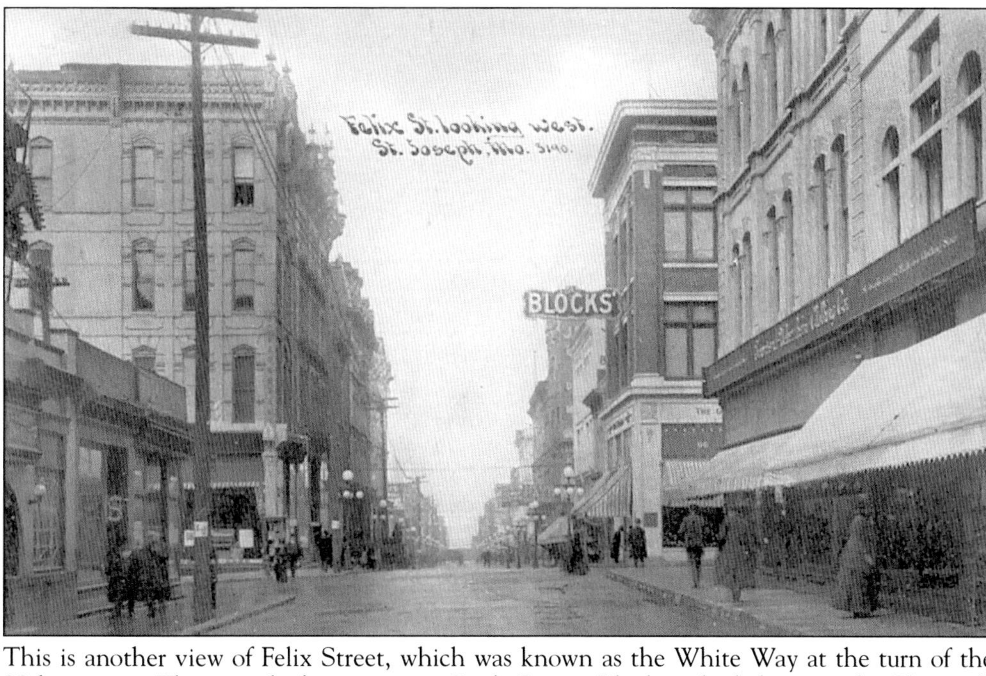

This is another view of Felix Street, which was known as the White Way at the turn of the 20th century. The view looks west, past Sixth Street. Blocks, which became the Plymouth Department Store, is the only building of the four in the foreground still standing. The buildings in the left foreground were torn down to make room for the Townsend-Ueberrhein Clothing Company. It became the United Department Store, which today is the United Antique Mall.

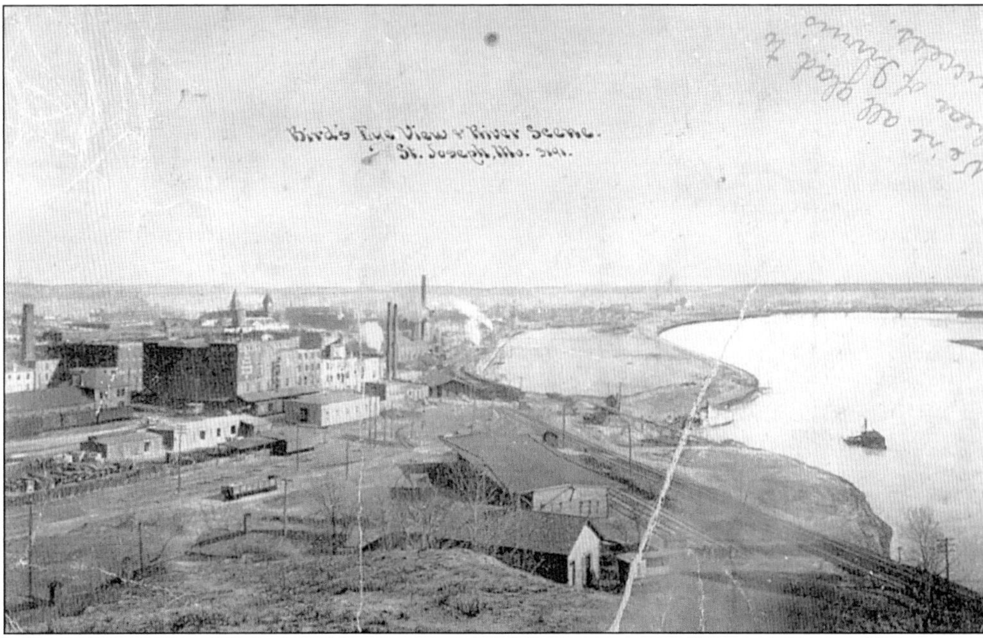

This bird's-eye view of the edges of St. Joseph and the Missouri River looks south from Prospect Hill. The photo could have been taken earlier than its 1909 date.

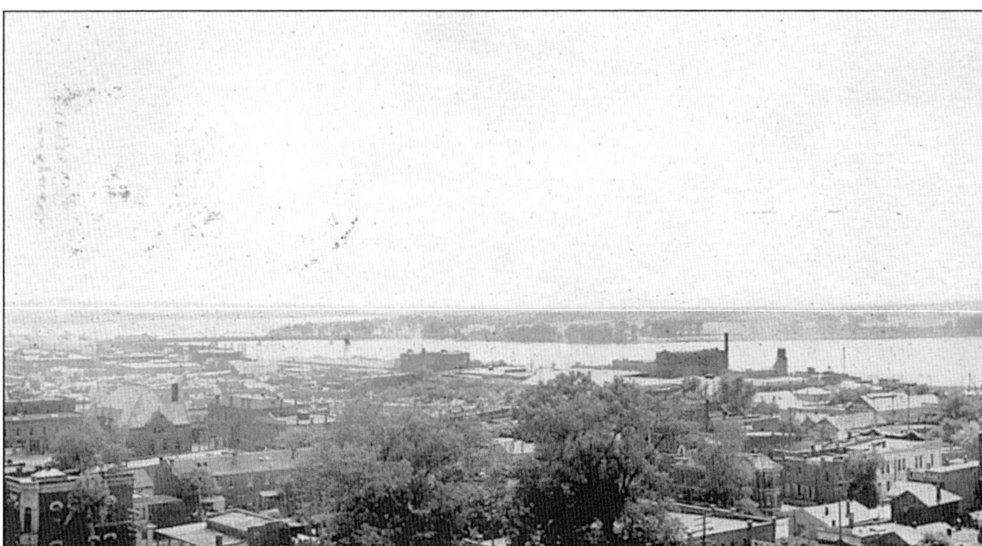

This view looks southwest from the old post office at Eighth Street. The Missouri River is in the background. Virtually all of downtown is visible.

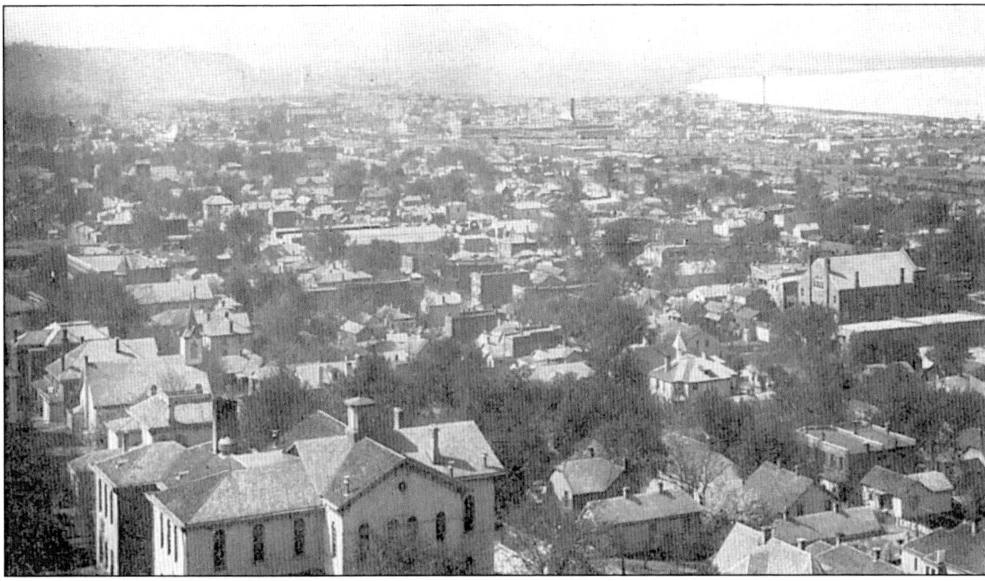

This bird's-eye view shows south St. Joseph. The stockyards are in the distance.

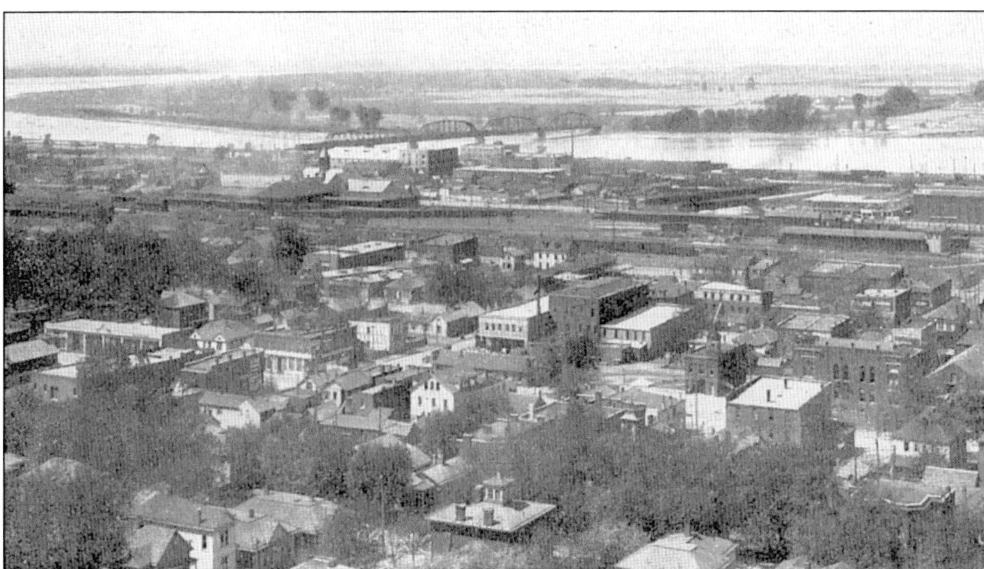

This western view of St. Joseph shows mostly commercial buildings, with the Missouri River running along the edge. At the time of this postcard, the river was more of a focal point as it was still used for commerce and was better connected to downtown than it is today.

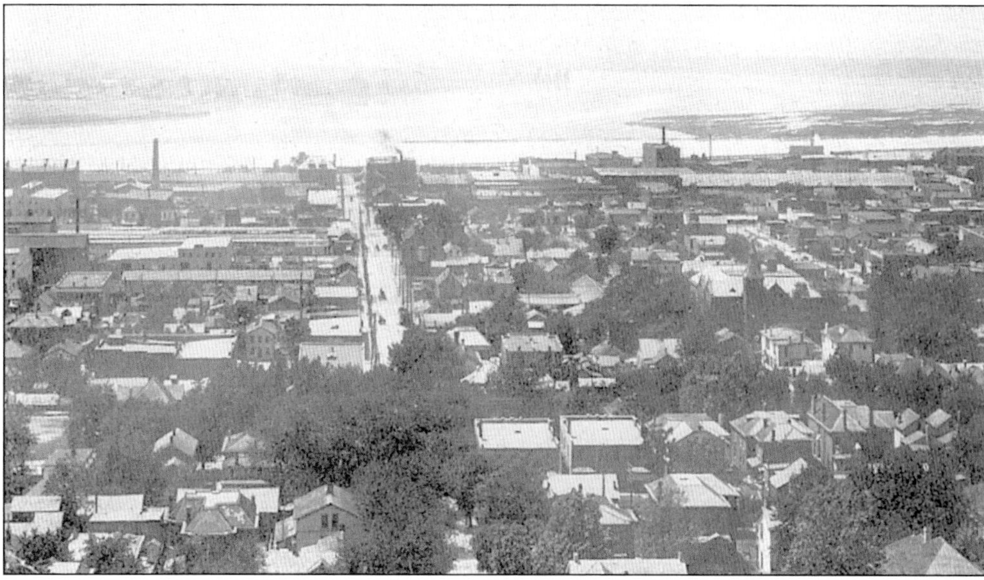

A panoramic view of St. Joseph shows the city west by north, again with the Missouri River in the background.

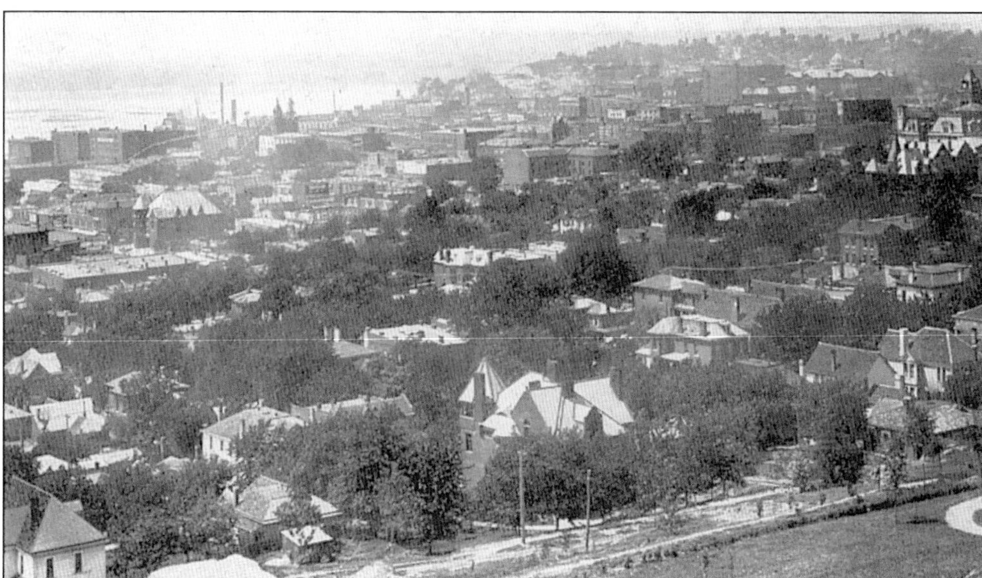

The downtown retail district of St. Joseph is visible in this bird's-eye shot, along with some of the city's more notable homes in the foreground.

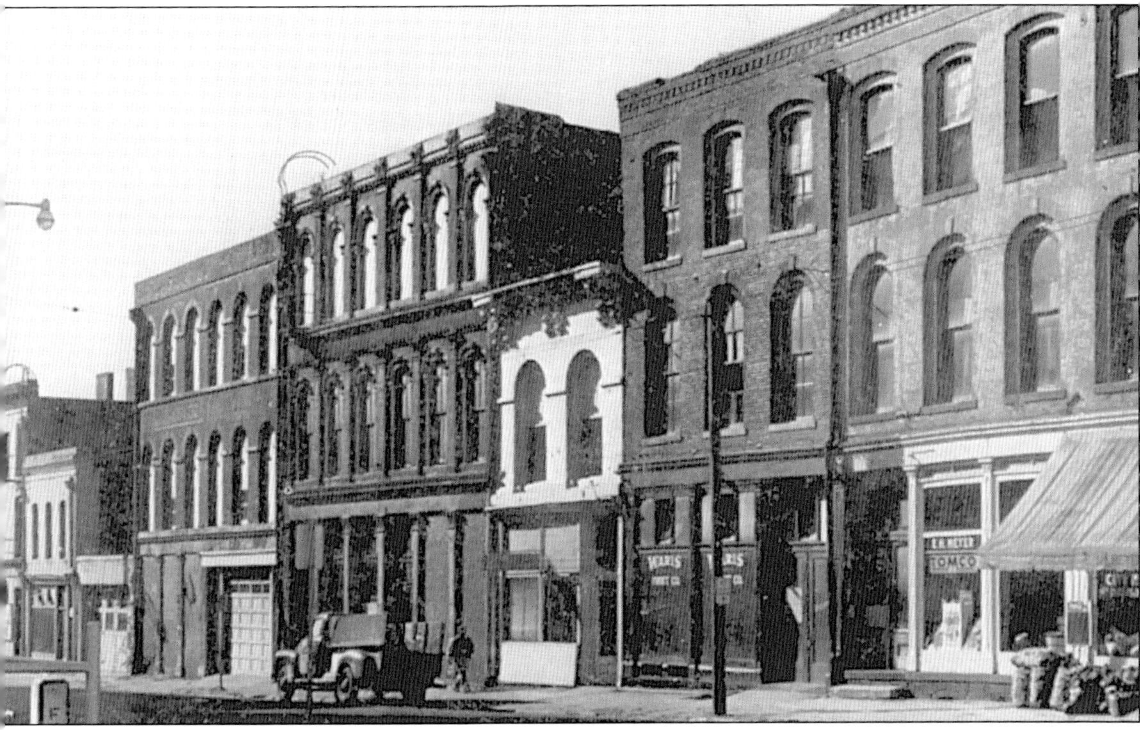

This photo shows the west side of Third Street, a portion of the wholesale district. Most of the buildings were offices and storage for wholesale grocery and fruit companies. The back side faced Market Square at the old city hall and later city market. A railroad spur ran through the area and produce could be shipped on railroad cars. These buildings were constructed from the 1870s through 1900 and lasted until urban renewal.

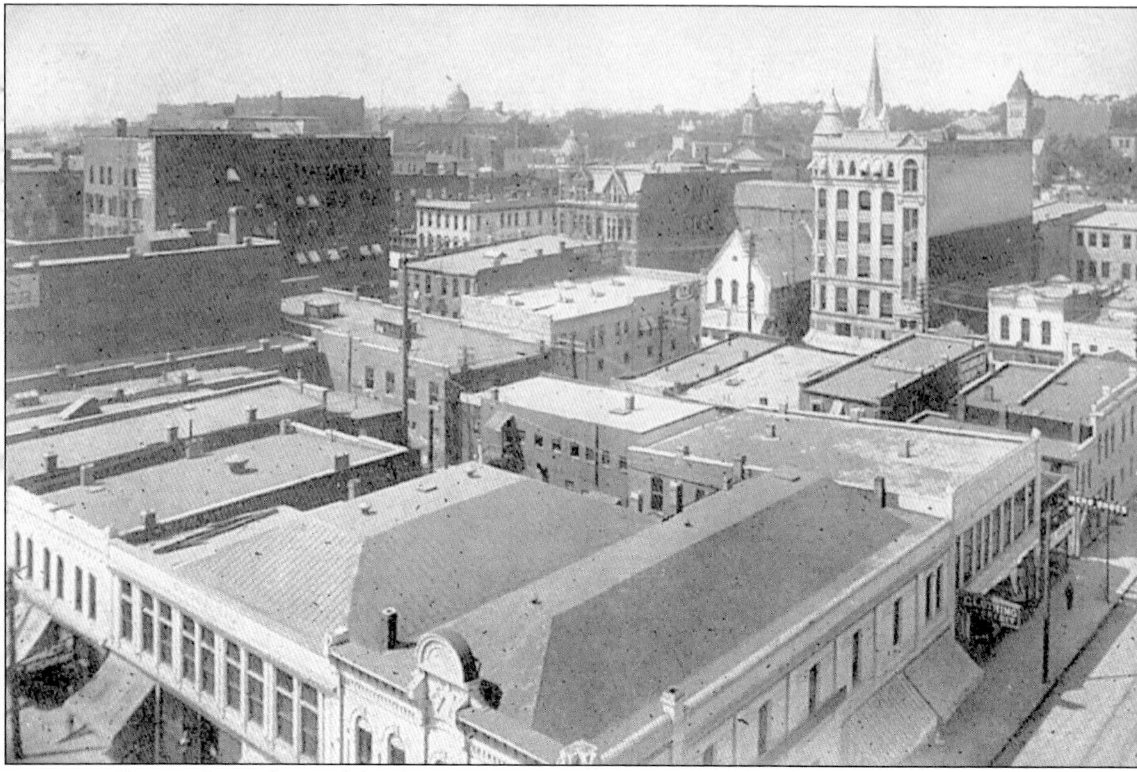

This is a later photo of the downtown retail district as seen from the tower of the old customs house and post office. The buildings in the foreground, at Eighth and Edmond Streets, were destroyed when the Missouri Theater complex was built in 1927. The only building to survive was the men's shoe store on Eighth Street, pictured on the right side of the card. Felix Street is the next street north. The buildings on the south side of Felix still stand. All of the buildings on the north side of Felix have been removed, and the area between Seventh and Eighth Streets is now Felix Street Square.

Three

PUBLIC BUILDINGS

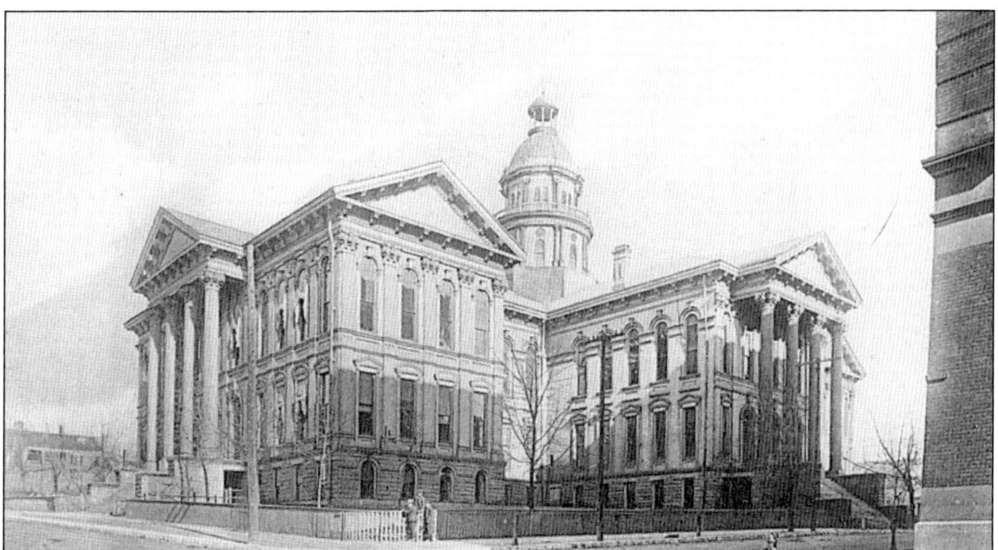

This is an 1880 photograph of the Buchanan County Courthouse from a postcard made c. 1905. The courthouse burned in 1885 and had no dome at the turn of the 20th century. Also note the chimney on the right side of the dome, the picket fence surrounding the building, and the stairs on the south side of the building.

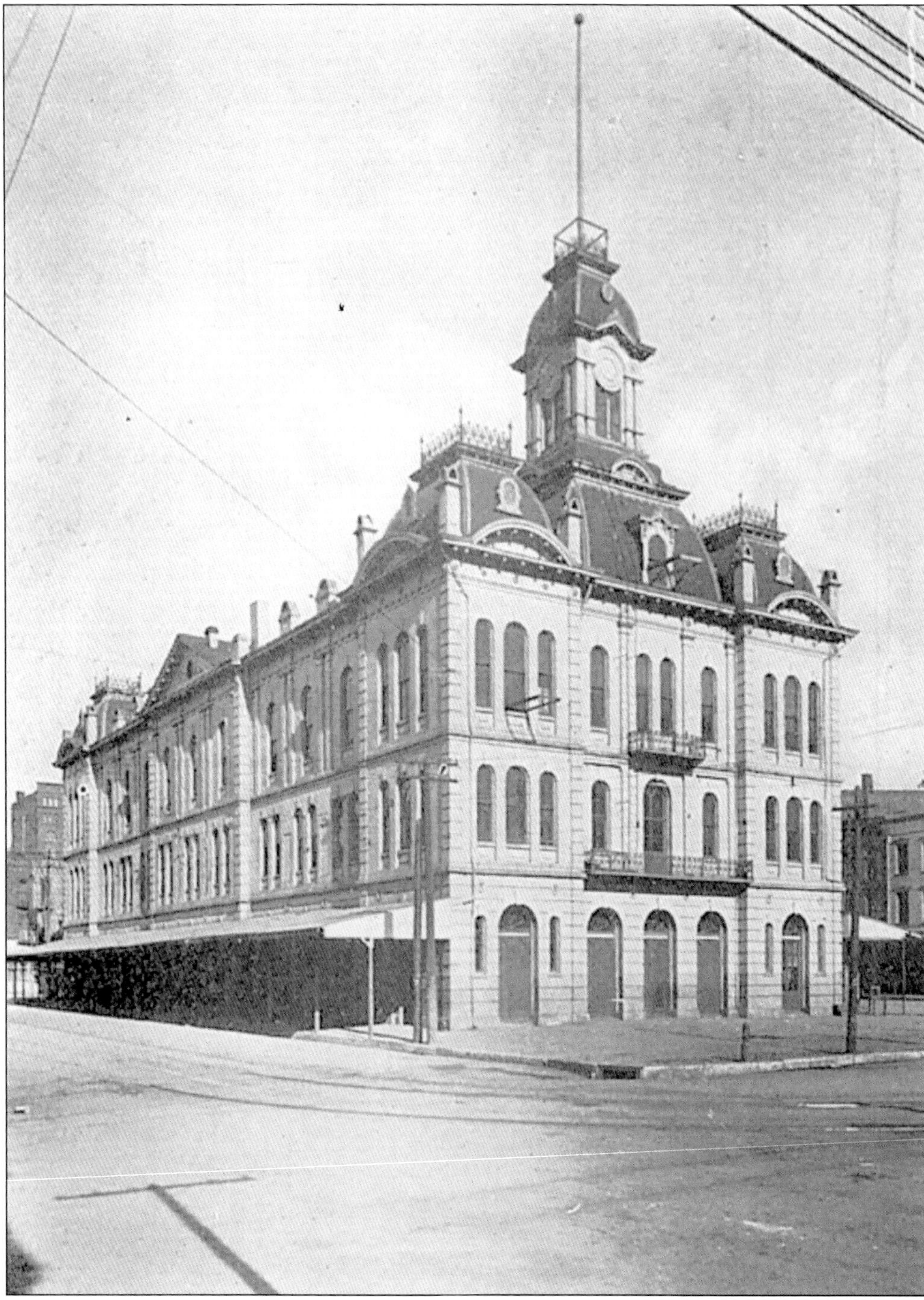

The old city hall at Market Square stood on Second Street, between Edmond and Felix Streets. The first floor was used as a city market. It was a three-story Second Empire-style building erected in 1873–74 and torn down just before World War II. At the time it was built, it was regarded as one of the most pretentious buildings in the West. The 1926 City Hall at Eleventh Street and Frederick Avenue replaced it.

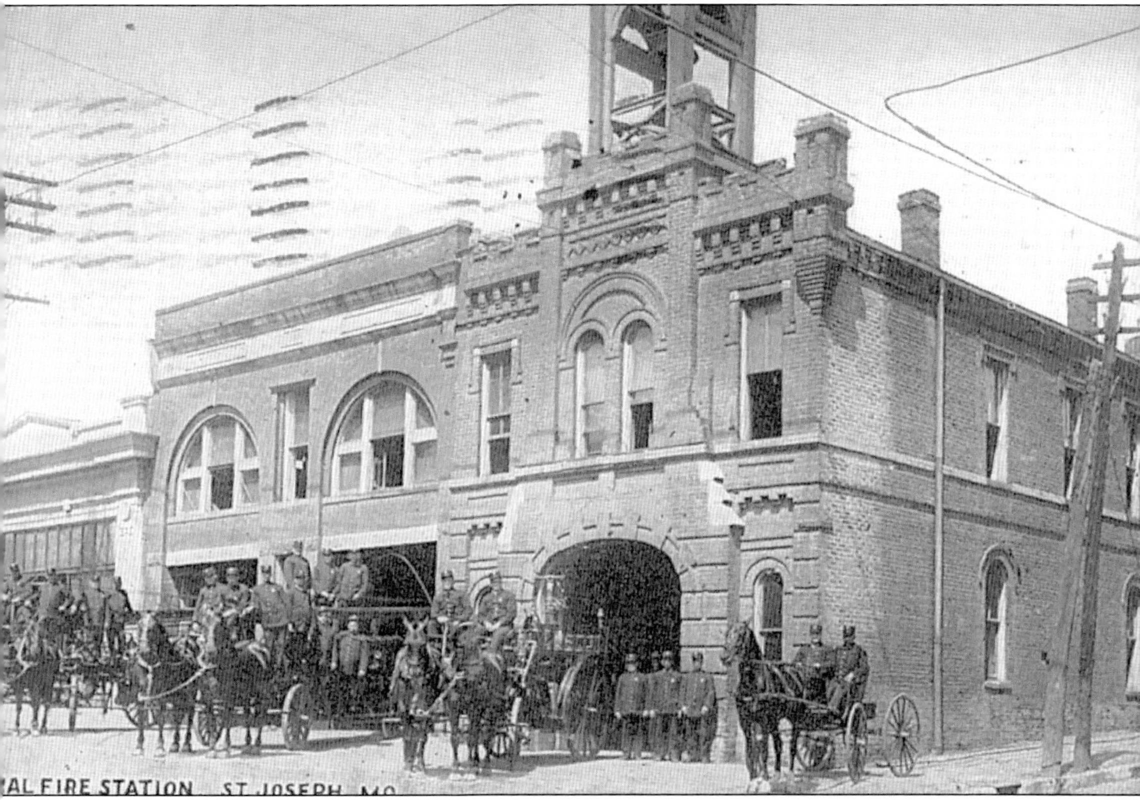

Central Fire Station was built *c.* 1890 at the corner of Charles and Seventh Streets, one block north of the current fire station. At that time, horse-drawn units were used to fight fires. The crews shown in this picture are believed to have battled the infamous center-city fire on September 26, 1893. The building no longer stands. It is the site of the state employment office.

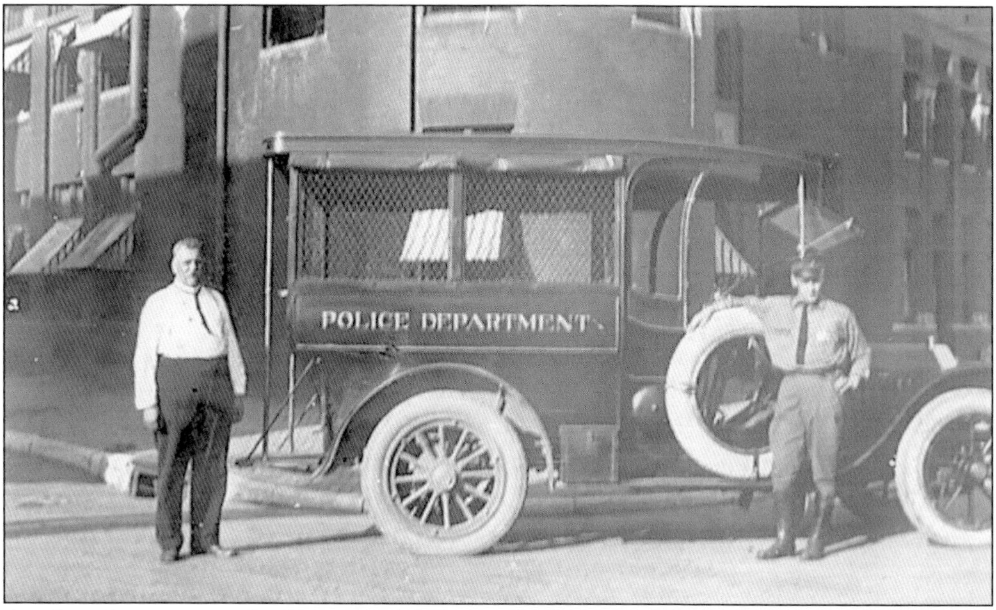

A police department vehicle is parked in front of the station at Seventh and Messanie Streets. The building was constructed in 1890 and enlarged in 1908. It is now used as the National Military Heritage Museum.

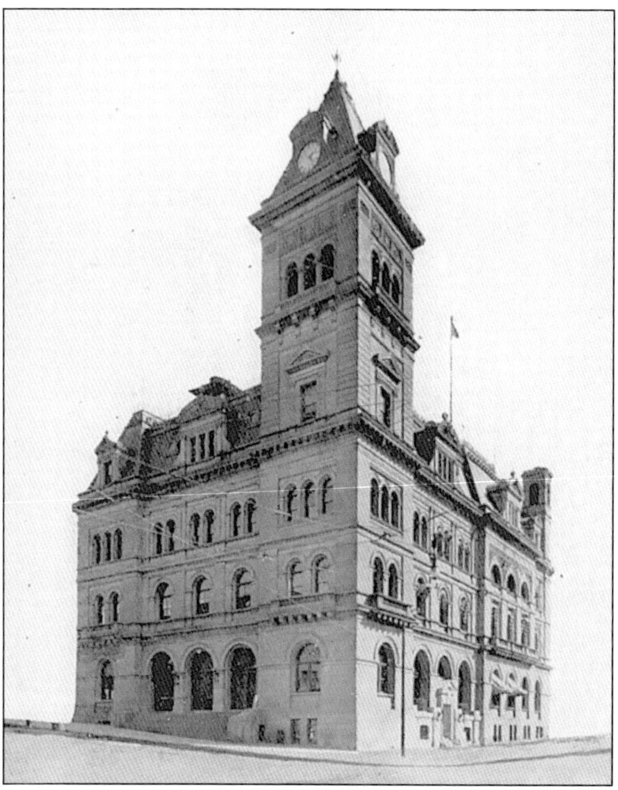

Construction on the post office and customs house began in 1883 and was completed in 1890. The construction took so long because the northwest corner at Eighth and Edmond Streets sank. Parts of the building had to be taken down and rebuilt after the foundation was strengthened. The entire structure was later torn down and replaced by a newer version in the same location. The right side of this building faces Eighth Street and the left side faces Edmond Street.

This is another view of the post office and customs house. This particular card was one of a series of 16 black-and-white postcards sold by the *St. Joseph News-Press*.

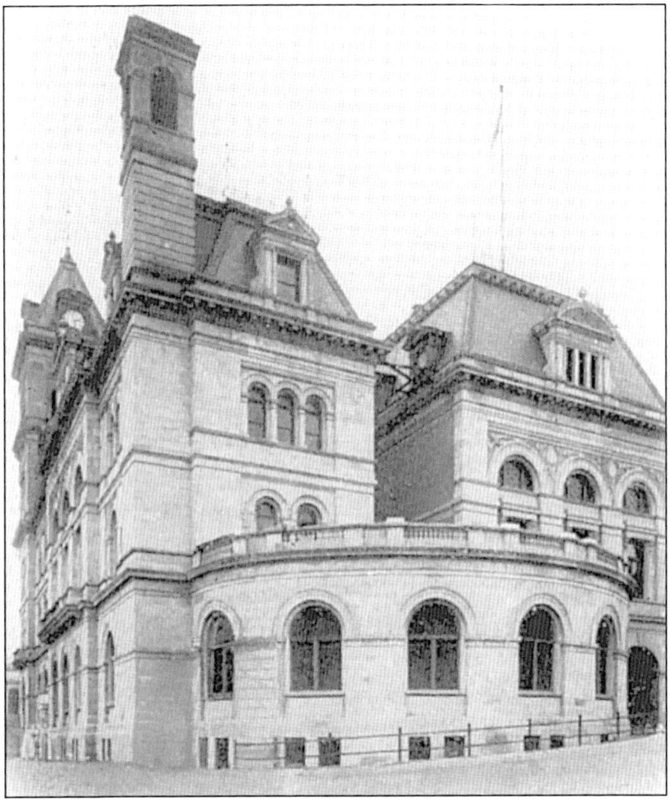

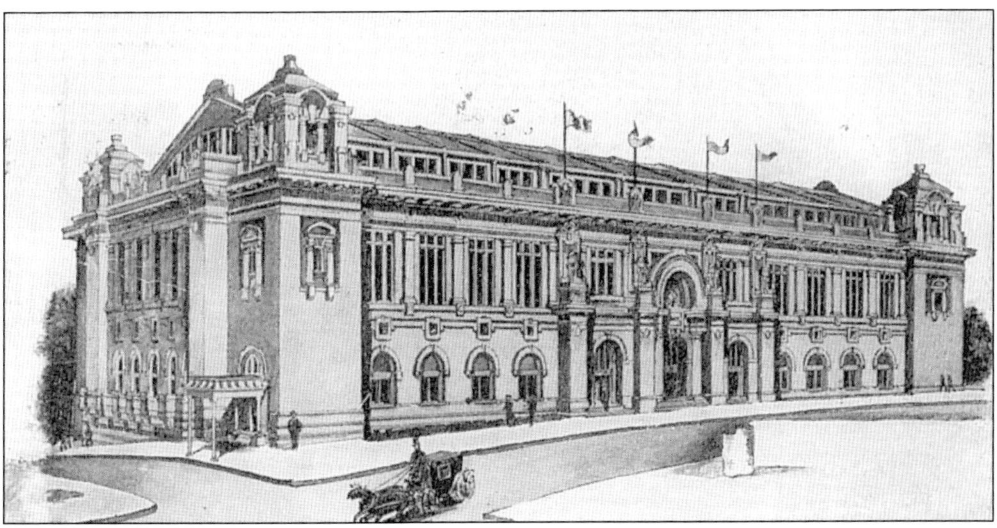

This architectural drawing of the St. Joseph Auditorium was sold by the Townsend and Wyatt Dry Goods Co. The auditorium opened in 1905 with a music festival. Arthur W. Brewster, postmaster, proclaimed at the opening of the auditorium, "Citizens of St. Joseph only can keep St. Joseph back. Omaha can't retard us, Kansas City can't impede."

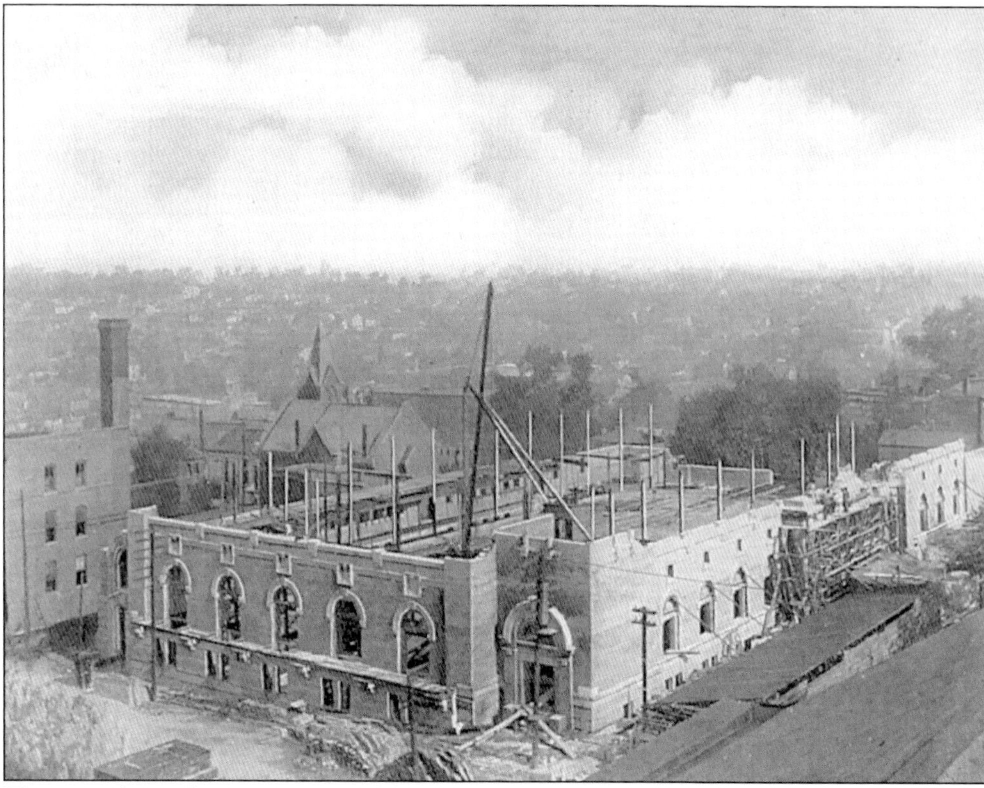

This view shows the construction of the city auditorium at Fourth and Faraon Streets.

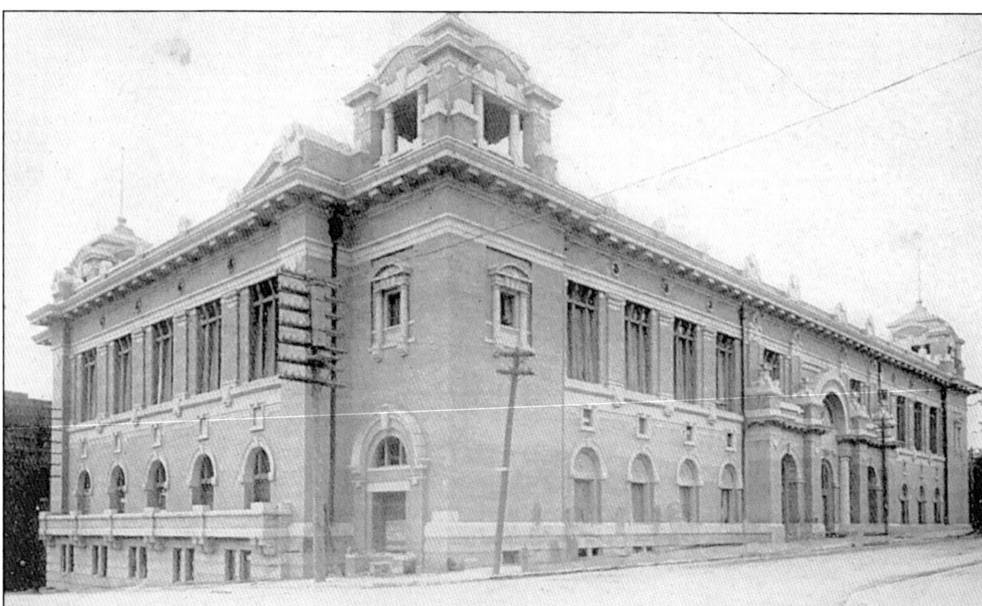

The auditorium was one of the city's finest buildings at the time of its completion. It stood on the west side of Fourth Street, between Faraon and Robidoux. When the civic arena was built downtown, the auditorium was demolished and the site became a parking lot.

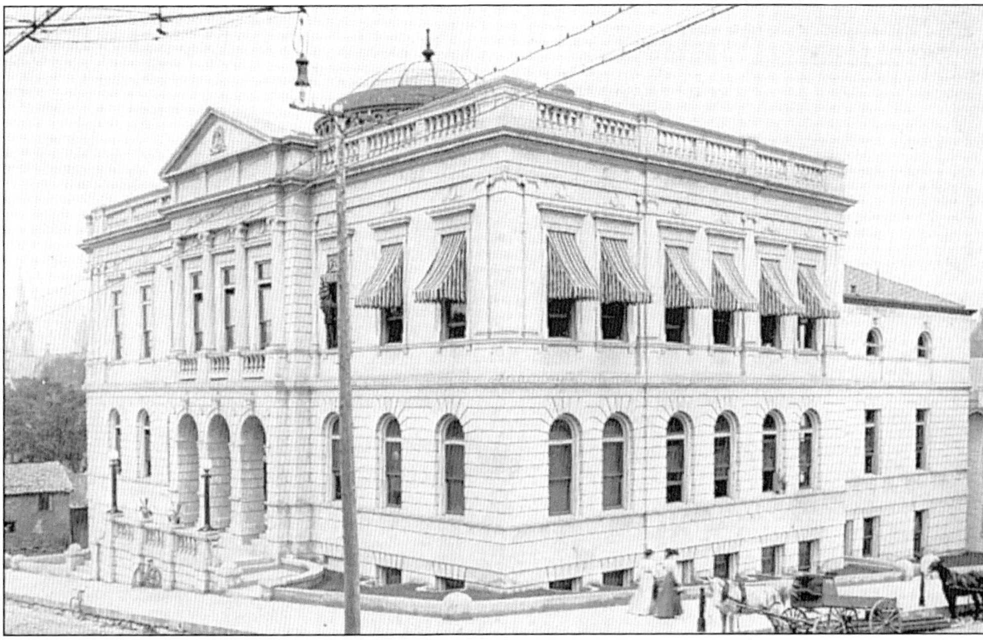

The St. Joseph Public Library has classic lines and a glass dome in the center, hallmarks of Edmond Eckel, the city's most notable architect. The library still stands at Tenth and Felix Streets. This image was captured *c.* 1904, as evidenced by the horse and buggy and the women wearing long-skirted outfits.

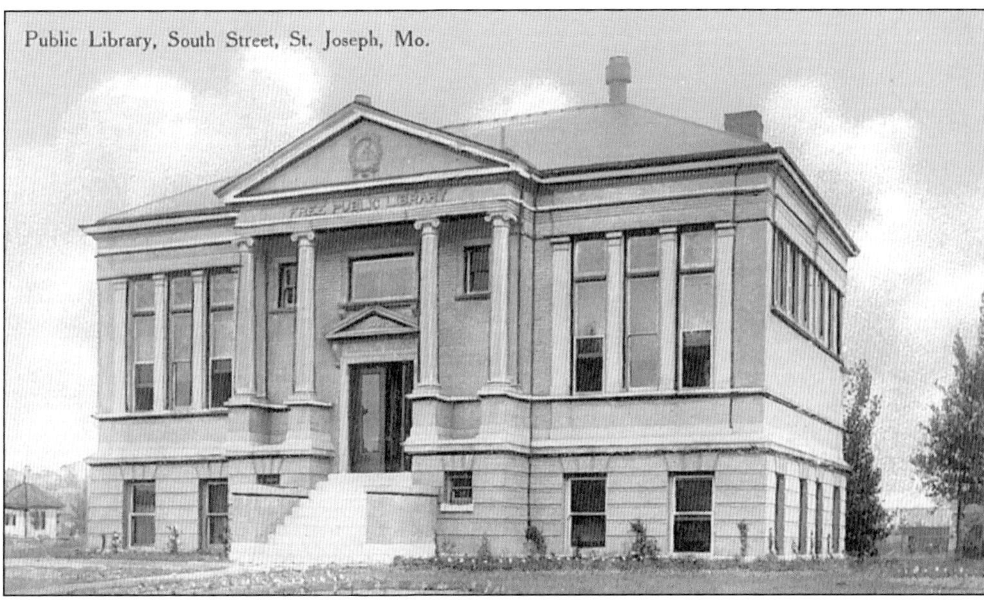

Col. John Donovan, a prominent resident of south St. Joseph, requested a $25,000 grant from Andrew Carnegie to build this library in south St. Joseph, a newly annexed area of the city at the turn of the 20th century. The people of St. Joseph agreed to pay $2,500 annually in maintenance fees, and the library was built. The Carnegie Public Library, 316 Massachusetts Street, was designed by Edmond Eckel, who chose a Classical Revival style. It was dedicated in December 1902.

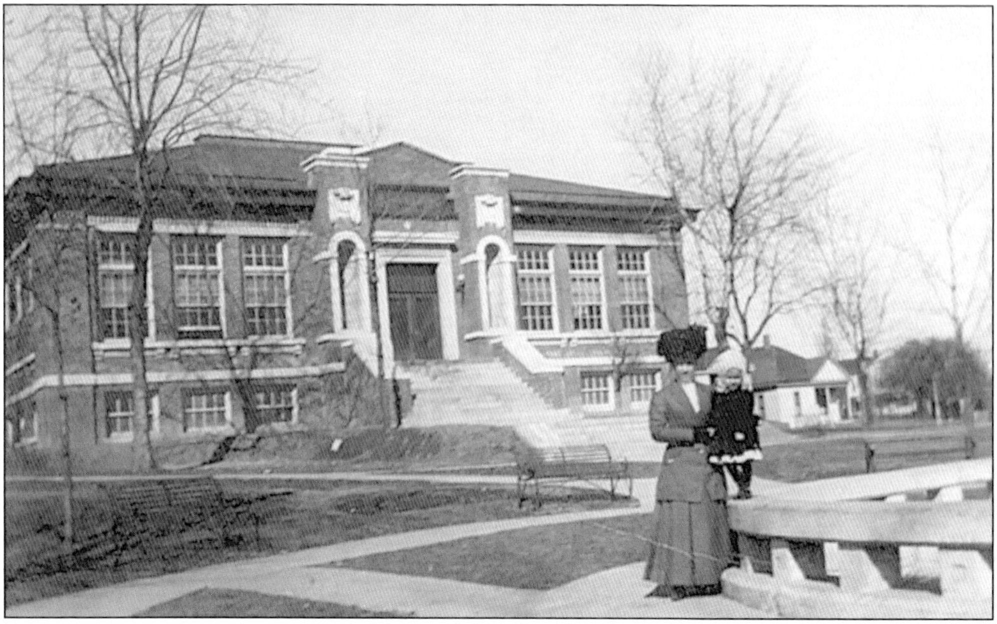

An unidentified mother and child stand by the fountain outside the Washington Park Library in 1911.

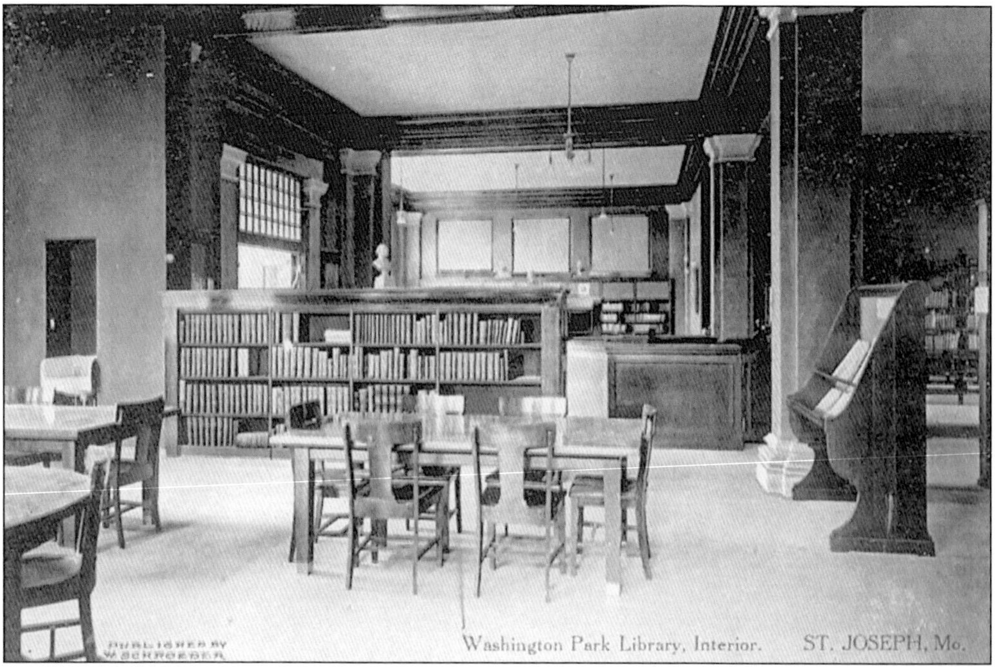

The interior of the Washington Park Library has changed very little since this photo was taken in 1910, when the building was constructed. It was designed by local architect Rudolph Meier at a cost of $26,000. Nearly all of its books and later additions were bought from a special subscription fund raised by nearby residents.

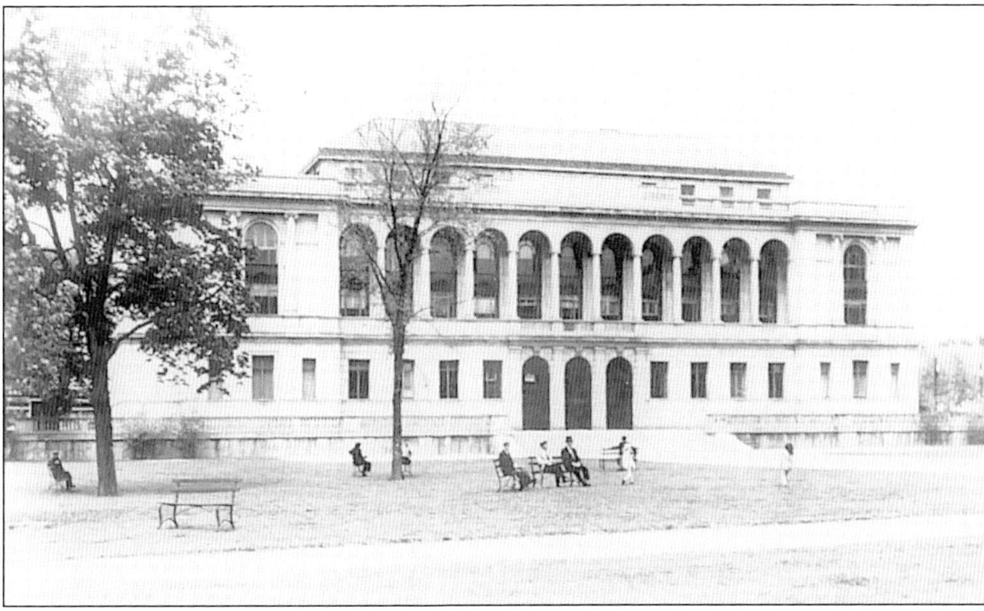

St. Joseph City Hall, built in 1926 and opened in 1927, is still one of the city's landmarks. It was designed by the architectural firm owned by Edmond Eckel, and his European training is evident in the building's classical lines. It stands at Eleventh and Frederick and is still used as the city's main municipal building. The interior lobby area and staircase remain largely as Eckel designed them.

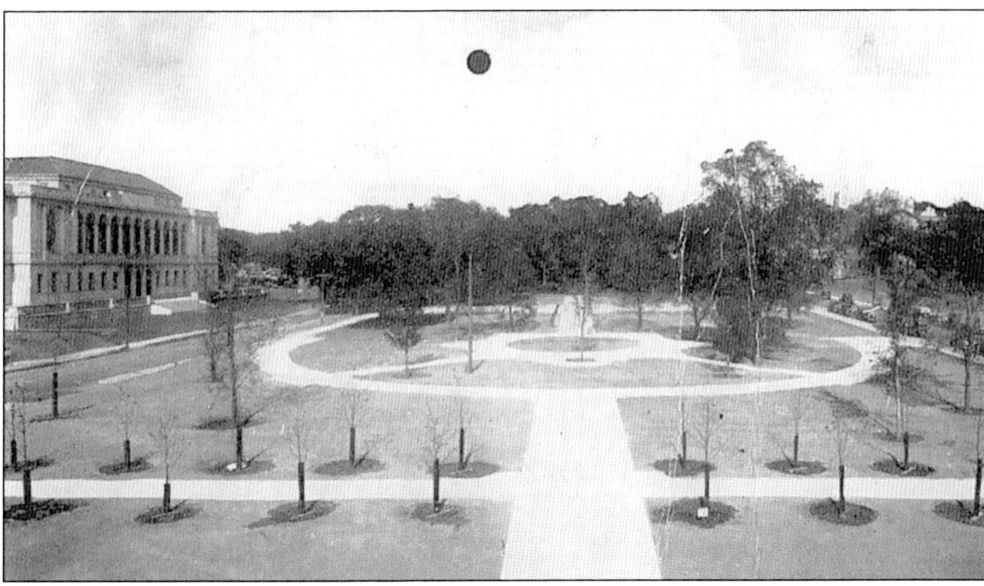

Civic Center Park was in its infancy when this photo was taken in 1926; the trees are merely twigs in this photo. The park was designed to show off the front of city hall, as patrons approached it from this angle rather than the Frederick Avenue side of the building, which is used today as the building's main entrance. Jules Street ran in front of the building, through Civic Center Park.

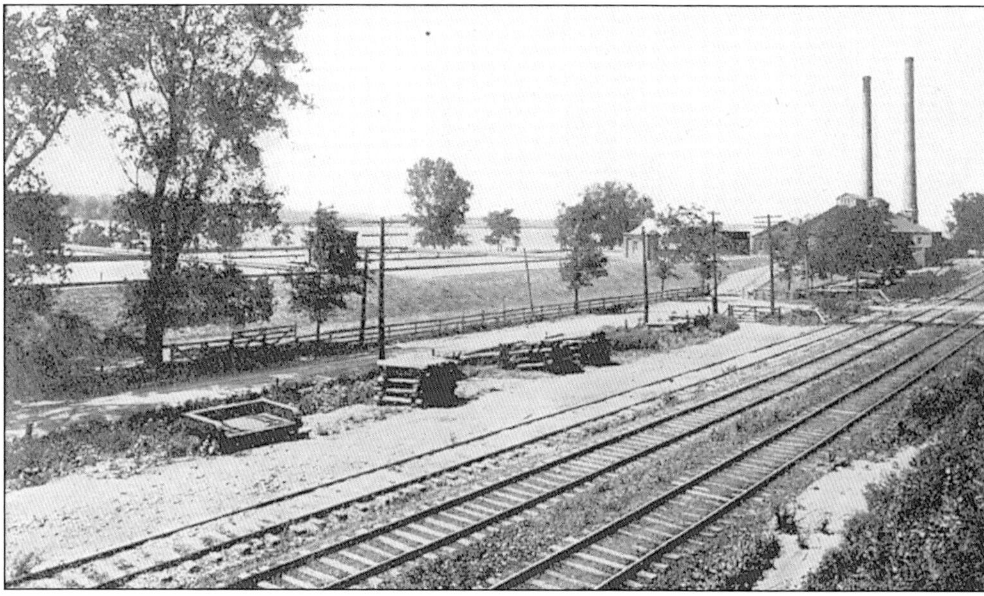

Railroad tracks ran near the St. Joseph Waterworks, the municipally-run water plant that supplied the city's residents. Now, the water system is privately operated.

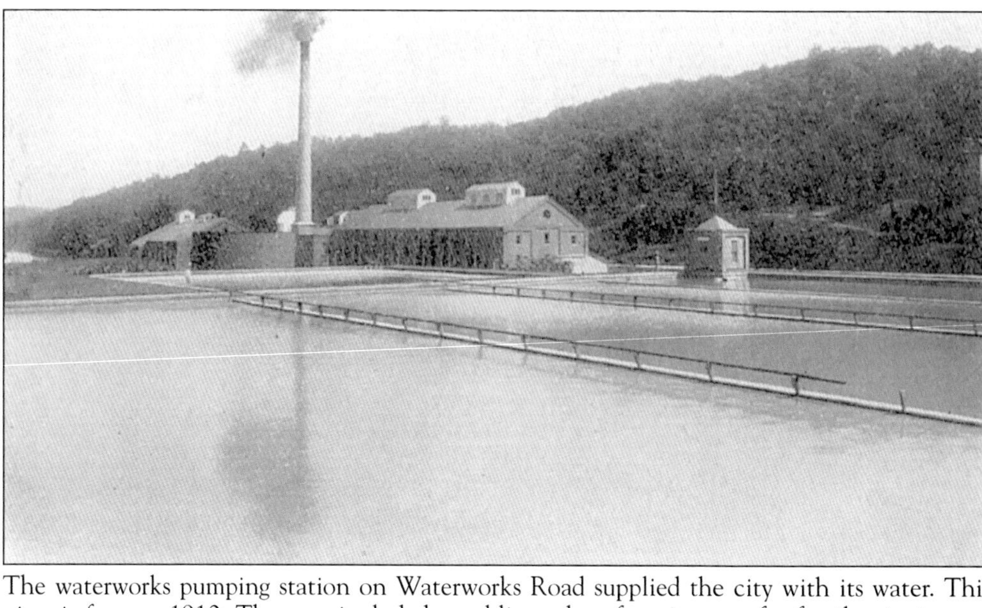

The waterworks pumping station on Waterworks Road supplied the city with its water. This view is from c. 1910. The area included a public park, a favorite spot for family picnics and views of the city.

Four

BUSINESSES

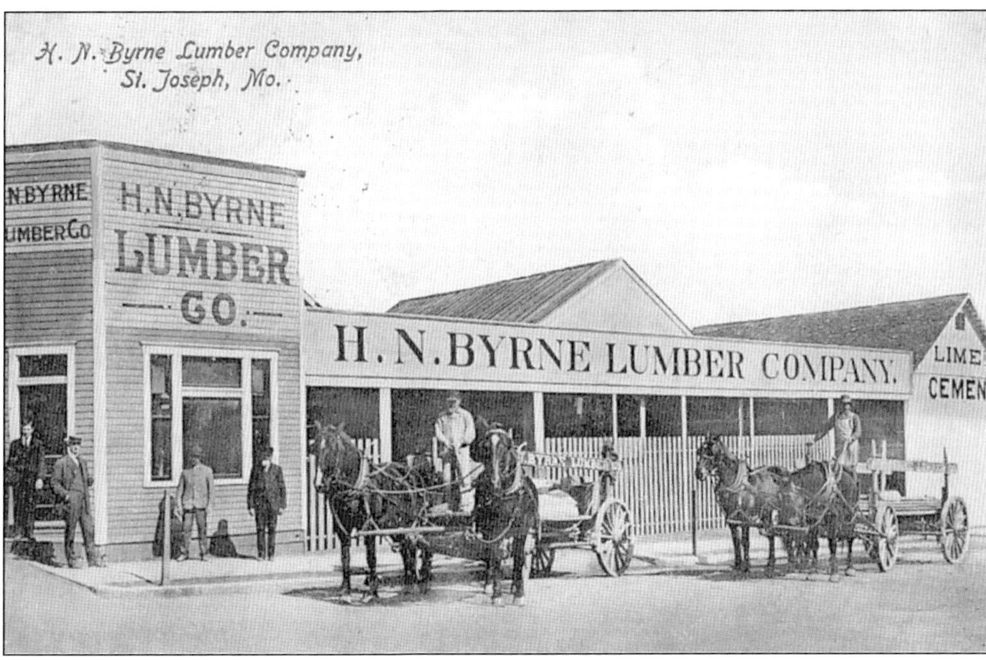

Lumber companies were vital to cities growing at the rate of St. Joseph at the turn of the 20th century. The Byrne Lumber Company, located at 1502 Middleton Street, was one such company. This card was likely used as an advertisement for the company, as the message hand-written on the back instructs the receiver to "Dial 29 for lumber."

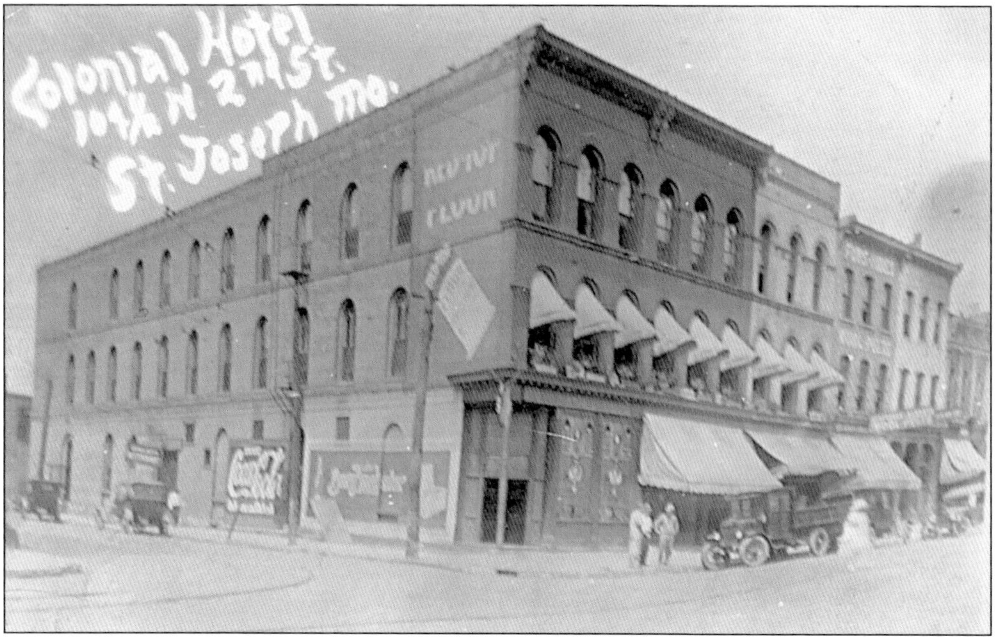

The Colonial Hotel at 104 North Second Street was one of many downtown hotels to serve the booming population here. This hotel stood near the market square and old city hall. The image was taken *c.* 1910.

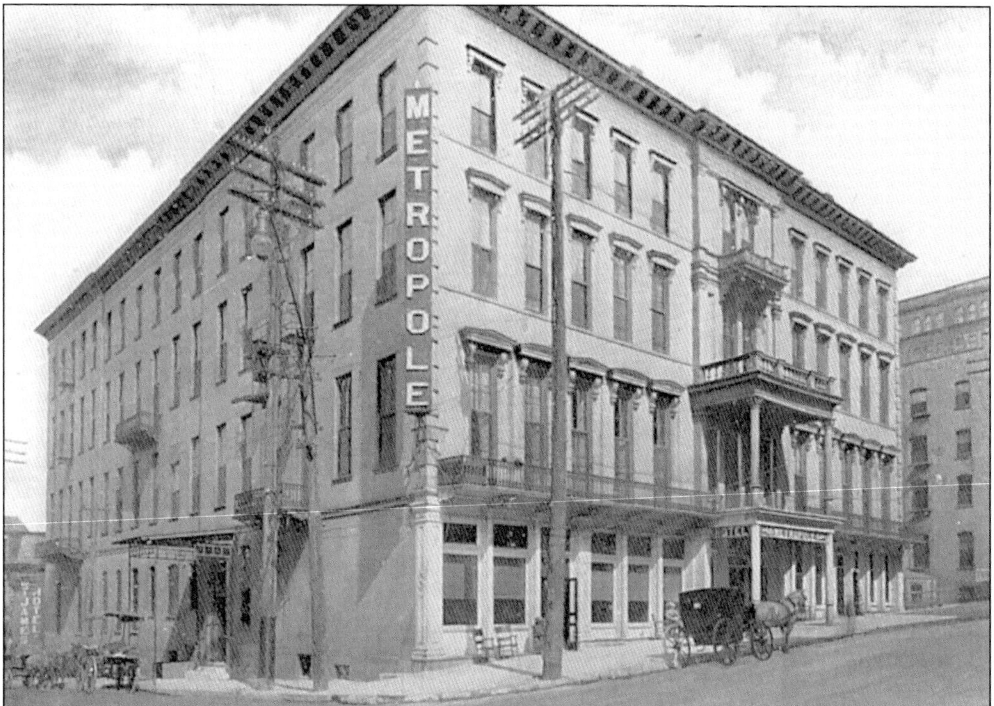

The Metropole Hotel at Third and Francis Streets had 75 rooms in 1900 and was congratulated for being one of the finest in the West. It wasn't sufficient to meet the growing city's needs, however; the Hotel Robidoux would replace the Metropole as the city's largest hotel.

The Tootle-Campbell Dry Goods Company at Fourth and Faraon Streets was a large department store that issued its own catalogs. Today, the building is owned by Hillyard, a chemical company. The first floor is leased by the Buchanan County government for office space.

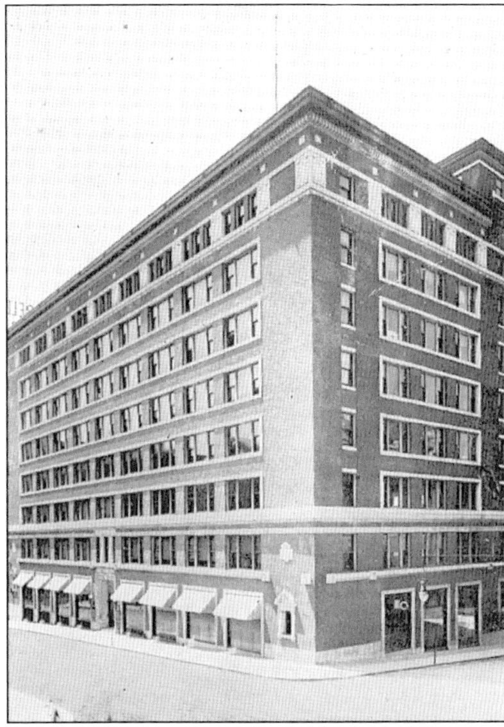

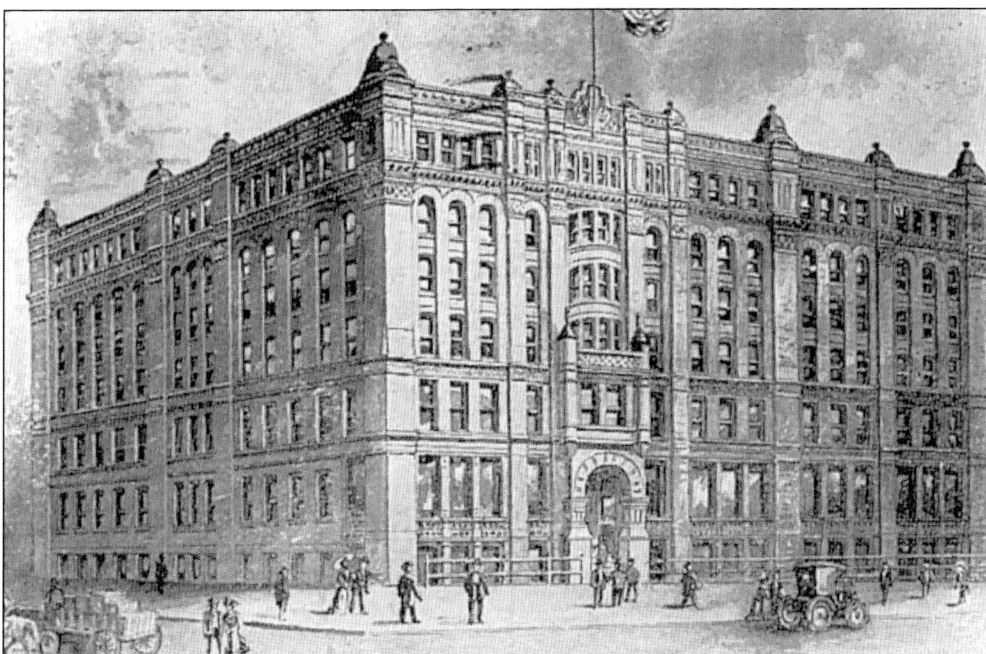

The Wheeler and Motter Mercantile Company building was no doubt one of the city's most impressive commercial structures. The business began in 1849, and the building pictured here, at the intersection of Fourth and Jules Streets, was built in 1889. The business is said to have carried the largest line of dry goods, notions, carpets, and furniture of any business west of New York. The building no longer stands.

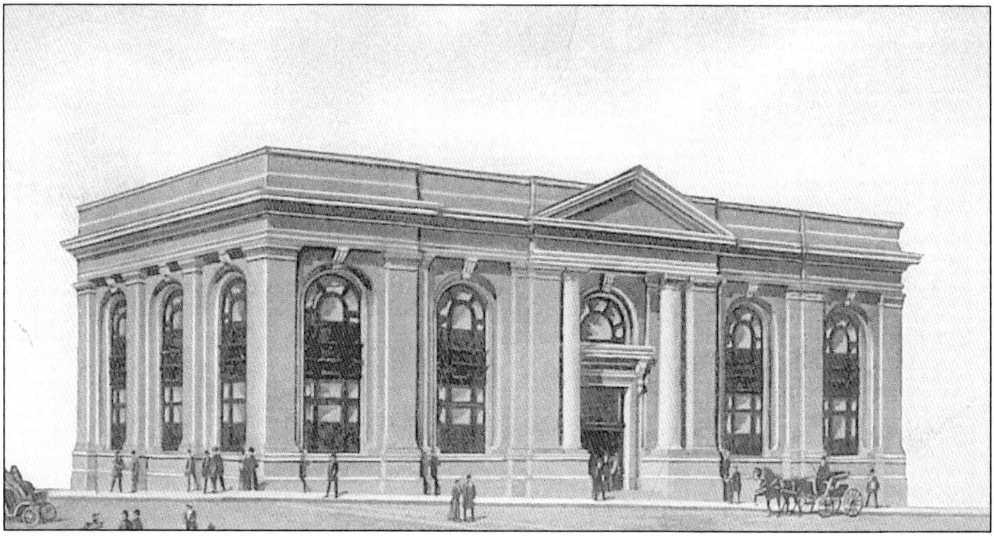

First National Bank at Fourth and Felix Streets represented the financial success of the city's entrepreneurs. The building is now used by Commerce Bank. From shortly after the turn of the 20th century through the Great Depression, they were a federally chartered bank that issued federal currency bearing the bank's name.

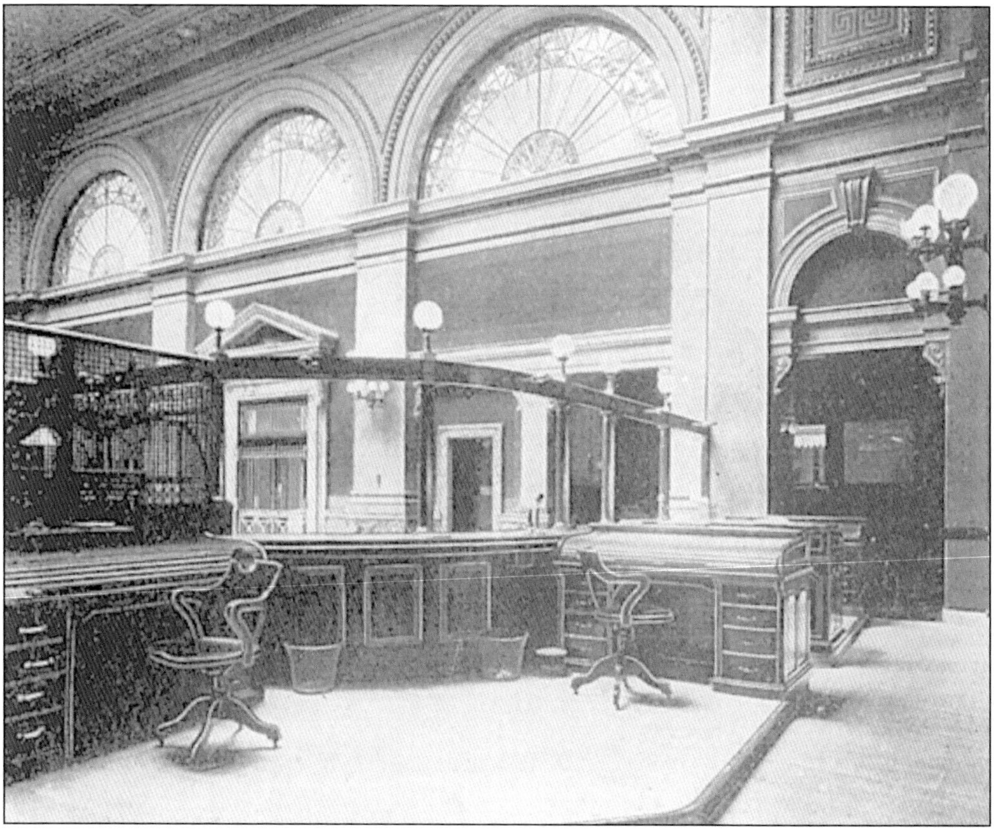

The impressive interior of First National Bank is largely the same, with many of the same architectural features remaining. This postcard shows the officer's desk inside.

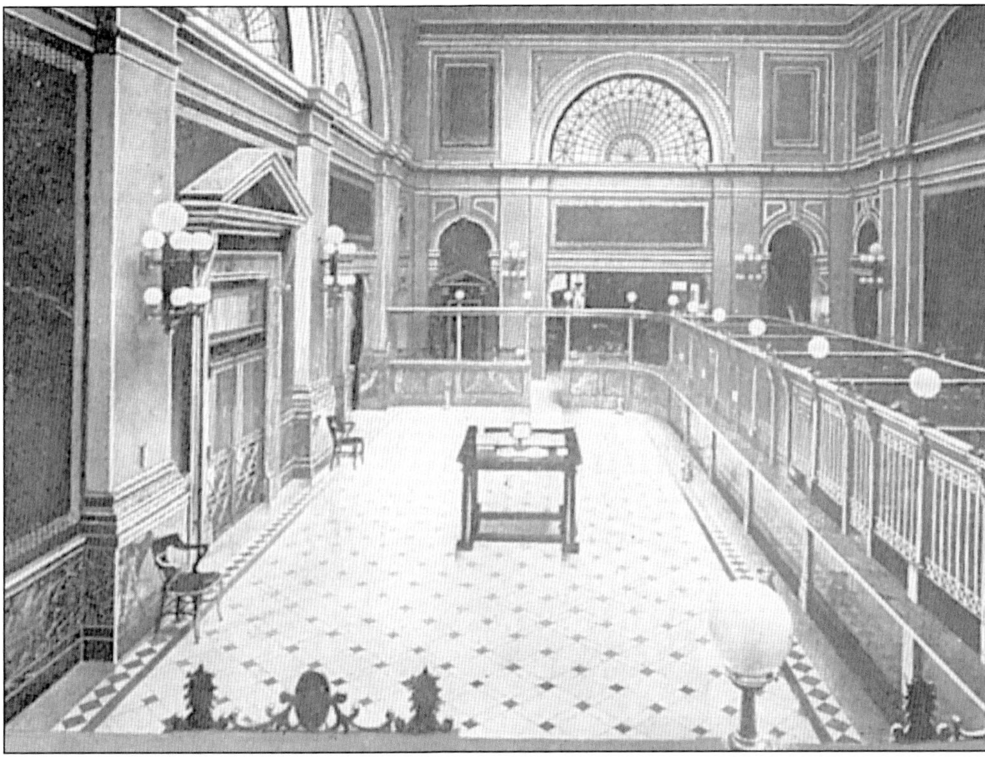

The main lobby of First National Bank is the view most residents would have seen at the turn of the 20th century. Most St. Joseph residents today will recognize the interior, despite the changes that have been made over the years.

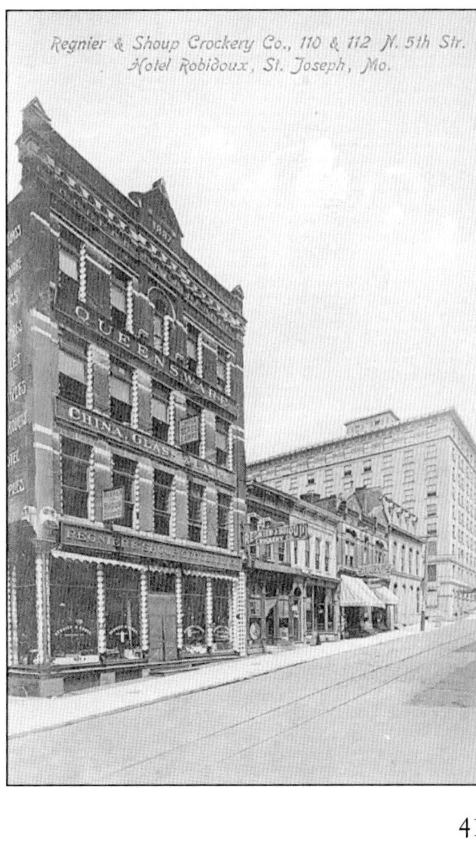

The Regnier and Shoup Crockery Co. at 110 and 112 North Fifth Street was located one block south of the Hotel Robidoux. The building was constructed in 1887. It was a prominent turn-of-the-20th century business that routinely ordered china from Germany, many pieces with St. Joseph scenes on them.

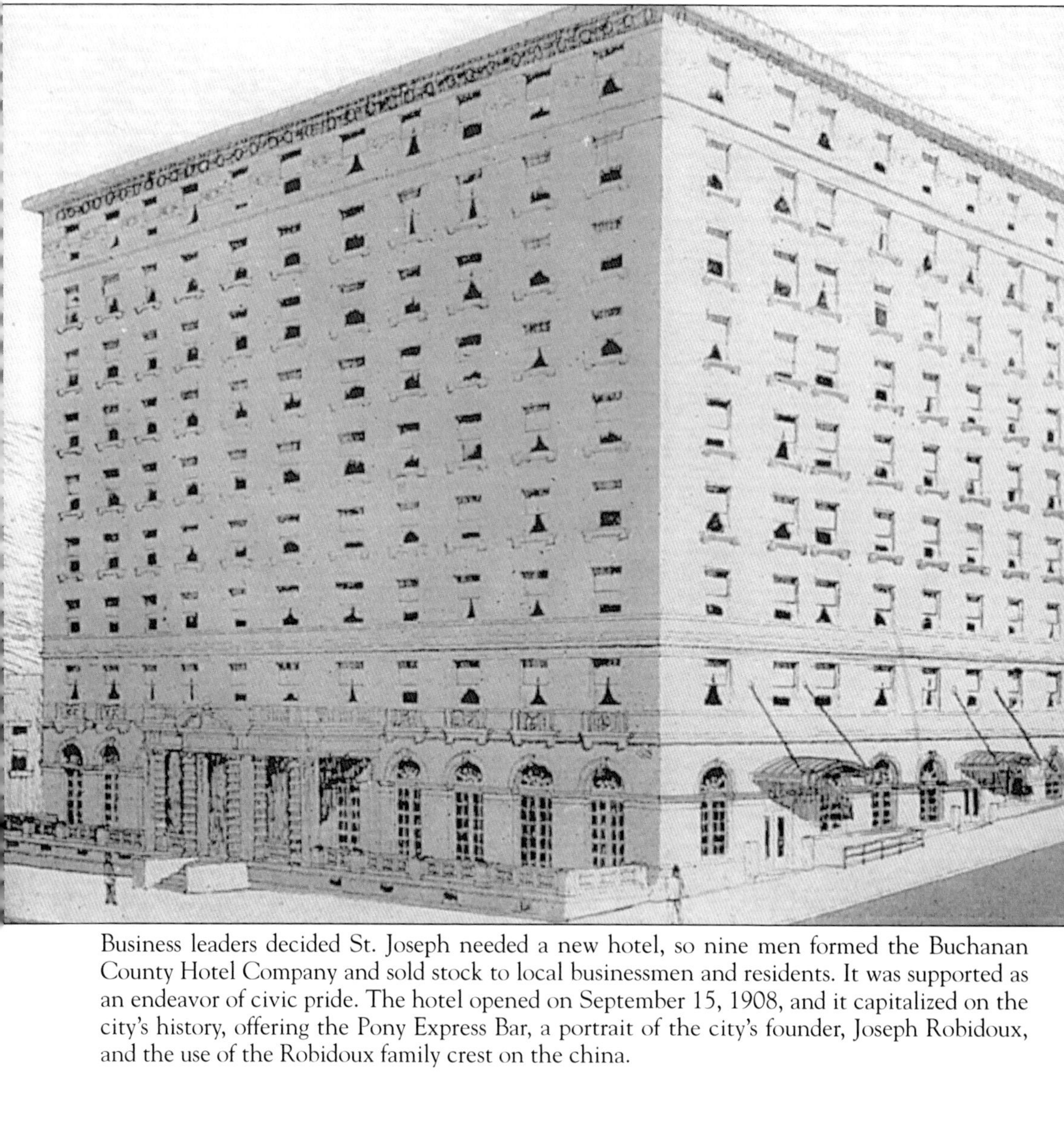

Business leaders decided St. Joseph needed a new hotel, so nine men formed the Buchanan County Hotel Company and sold stock to local businessmen and residents. It was supported as an endeavor of civic pride. The hotel opened on September 15, 1908, and it capitalized on the city's history, offering the Pony Express Bar, a portrait of the city's founder, Joseph Robidoux, and the use of the Robidoux family crest on the china.

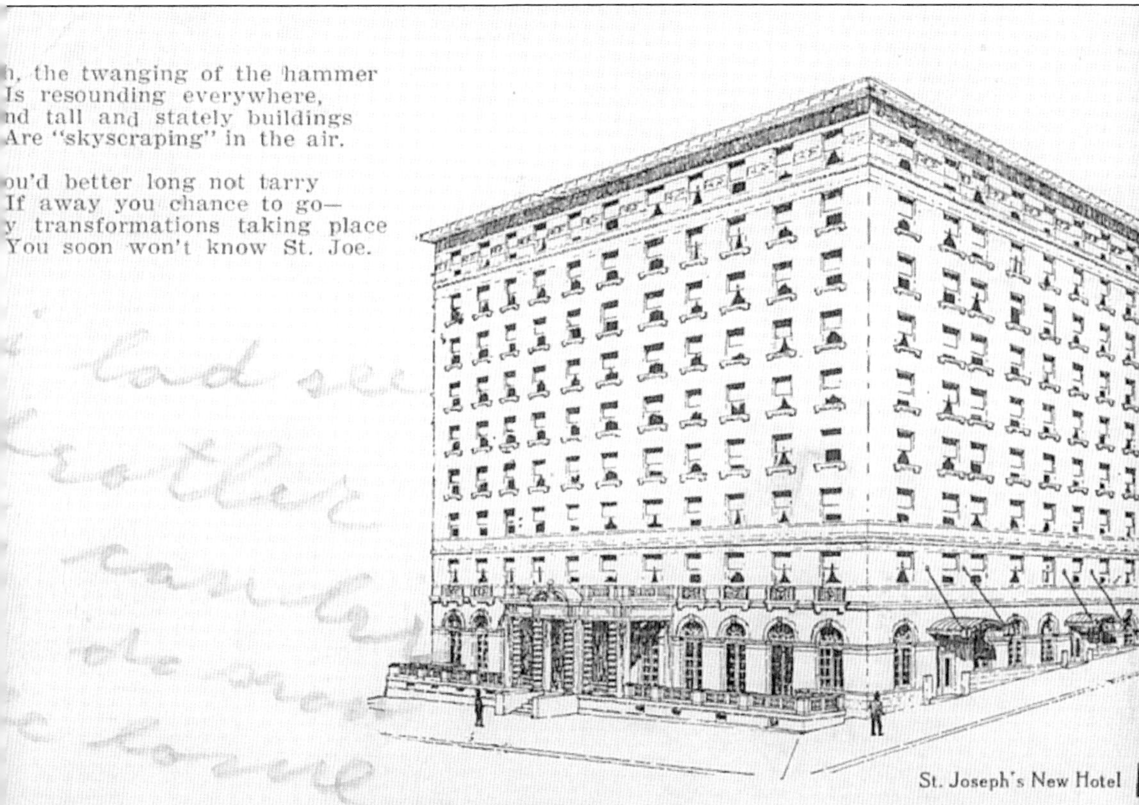

The Hotel Robidoux was a prominent fixture in the community. Residents came here for celebrations, family occasions, holidays, and major social events. But 68 years later, on June 13, 1976, the hotel was imploded. The majestic structure was deemed unfeasible for renovation and became a victim of urban renewal. A film of the implosion was used in a popular beer commercial.

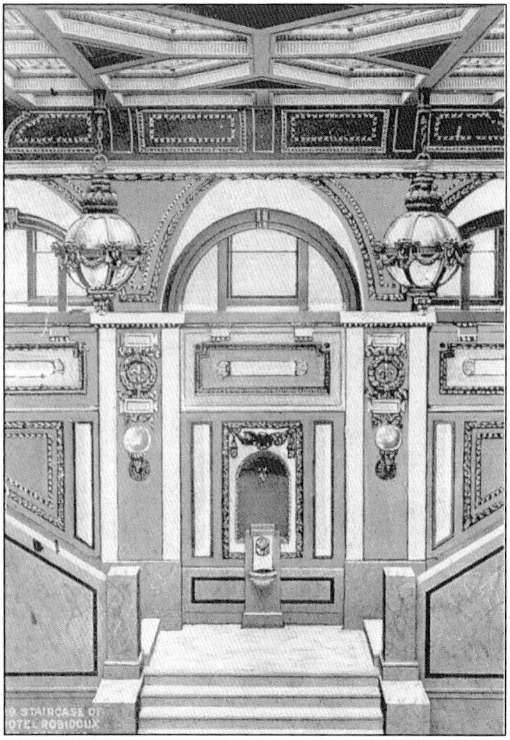

Some of the Hotel Robidoux's fixtures were auctioned off, and a bank building built some years later on the site incorporated the chandeliers from the hotel. This view shows the main staircase, which was made of marble.

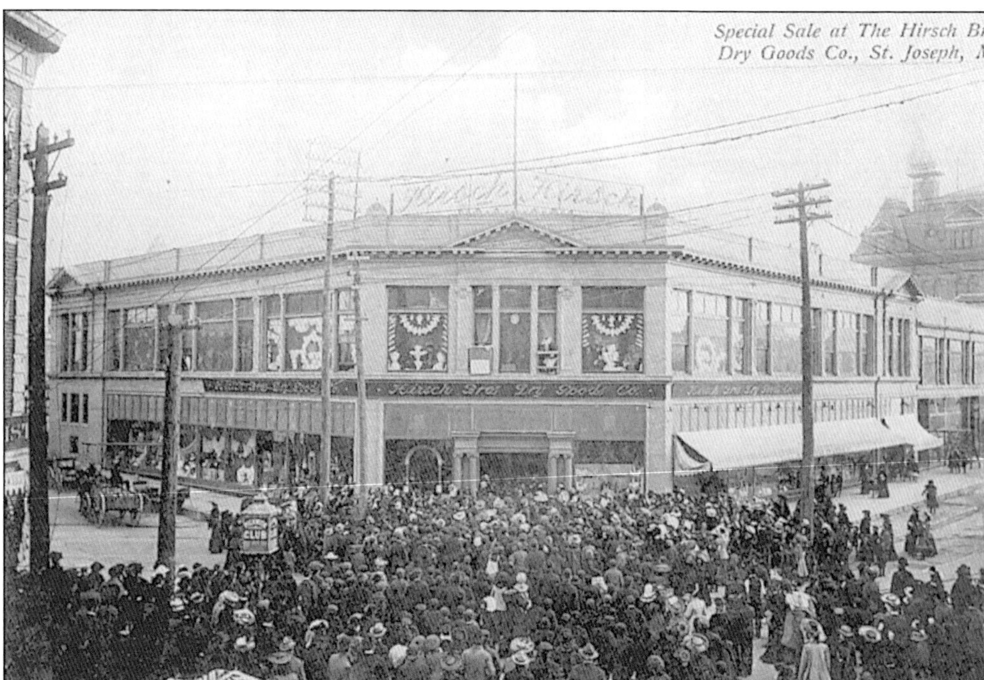

The Hirsch Brothers Dry Goods Company could apparently draw a crowd. This photo is captioned, "a special sale at the Hirsch Brothers Dry Goods Co." Today, the site of the store is a parking lot for the *St. Joseph News-Press*.

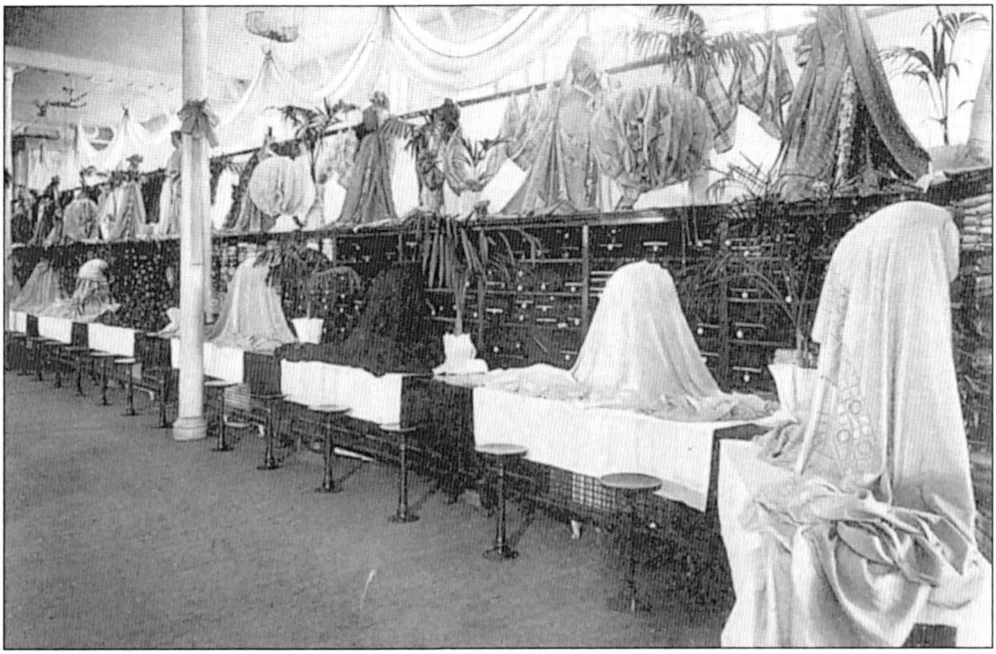

This interior view of the Hirsch Brothers Dry Goods Co. shows the silk and dress goods section of the store *c.* 1905. The store was one of the most opulent in St. Joseph.

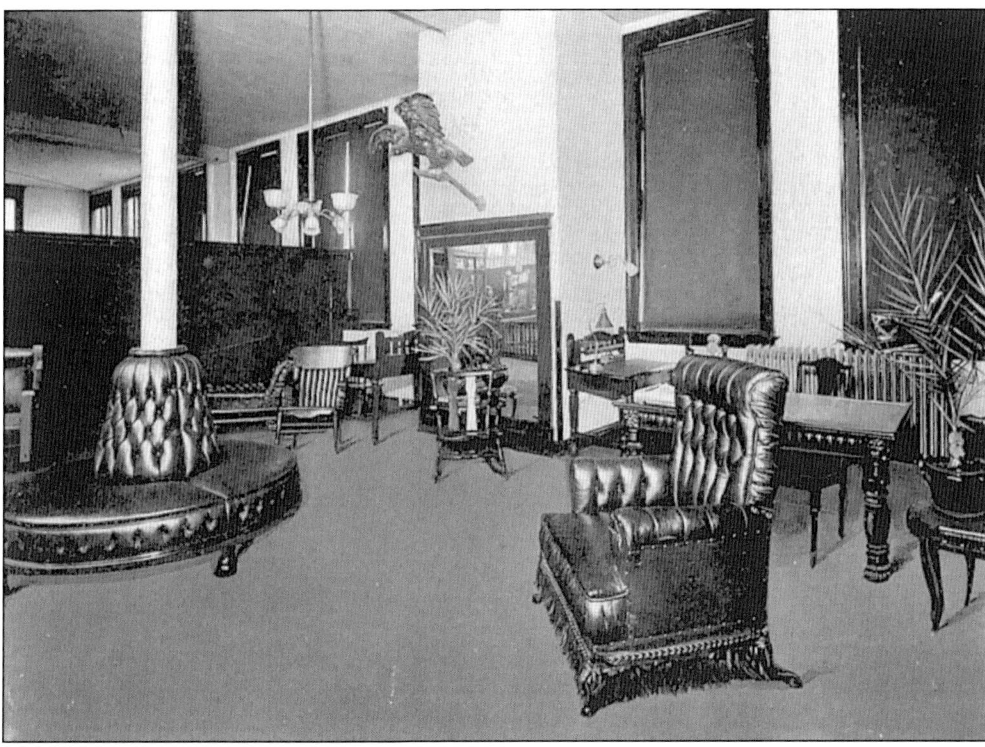

Even the ladies' restroom at the Hirsch Brothers Dry Goods Co. was considered pretty enough for a postcard. Note the leather chairs, potted palm plants, and the amount of space allotted to it.

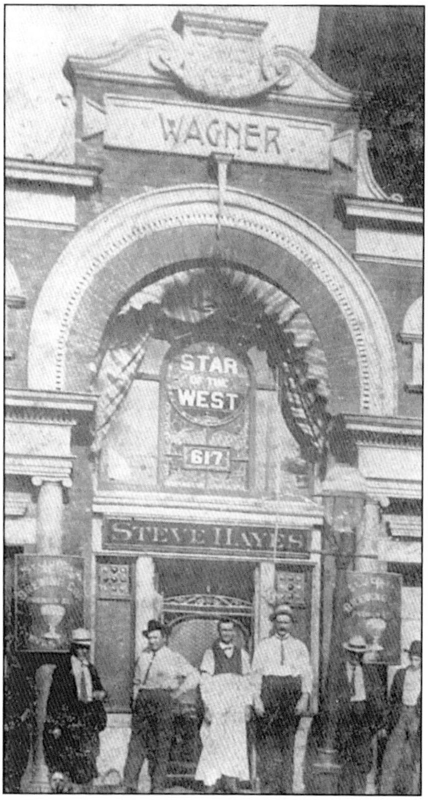

At the turn of the 20th century, this establishment at 617 South Eighth Street was known as the Wagner Saloon. The building was constructed in 1877 and is noted on the back of the postcard as being "a rare brick and iron front building being restored as an operating saloon." It has since been demolished.

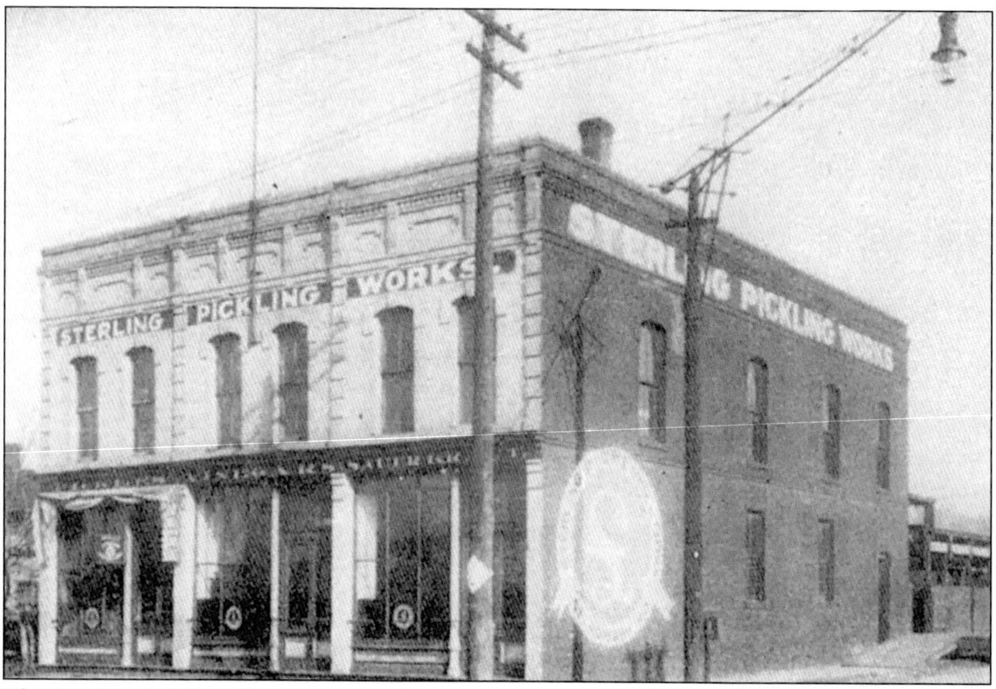

The Sterling Pickling Works stood on Seneca Street. From 1901 to 1953, the firm was operated by M.J. and Charley Heerlein.

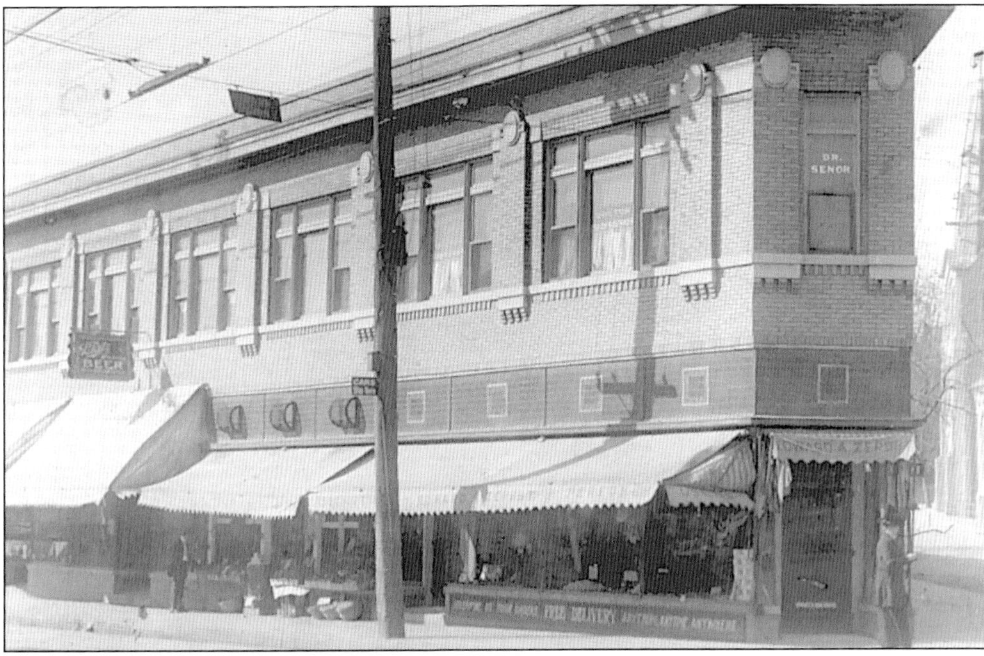

The Howard A. Zerbst Pharmacy once stood at the intersection of Ninth Street, Francis Street, and Frederick Avenue. This image was taken *c.* 1910. The advertising on the side of the building reads, "Telephone us your order. Free Delivery. Anything, anytime, anywhere." The window at the top right advertises Dr. Senor. The sign to the left, above the awning, advertises Blatz Beer. Christ Episcopal Church is in the background, on the right.

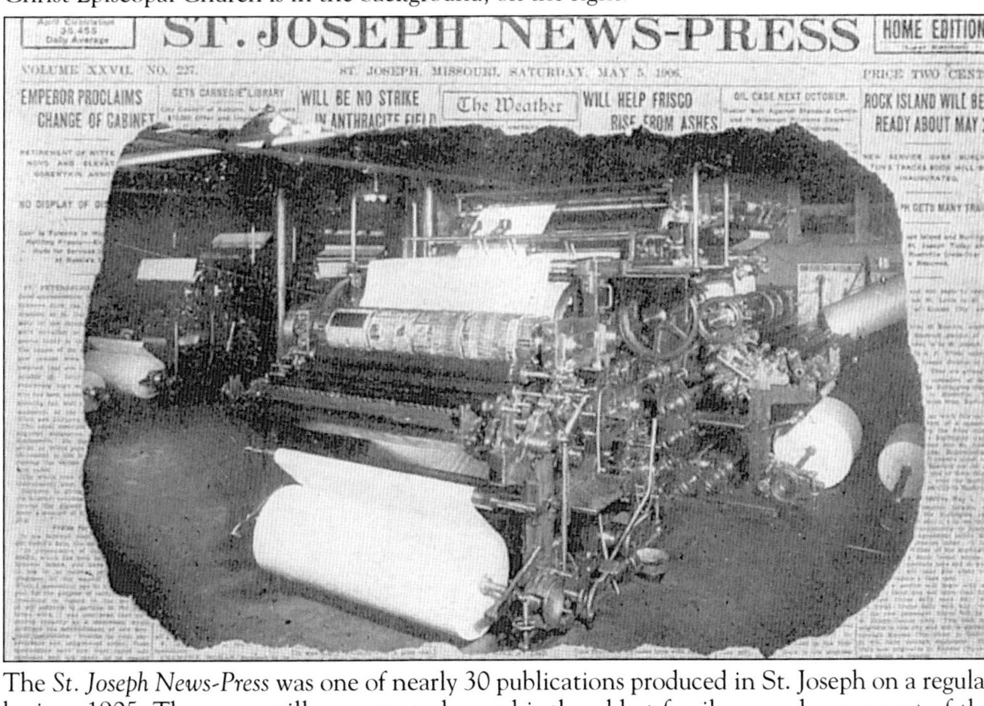

The *St. Joseph News-Press* was one of nearly 30 publications produced in St. Joseph on a regular basis *c.* 1905. The paper still operates today and is the oldest family-owned paper west of the Mississippi. It is also the city's oldest publication, having started in 1845.

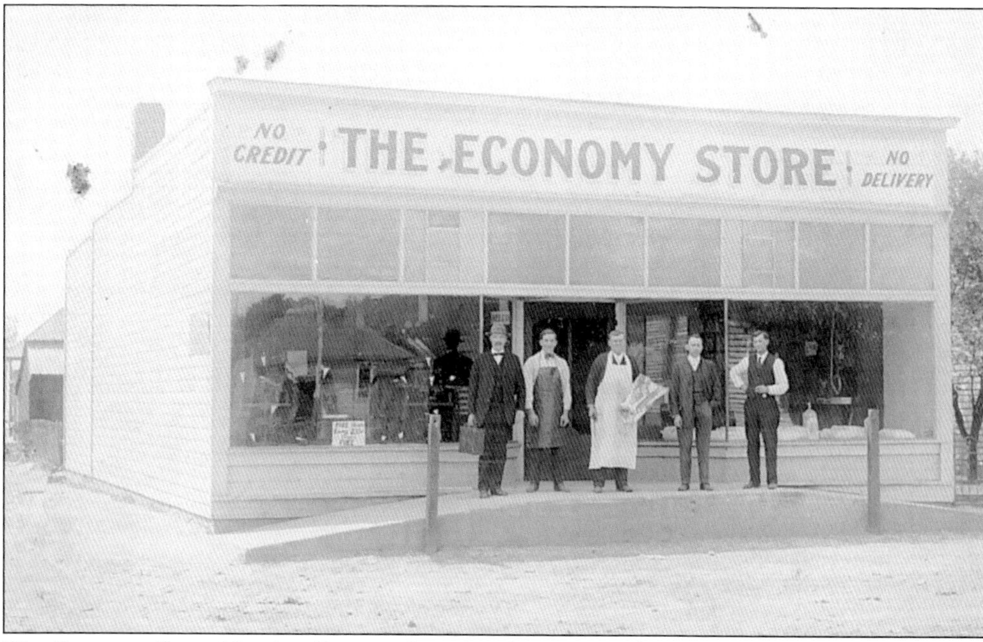

The Economy Store Number 7 was a short-lived commercial enterprise with good intentions. The sign along the top advertises "no credit" and "no delivery," perhaps in an effort to keep costs down. The store was located at 6220 Sherman Street and was owned by O.C. Miller. It is believed to have been in operation for one year.

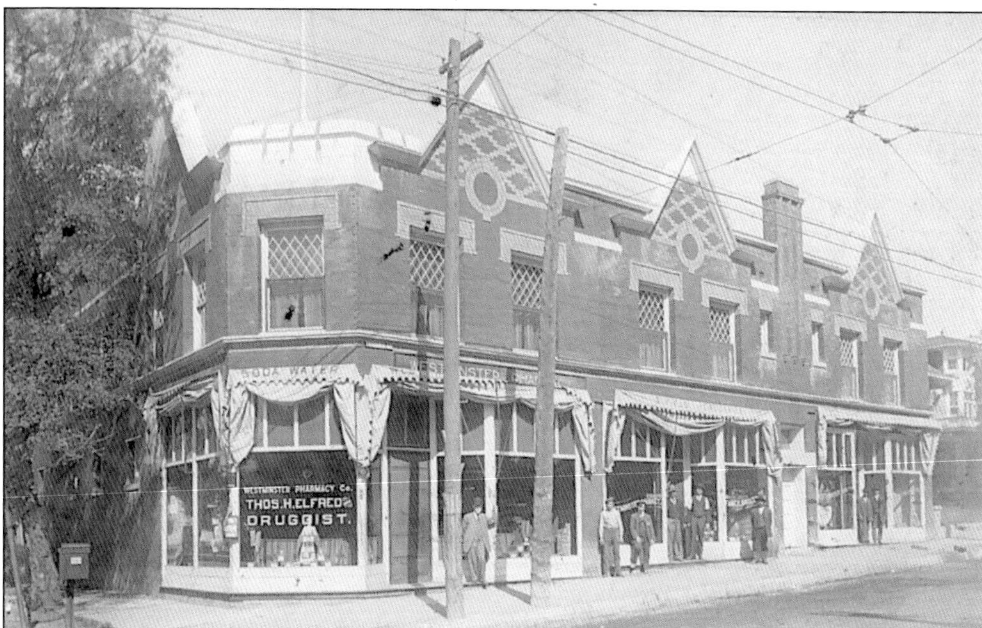

The building that housed the Westminister Pharmacy Co. still stands on Frederick Avenue, at the intersection of Twenty-sixth Street. The businesses housed in these buildings were Thomas H. Elfred, Druggist on the corner, Westminister Market in the next storefront, and the Eastside Market in the third storefront. Westminister Market sold fancy groceries. Today, Zercher Photography operates in the corner storefront.

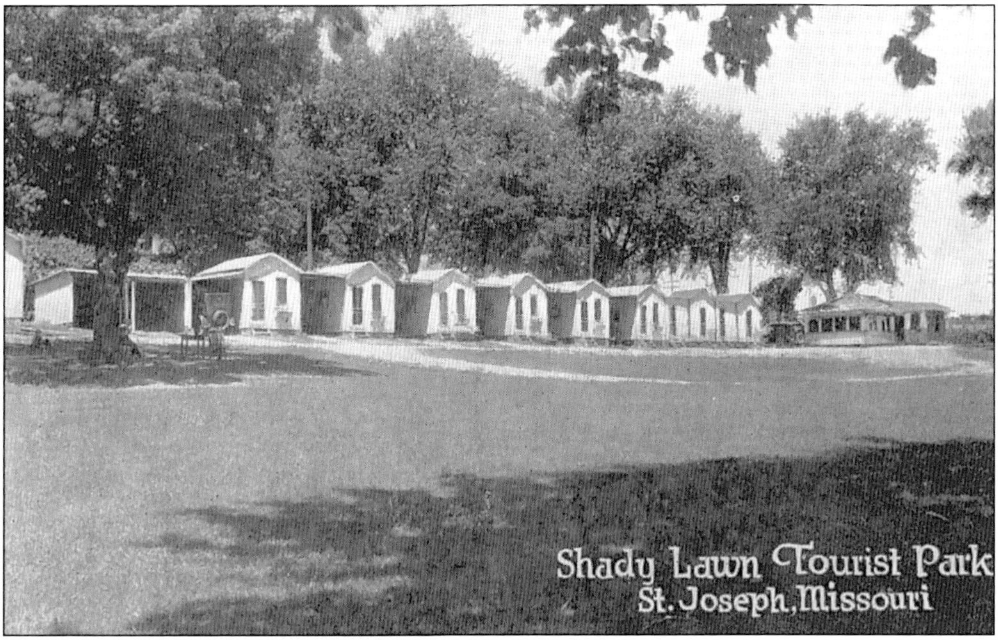

Tourist parks became popular as cheap overnight accommodations when the automobile gained favor following World War I. This tourist park was located just east of the city, at the intersection of U.S. 36 and Missouri 6, which were main thoroughfares through St. Joseph at the time.

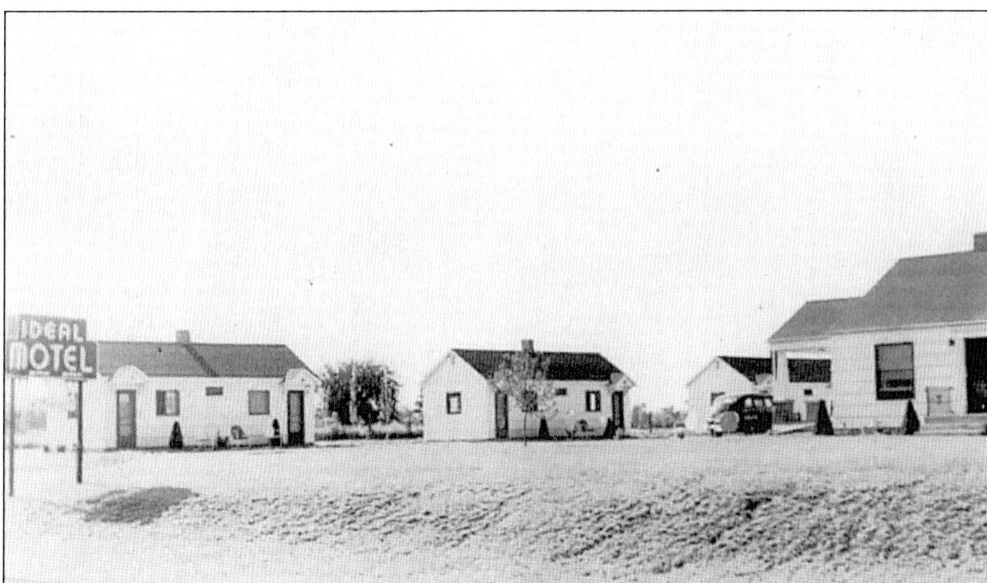

The Ideal Motel on U.S. 36 served motorists in the 1920s. Its units appear a bit more spacious than the Shady Lawn Tourist Park, but they were still modest accommodations for travelers.

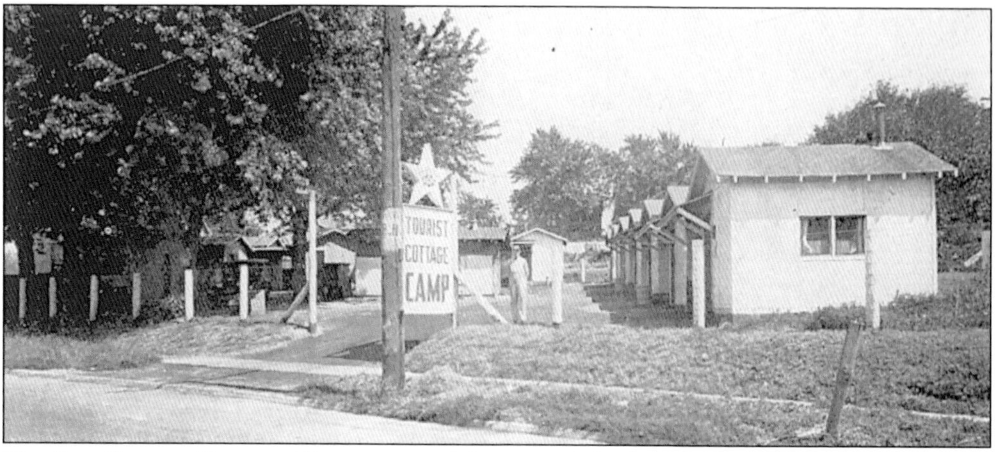

The Star Cottage Camp at Twenty-second Street and Garfield Avenue emphasized its shady lots, its cleanliness, and free showers, as well as the nearby location of grocery stores and gas stations. This business served motorists c. 1926.

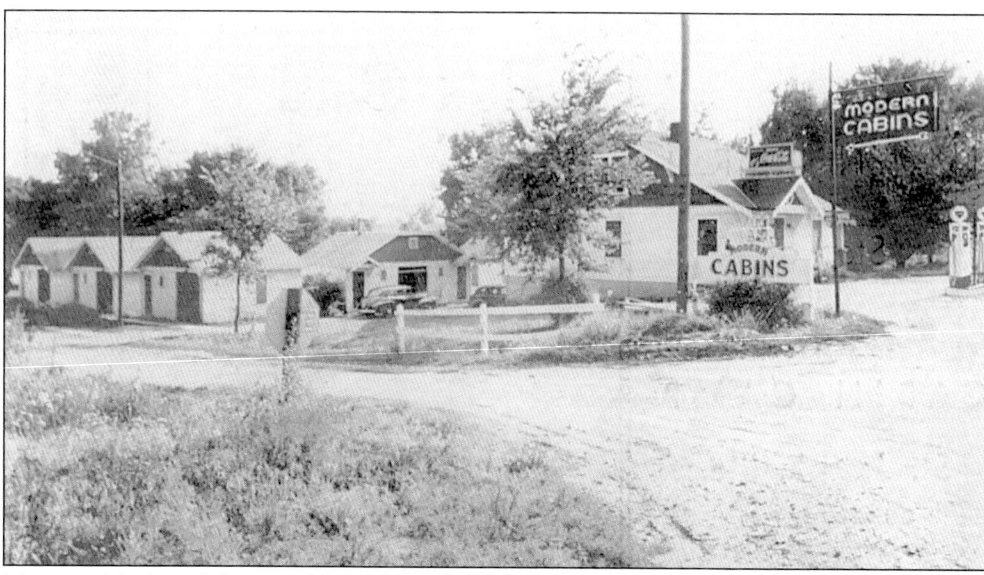

Mettings Modern Cabins on U.S. 36 was located three blocks east of the junction of U.S. 36 and U.S. 71, a major interchange in the early 20th century. The postcard doesn't give a date, but the tourist camps are believed to have been established after the end of World War I.

Five

The Stockyards

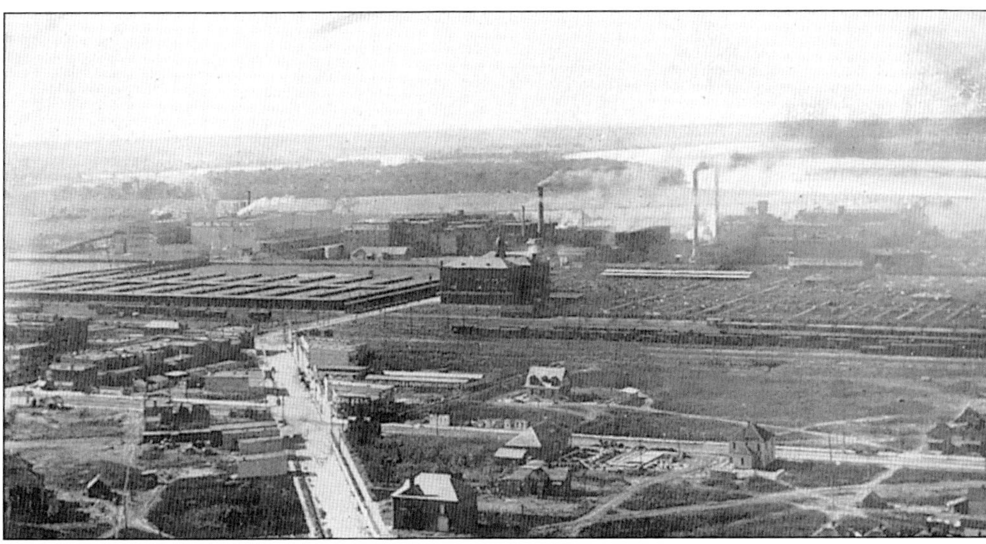

The stockyards area in south St. Joseph was once lined with meat-packing plants, including Swift, Armour, and Monfort Pork. The area around the stockyards was largely comprised of housing for the hundreds of workers employed in the industry and their families. Monfort Pork, the last of the meat-packing plants, closed in 1993. The stockyards still operate as a place for farmers to buy and sell cattle and hogs, but much of the industry around it is gone. Seitz, owned now by Sara Lee, is the only meat production plant still operating in St. Joseph today.

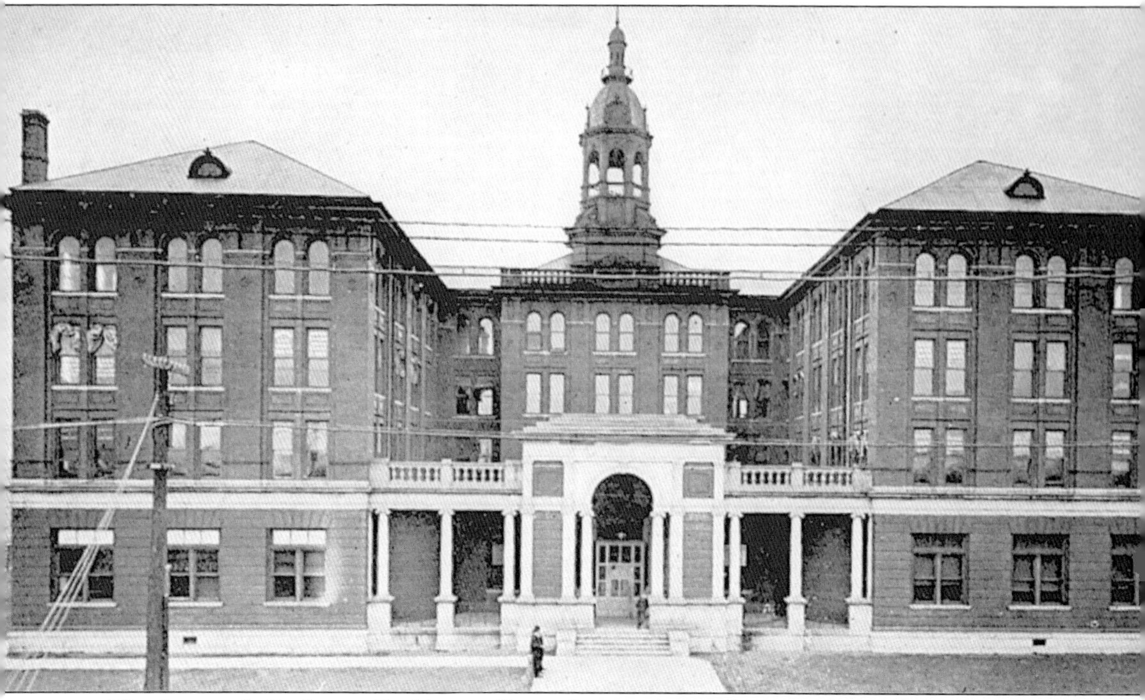

The Livestock Exchange Building still stands near the working stockyards but has fallen into disrepair. Its first day of business was June 9, 1899. It was a proud landmark in St. Joseph, advertising 105 rooms, all with outside exposures, and served by electric elevators. It cost $100,000 to build, which was considered a bargain then. Among the offices inside were the stockyards office, a post office, the First Stock Yards Bank, and a barber shop. With nearby restaurants and hotels, it was an integral part of what could function as a self-contained community.

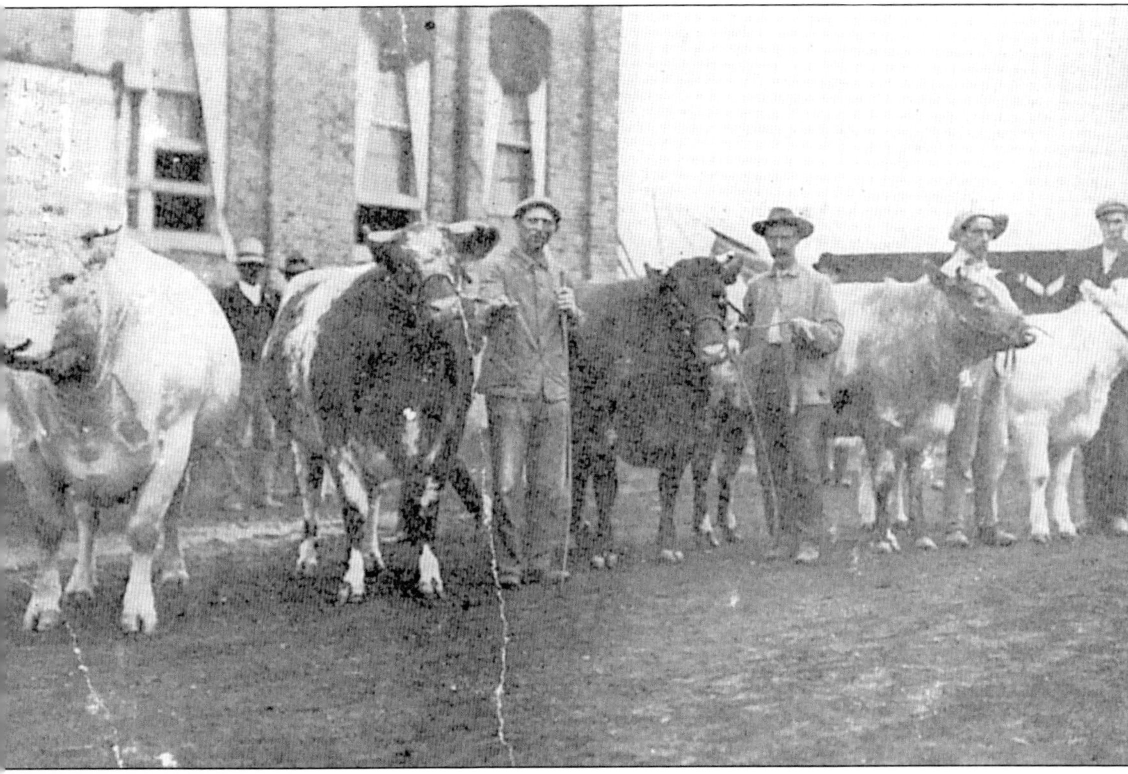

This postcard advertises the Inter-State Live Stock Show, set for September 21–16, 1908. The message side of the card is an advertisement for the *St. Joseph Star*, which charged $1 for a year's subscription.

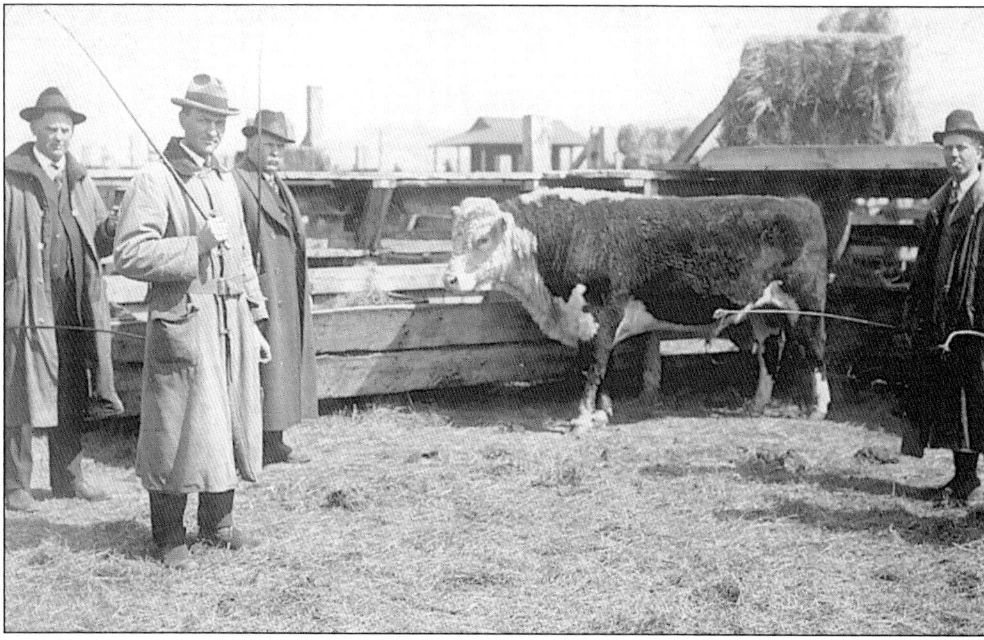

Mr. Wiley Webb is pictured on the far right on this card. He's selling his prize bull at the stockyards. The card is not dated.

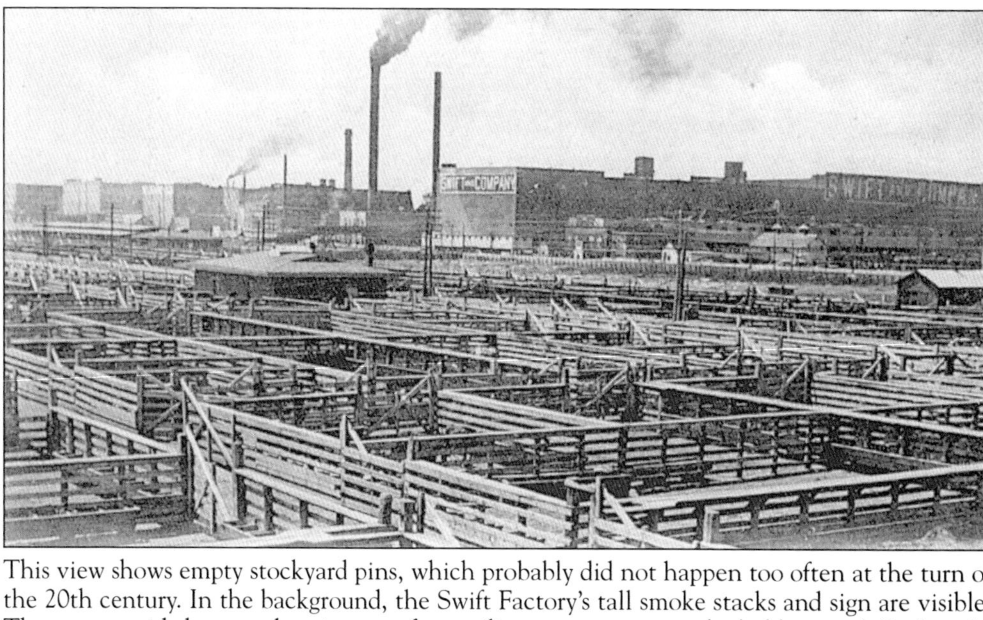

This view shows empty stockyard pins, which probably did not happen too often at the turn of the 20th century. In the background, the Swift Factory's tall smoke stacks and sign are visible. The message side has an advertisement for a military tournament to be held in south St. Joseph, September 23–28, 1907.

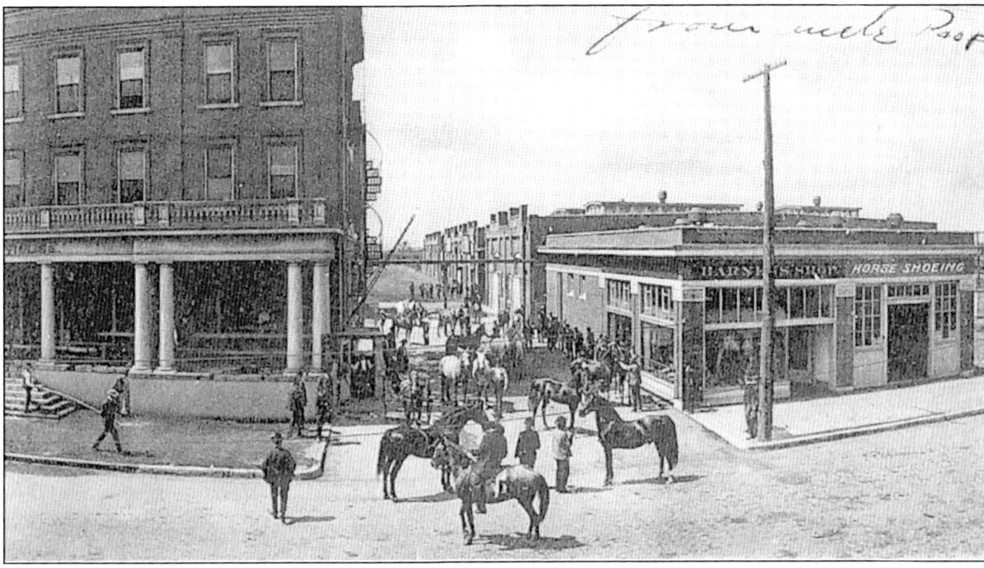

The Horse and Mule market in south St. Joseph was near the Transit House hotel at 416 Illinois Avenue.

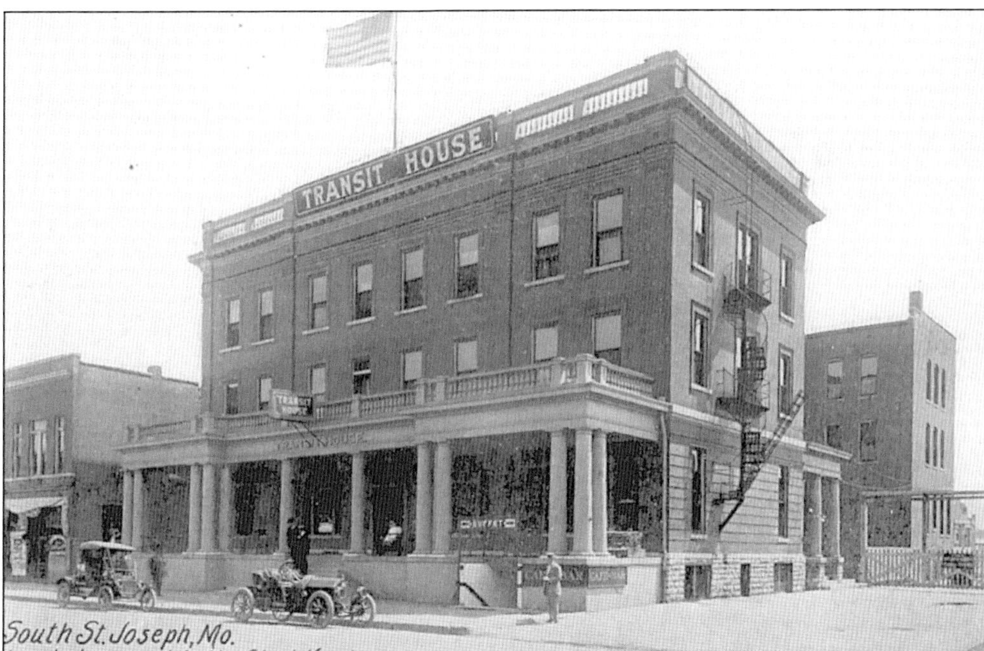

This is a closer view of the Transit House, a hotel built near the stockyards in 1902. In the early 20th century, the area had a number of hotels and restaurants to house and feed those en route to the larger cattle towns of Kansas City or Chicago.

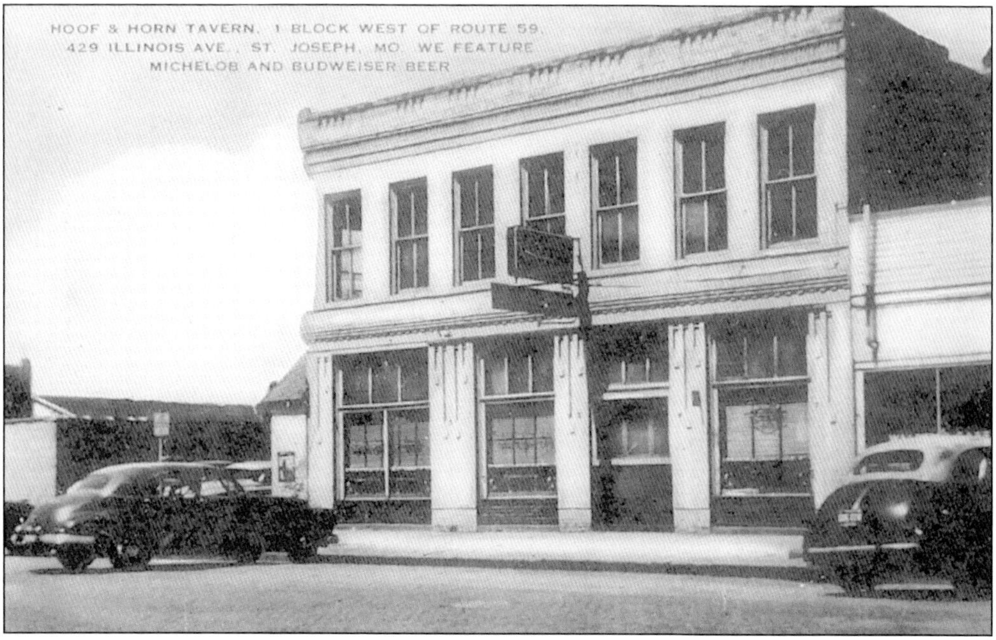

The Hoof and Horn at 429 Illinois Avenue catered to the men working in the stockyards and to travelers just passing through. It was started *c.* 1900 but was later purchased by a police officer, who cleaned up the establishment's reputation and turned it into a tavern. Today, it is the oldest restaurant in St. Joseph, having only closed once—in the 1980s, between owners.

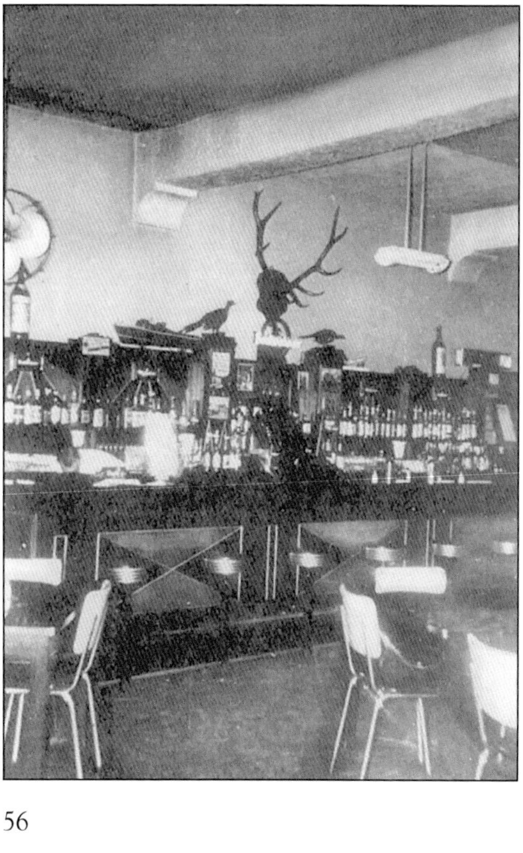

The Hoof and Horn still looks like it did in this photograph. Sets of horns from great beasts line the walls, and a mural depicting the Old West is on one wall. The restaurant eventually expanded, but little else about it has changed.

Six

ADVERTISING CARDS

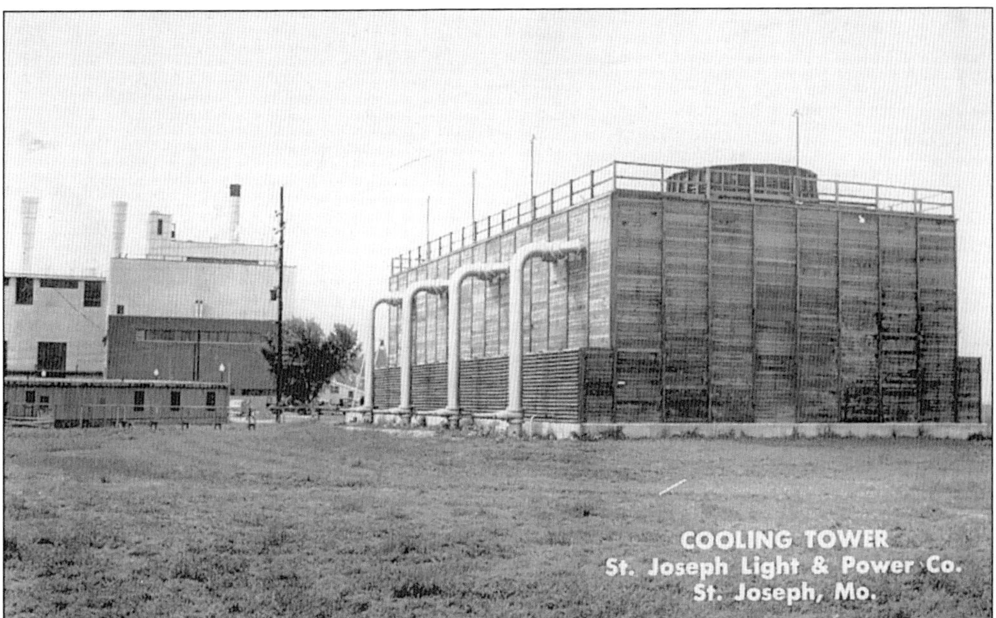

The cooling tower for the St. Joseph Light & Power Company had a capacity of 21,400 gallons per minute. The card was issued by J.F. Pritchard & Co. of Kansas City, Missouri, designers and constructors of the tower. The caption on the card reads as follows: "Here is an example of the foresight and sound engineering planning employed by the St. Joseph Light & Power Company officials in designing this power plant to better serve the best interests of the community."

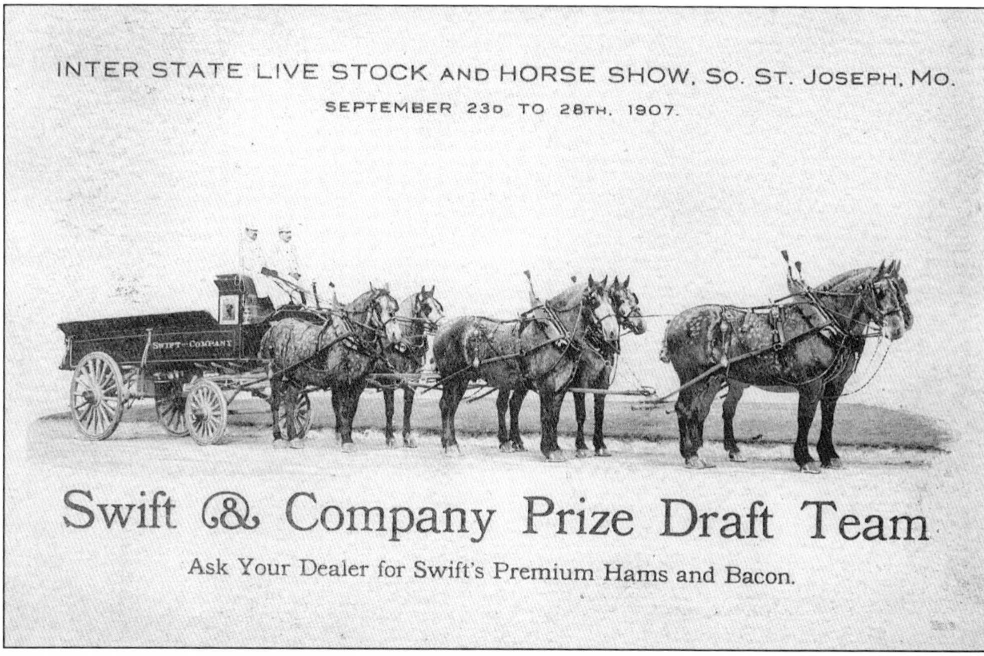

The Swift and Company Prize Draft Team was an advertisement for Swift. The team was scheduled to appear at the Inter-State Live Stock and Horse Show in south St. Joseph on September 23–28, 1907.

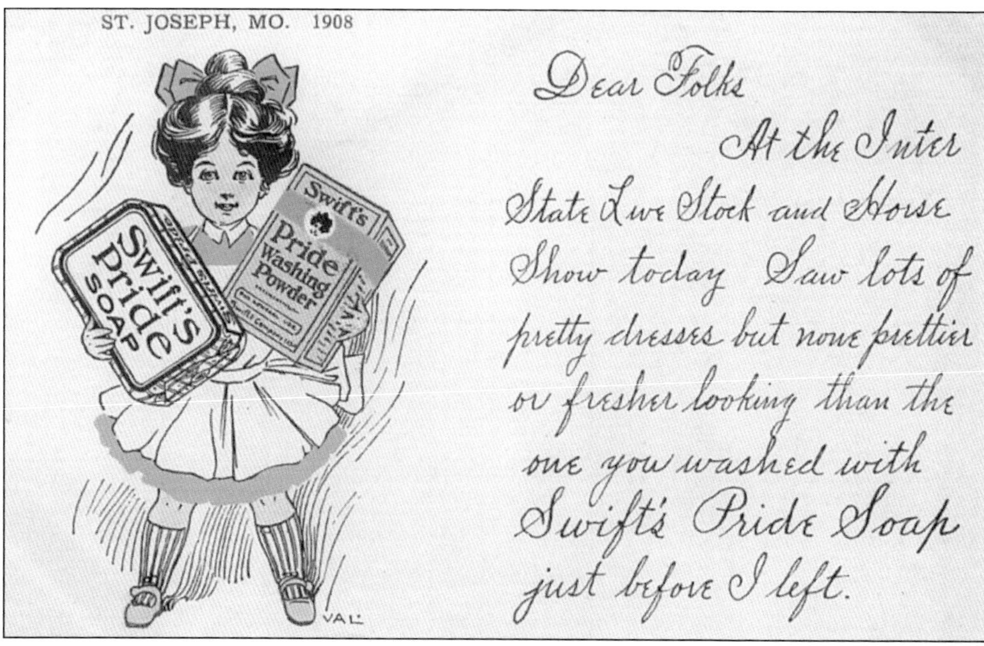

Another ad for the Inter-State Live Stock and Horse show also advertises the Swift's Pride Soap and Washing Powder.

Some companies issued advertising calendar cards. The St. Joseph Transfer Co. was one such company. The company's office, warehouse, and stables were located at Third and Charles Streets, and its phone number was 341. The calendar was for 1909.

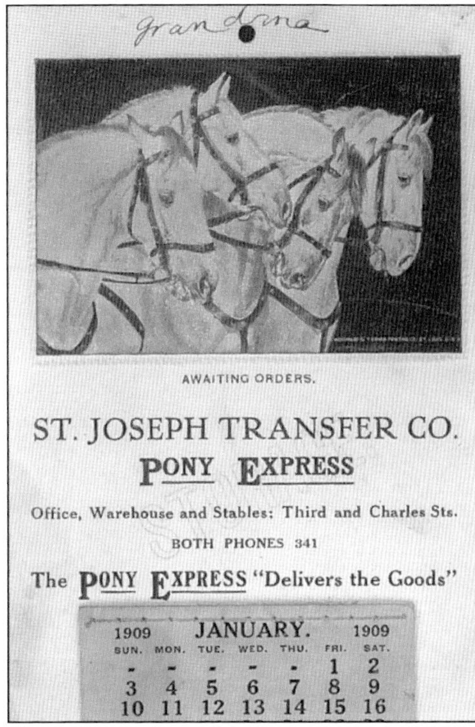

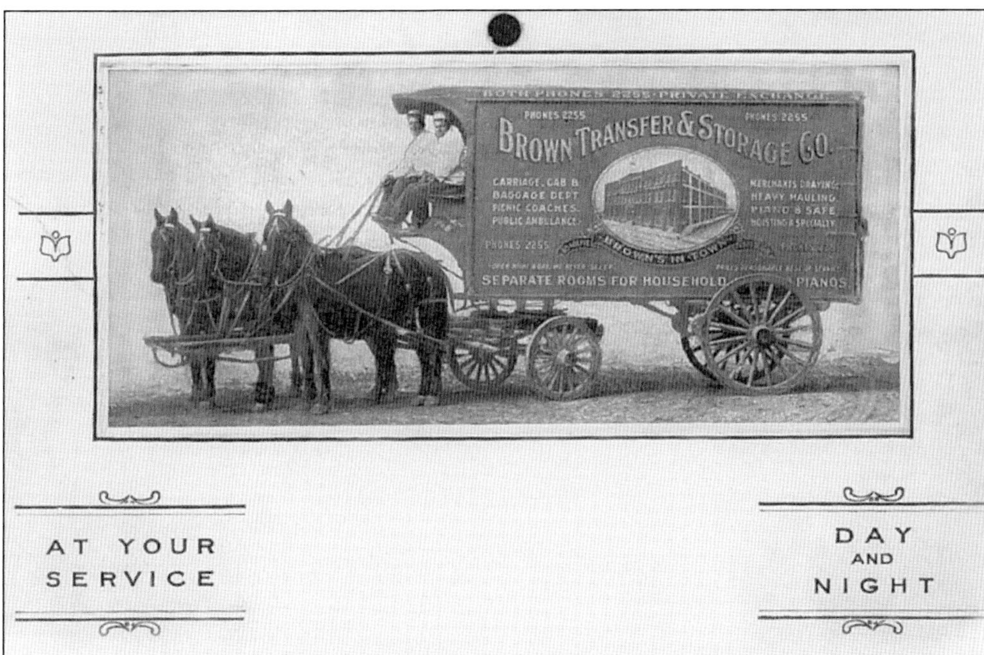

This card from the Brown Transfer and Storage Co. shows their three-hitch team. The company was located on South Sixth Street, and its stables were located at the northeast corner of Fifth and Olive Streets. The company has since moved; it no longer uses horses but is still in operation as one of the oldest businesses in St. Joseph.

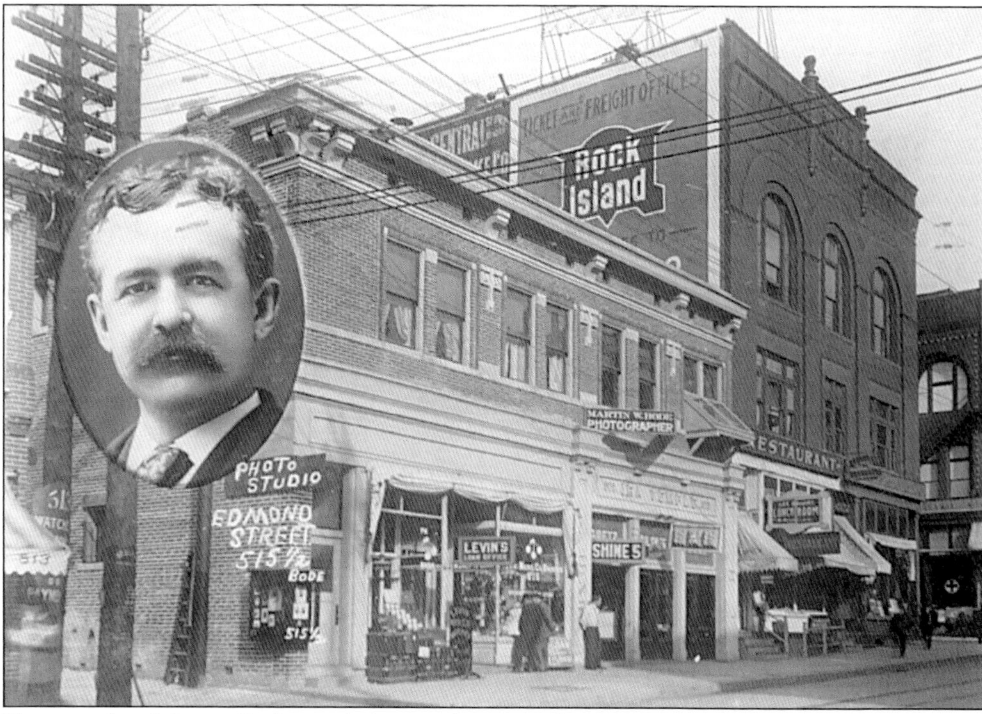

Photographer Martin Bode used this card as an advertisement for his business, located at 515 1/2 Felix Street. The card also shows the street scene, with an ad for the Rock Island Railroad on one building and a restaurant below it.

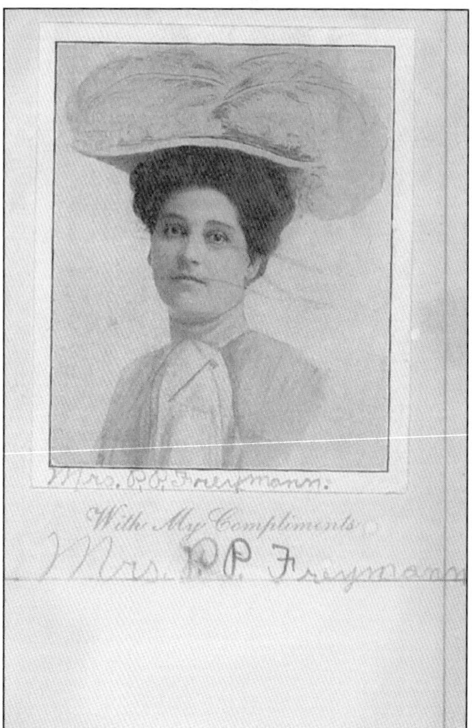

This card is an advertisement for Mrs. P.P. Freymann at the American Calendar Co. Office at 620 Felix Street. The calendar was removed from the card, but it dates to c. 1905. The back reads, "Thanking you for past patronage and earnestly soliciting your future trade, I beg to state my line of Spring Millinery will excel all showing in the city."

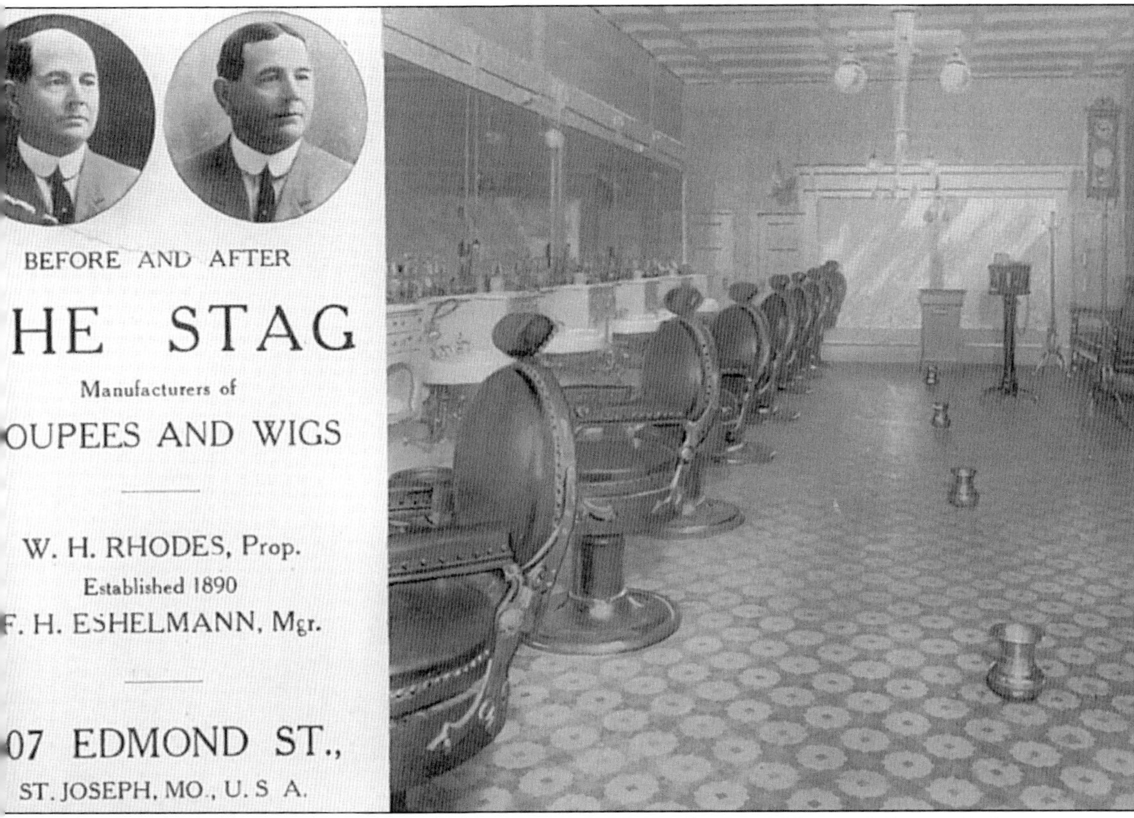

W.H. Rhodes used this card to advertise his toupees and wigs for men. The card shows a before-and-after view of a man with a toupee (upper left corner). The business, established in 1890, was located at the corner of 607 Edmond Street. A Kansas City company made the postcards for Mr. Rhodes.

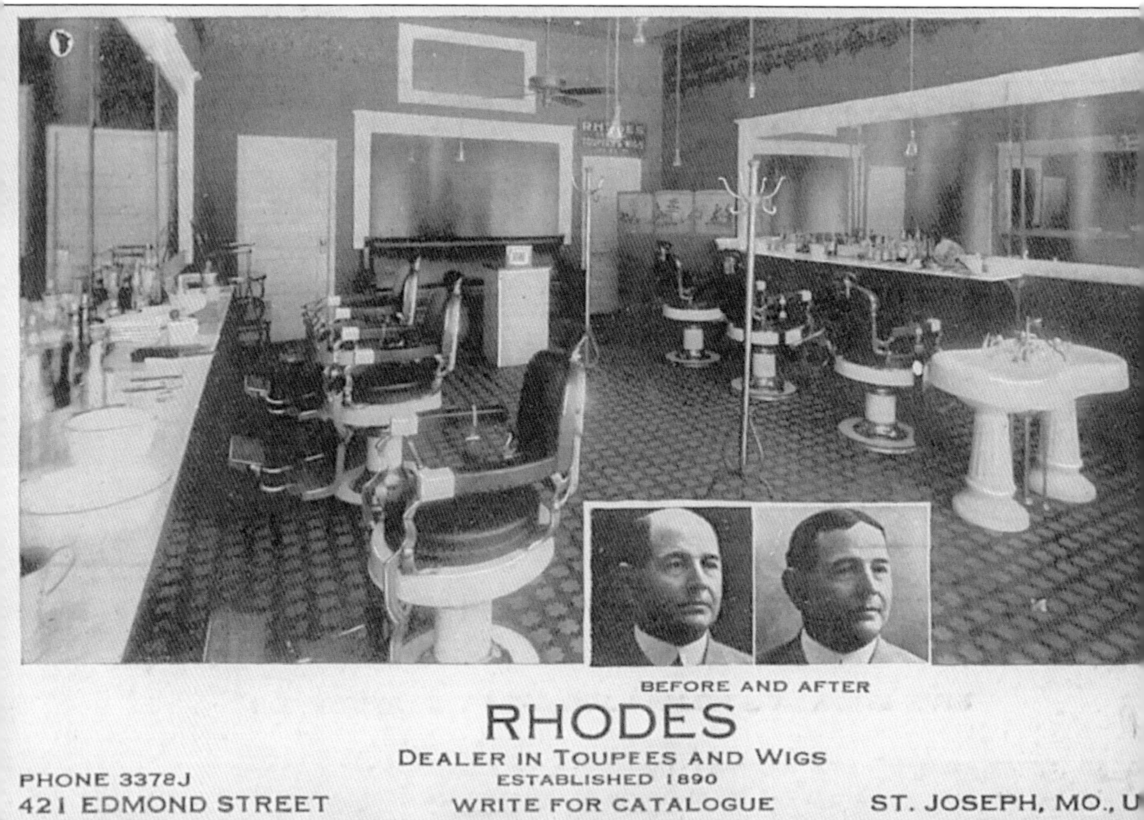

This is a more extensive advertisement for Mr. Rhodes, who apparently moved his shop to 421 Edmond Street. The postcard folds out to show two before-and-after photos, and reminds men, "women do not like to trade with a bald clerk." The last sentence reads, "If not interested, please send to some bald headed man."

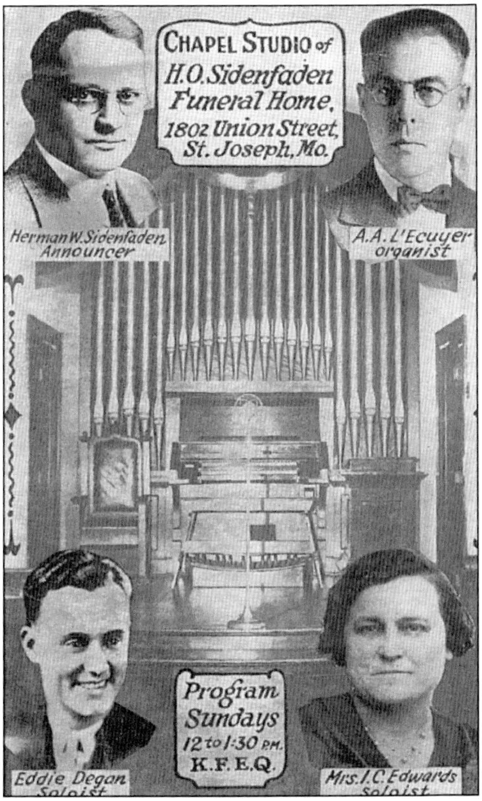

The H.O. Sidenfaden Funeral Home, the oldest in St. Joseph, once advertised its weekly radio show with a postcard. The funeral home was located at 1802 Union Street. The program was broadcast on radio station KFEQ from noon to 1:30 p.m. on Sundays. Pictured on the card are Eddie Degan, soloist; Mrs. I.C. Edwards, soloist; A.A. L'Ecuyer, organist; and Herman W. Sidenfaden, announcer.

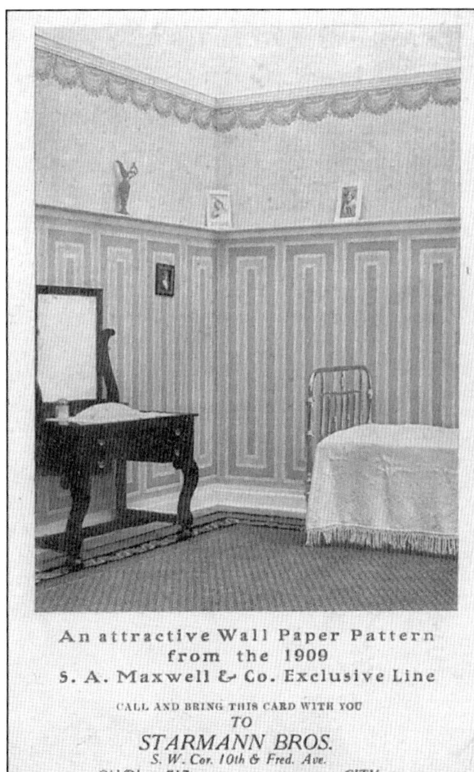

This color postcard from 1909 was an advertisement for Starman Brothers, located at Tenth Street and Frederick Avenue. The business sold wall paper and was advertising its S.A. Maxwell & Co. exclusive line.

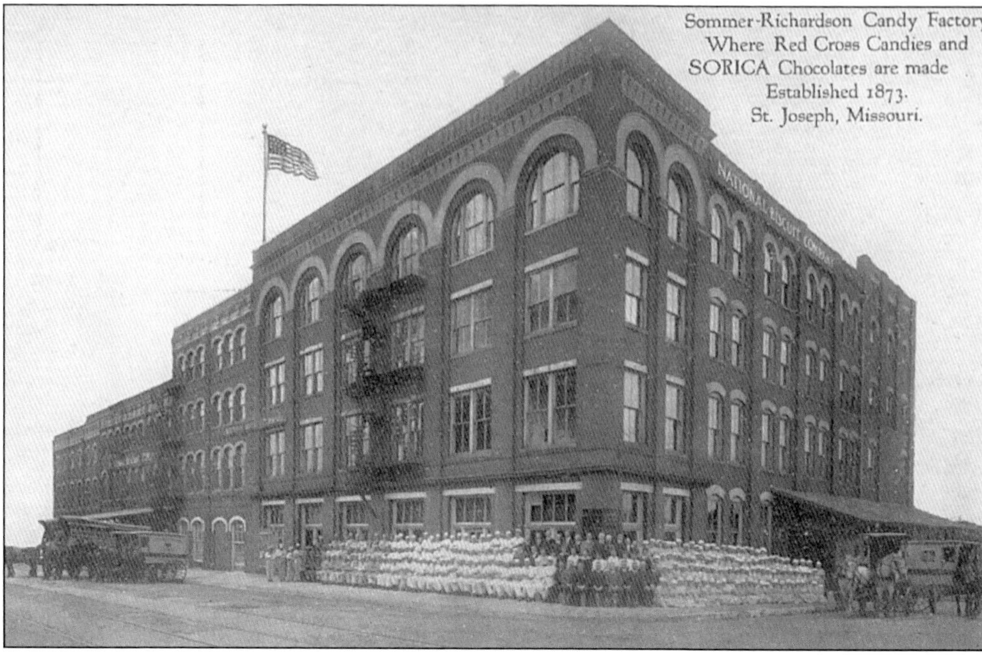

The Sommer-Richardson Candy Factory was one of several that operated in St. Joseph at the turn of the 20th century. The company, established in 1873, made Red Cross candies and chocolates. Notice the employees in white uniforms and white hats lined up in front of the factory and the horse and buggy on the right side. The building was later sold to the National Biscuit Company, which became Nabisco. Today, Nabisco has no presence in St. Joseph.

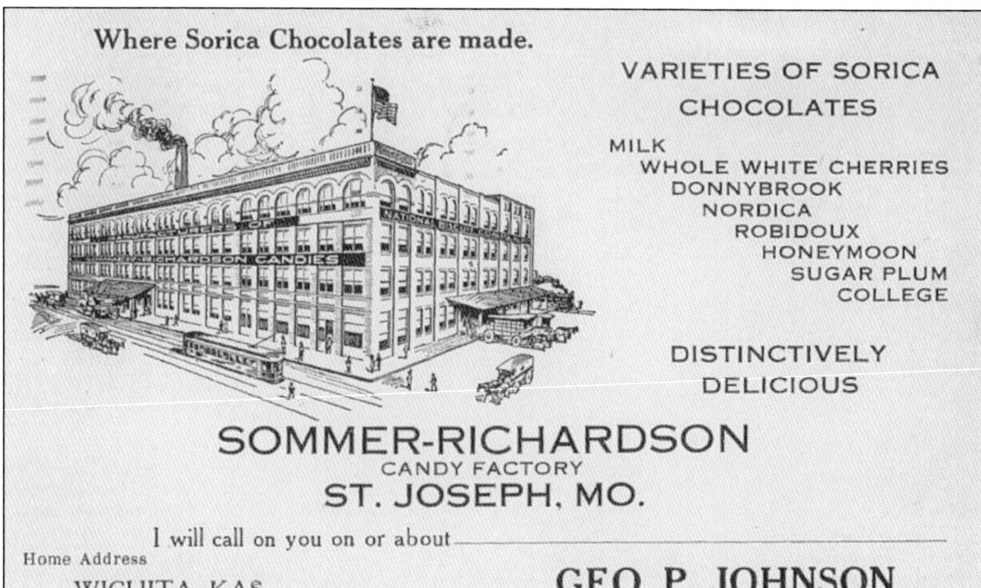

This was a salesman's card advertising Sommer-Richardson's products. The factory was located at 202–224 Main Street, and the building still stands. This postcard was mailed from Wichita, Kansas, where the salesman lived.

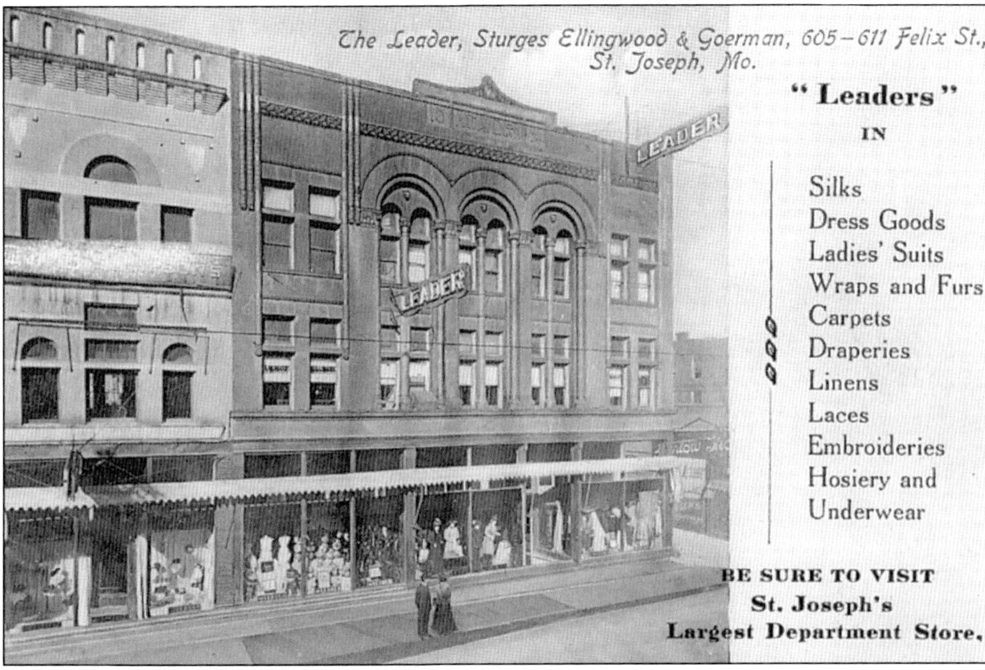

The Leader, Sturges Ellingwood & Goerman, located at 605–611 Felix Street, advertised itself as St. Joseph's largest department store. The store billed itself as the leader in silks, dress goods, ladies' suits, wraps and furs, and linens and laces, among other items. It moved to St. Joseph from Atchison, Kansas, in 1894. In 1900, it employed 35 people.

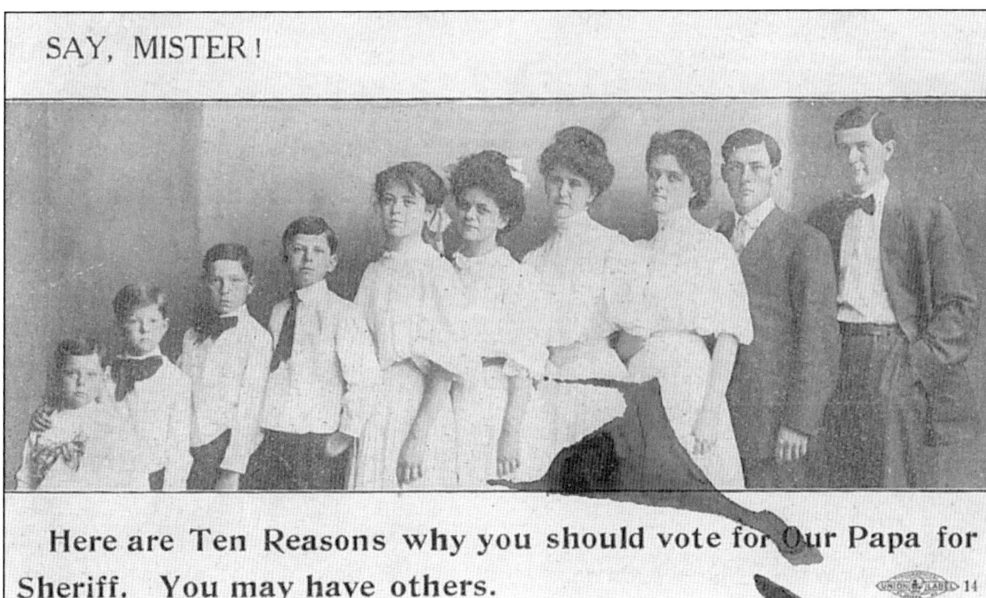

Political candidates also used postcards as a means of advertising. Robert I. Young, a 1908 Democratic candidate for sheriff, mailed out this postcard to garner support. He lost the primary to Otto Theisen, who is pictured on the next page.

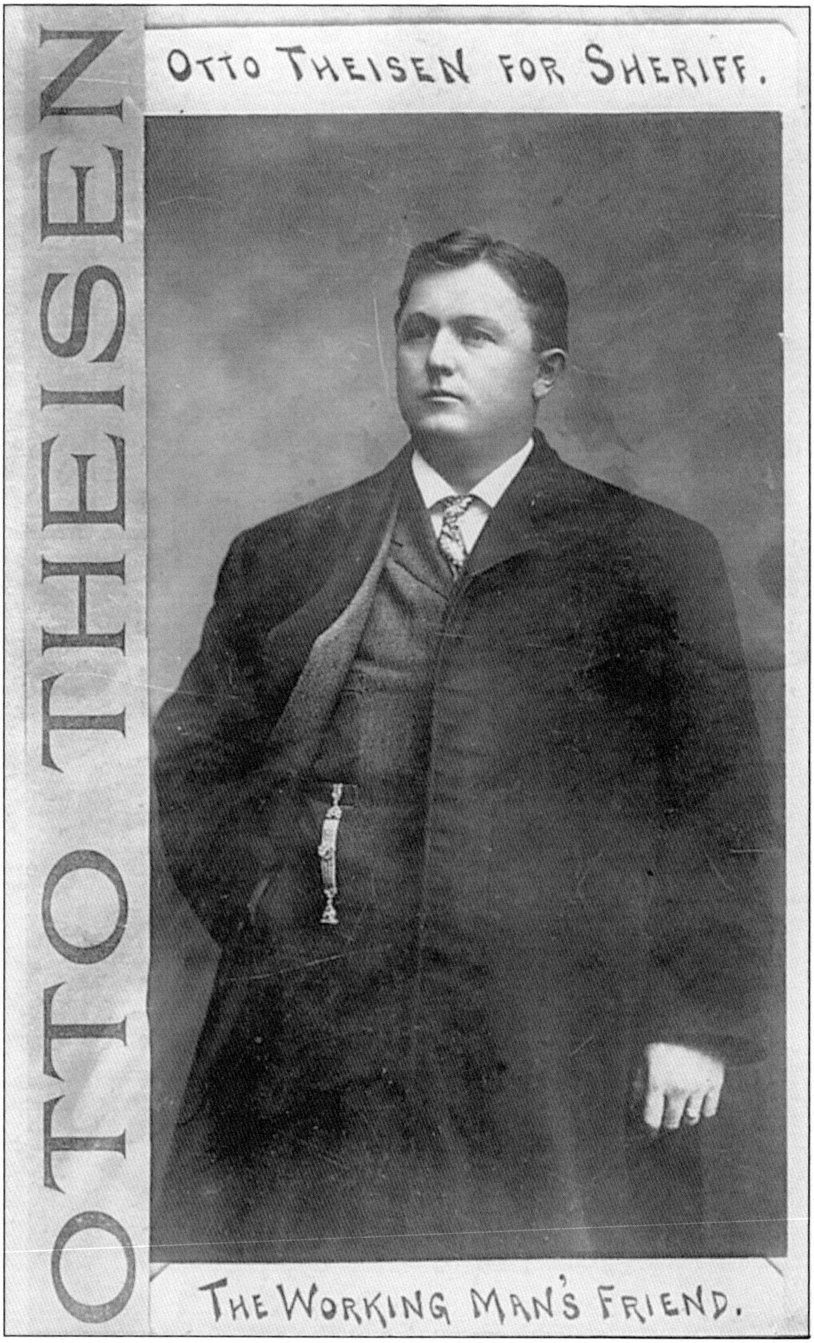

Otto Theisen used this distinguished looking portrait of himself to gather votes in 1908, the first year he was elected sheriff. This postcard is undated but was apparently mailed with the note, "Don't forget to vote for him the 3rd. He is OK." This was one of his early runs for the position of sheriff of Buchanan County; he was also sheriff on November 28, 1933, when an angry mob stormed the jail and demanded release of a black prisoner who had been accused of rape. Mr. Theisen turned the man over to the mob, saying he thought they would lynch other inmates if they couldn't get to the inmate they sought.

Seven

ENTERTAINMENT

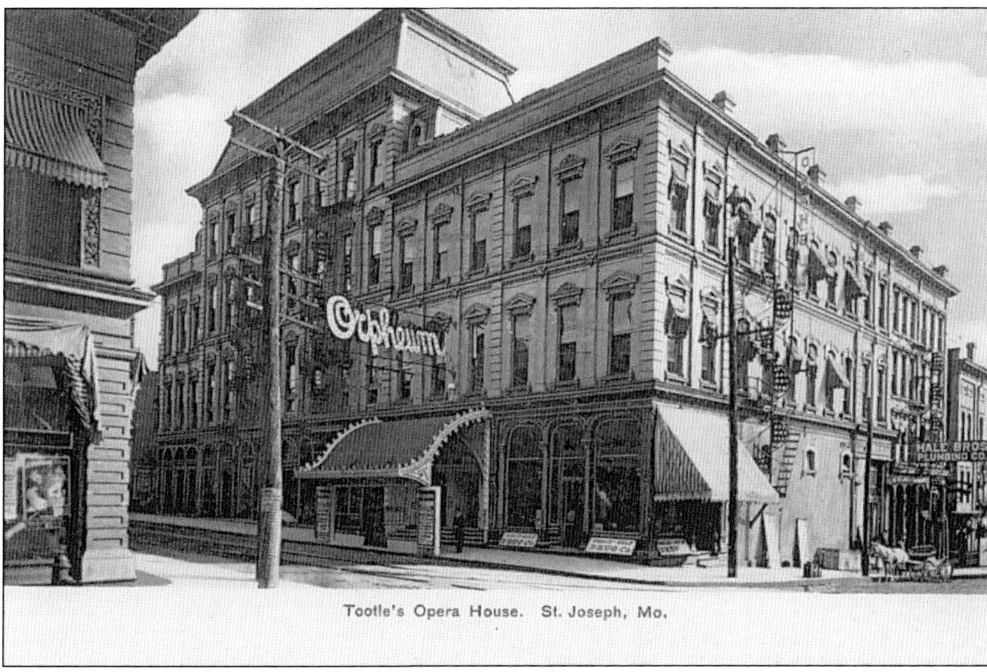

Tootle's Opera House. St. Joseph, Mo.

The Tootle Opera House was built in 1872 and still stands today, though the building was altered in 1932 to make room for office space. It is now known as the Pioneer Building. The opera house was built by Milton Tootle, a banker, at the corner of Fifth and Francis Streets. The cost of the building was $165,000, and its architect was W. Angelo Powell of St. Joseph. From the day the theater hosted its first performance on December 9, 1972, Mr. Tootle was said to have rarely missed a performance. He died 14 years later. At the time of its completion, the theater was regarded as among the most elegant venues west of the Mississippi River.

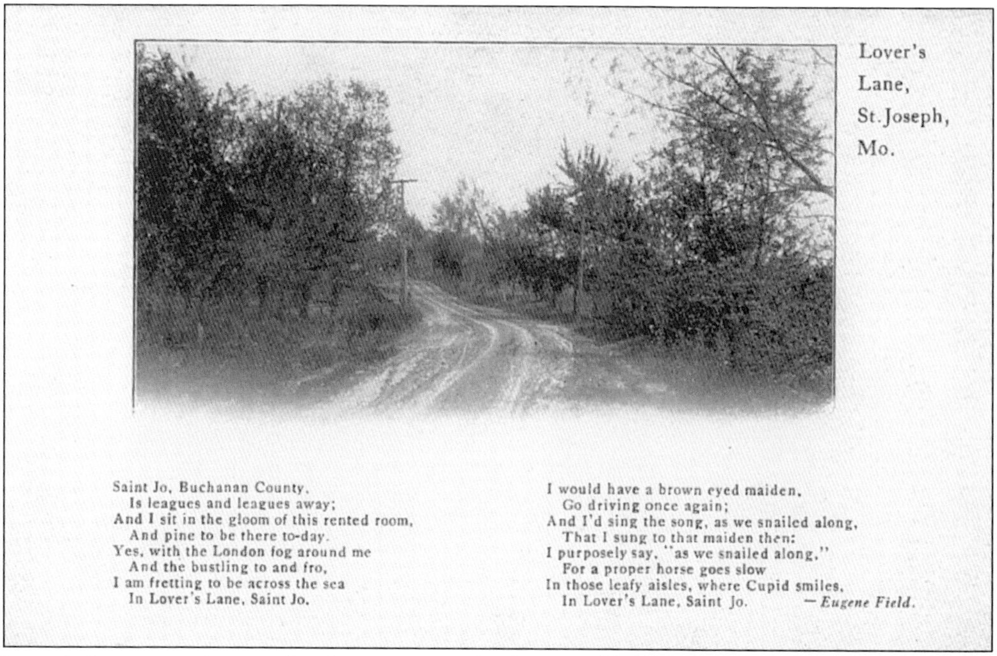

Lover's Lane was immortalized in a poem by Eugene Field, who worked for a St. Joseph newspaper and met his bride here. Field penned the poem in 1899 while living in London; he was somewhat homesick for Missouri.

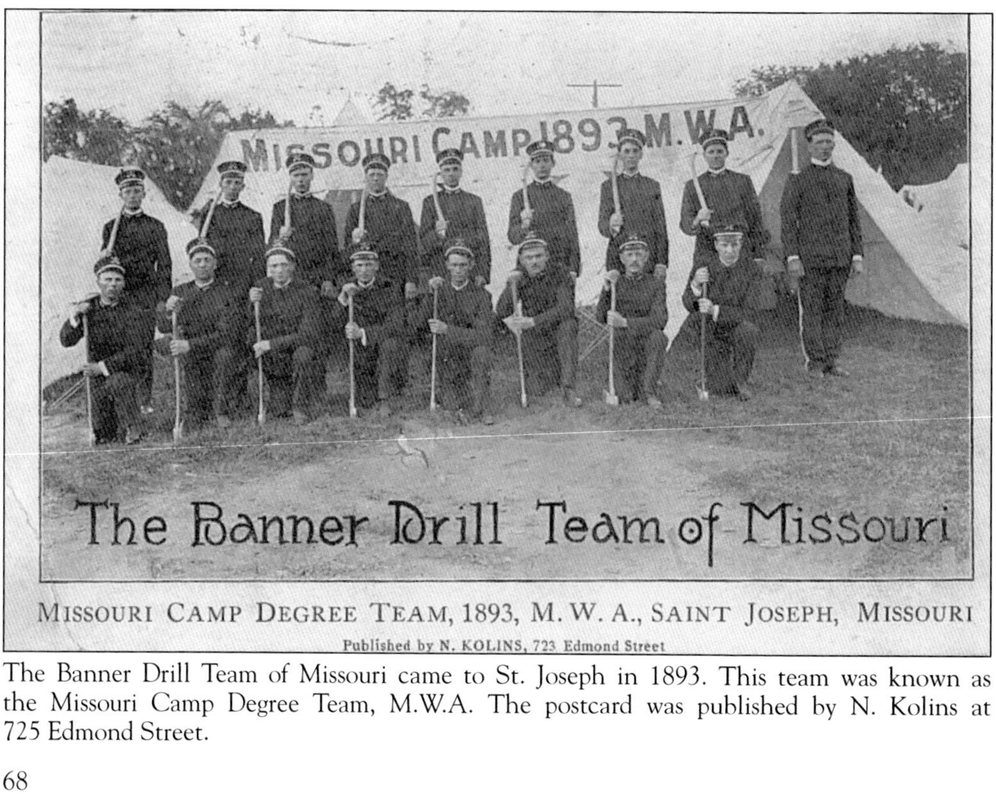

The Banner Drill Team of Missouri came to St. Joseph in 1893. This team was known as the Missouri Camp Degree Team, M.W.A. The postcard was published by N. Kolins at 725 Edmond Street.

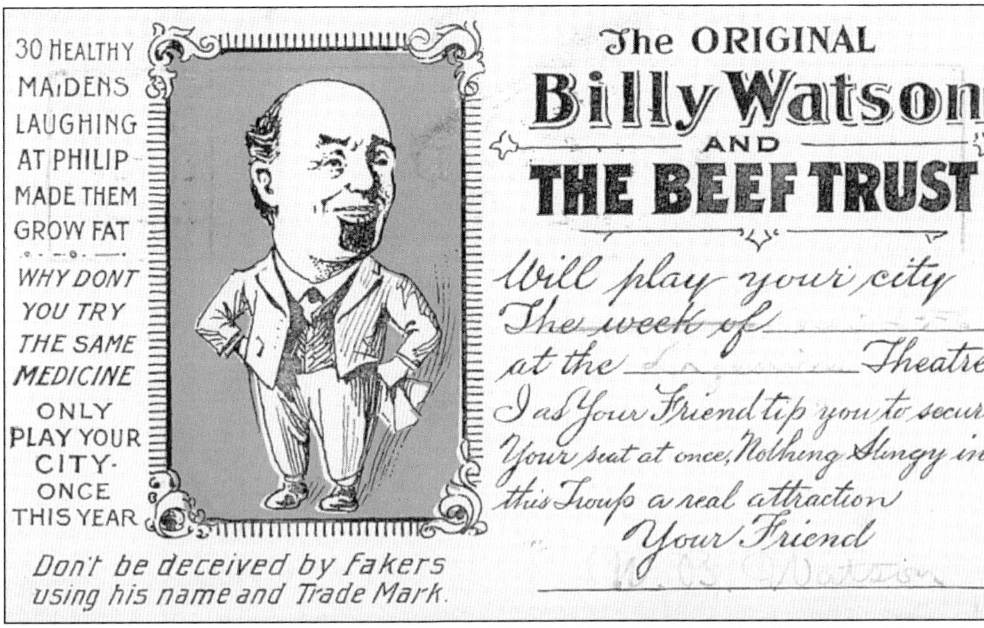

Billy Watson and the Beef Trust was a vaudeville act that played in St. Joseph on November 4–6, 1909, at the Lycium Theater. The ladies in the show were said to be quite large.

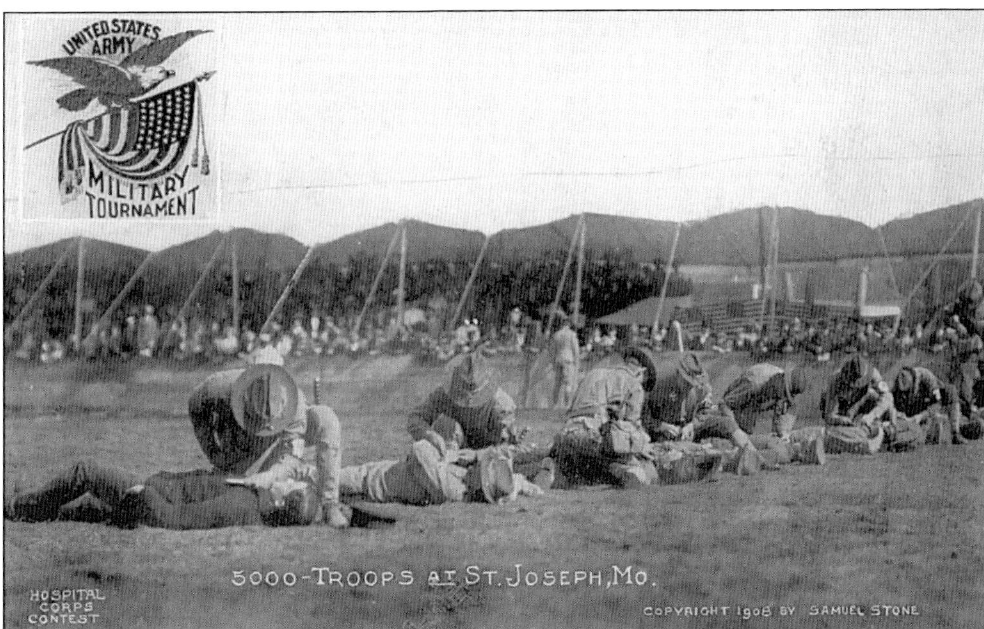

The U.S. Army Military Tournament brought 5,000 troops to St. Joseph in 1908. At the time, it was the largest military tournament ever held in the United States. President William Howard Taft attended during his campaign. A dirigible was test-flown during the event. Among the contests held was the hospital corps contest, shown here.

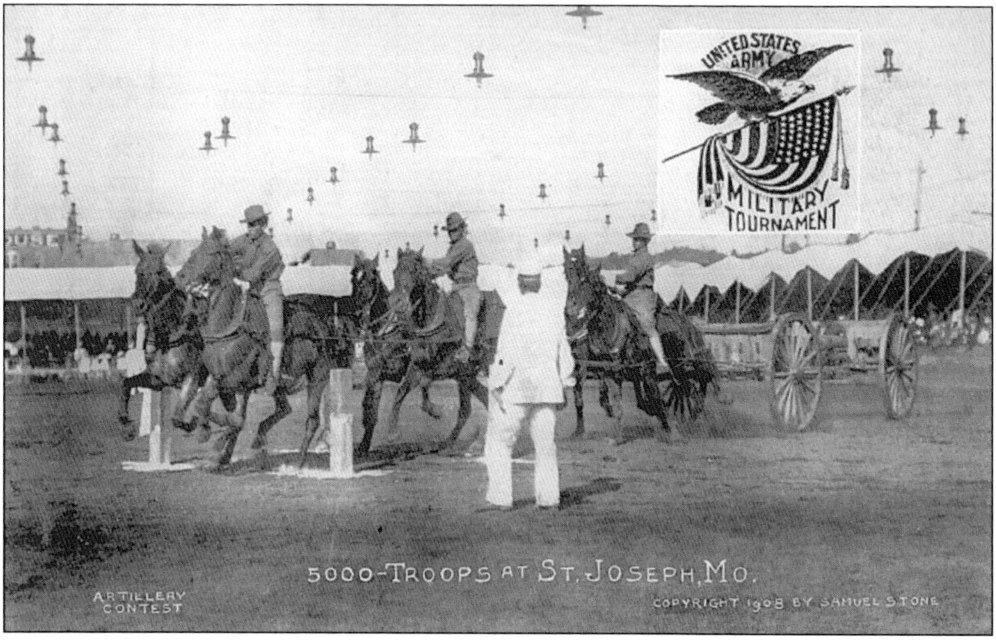

The tournament's other events included this artillery contest. Note the spectators under the tents surrounding the field.

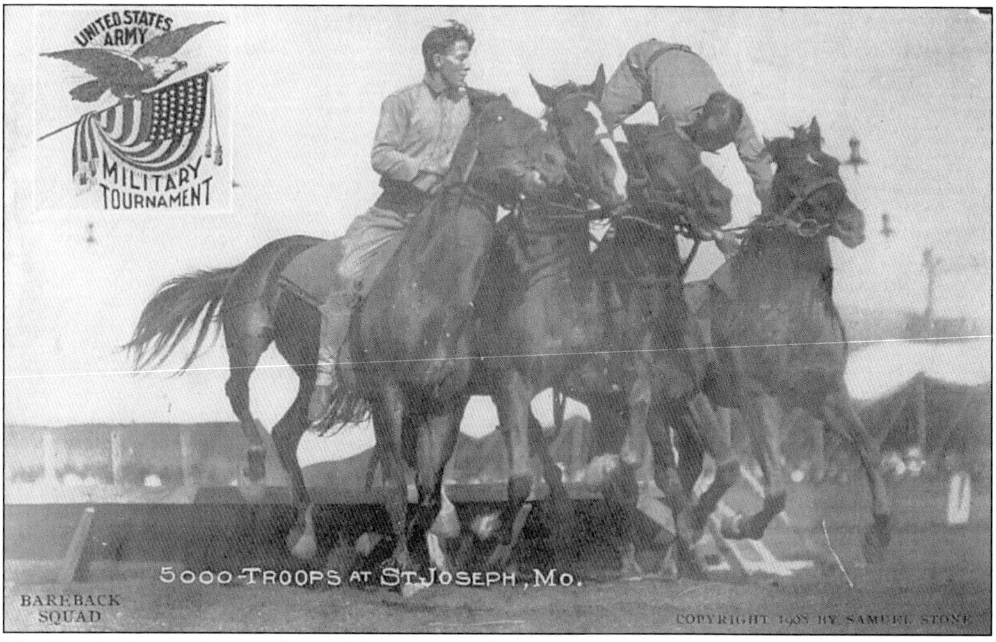

The bareback squad is caught mid-leap in another tournament event.

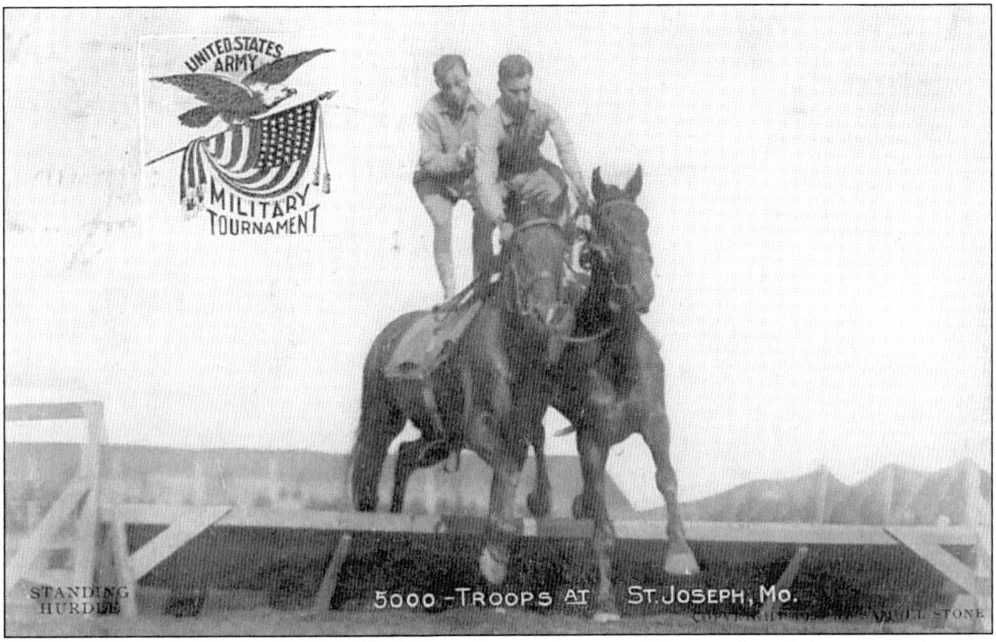

The standing hurdle event was held during the tournament. The sender of the postcard wrote that the troop was "in St. Joseph last week," and the card is postmarked September.

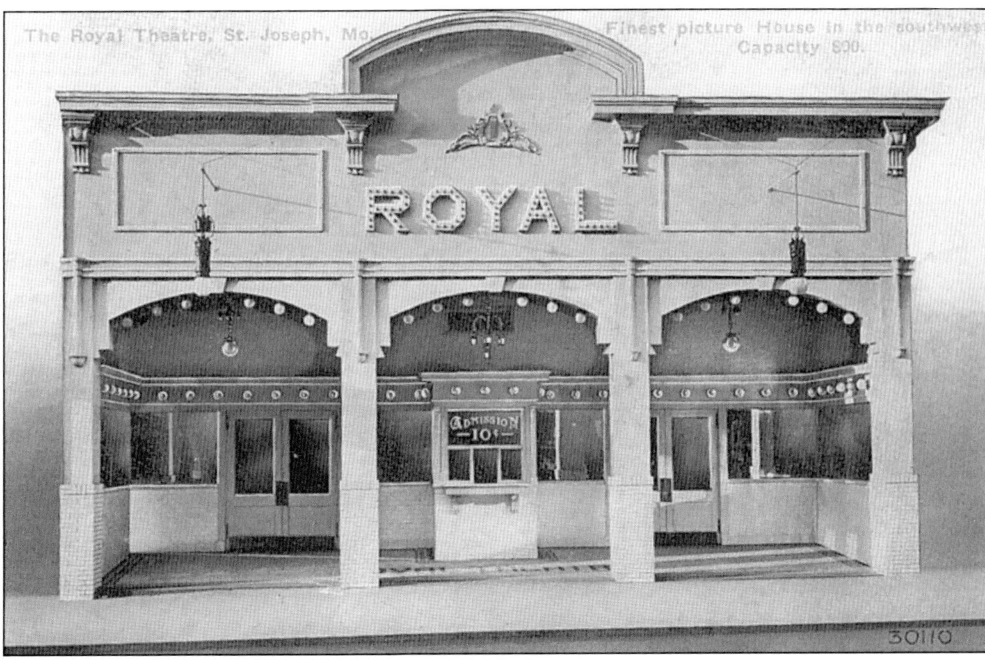

The Royal Theater offered entertainment for 10¢. It was located at 614–16 Edmond Street. The postcard refers to it as the "finest picture house in the Southwest." Its capacity was 800.

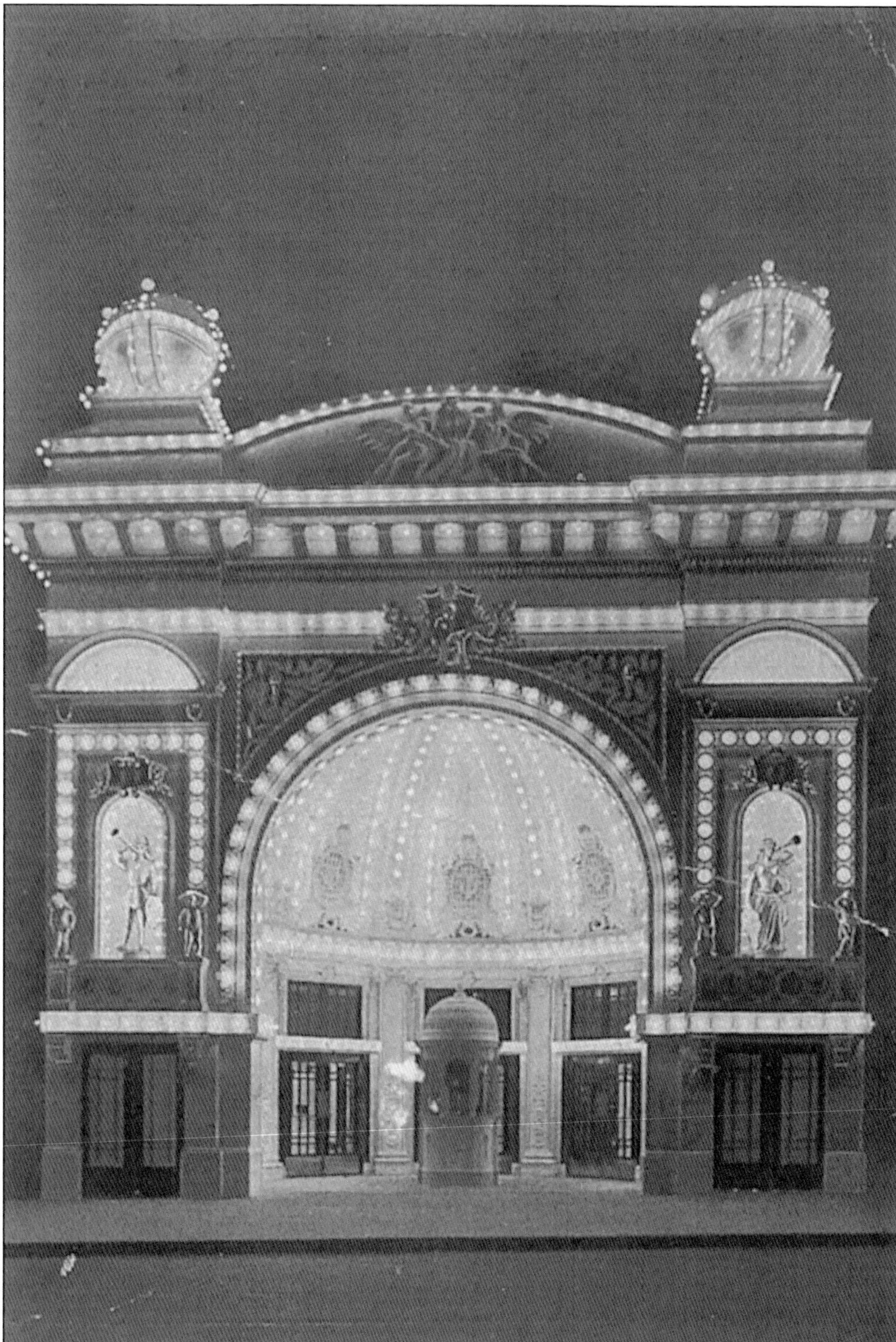

The Saxe's Orpheum Theater was one of the gems of downtown. It was located at Fifth and Edmond Streets, but is no longer standing. The theater was brightly lit at night.

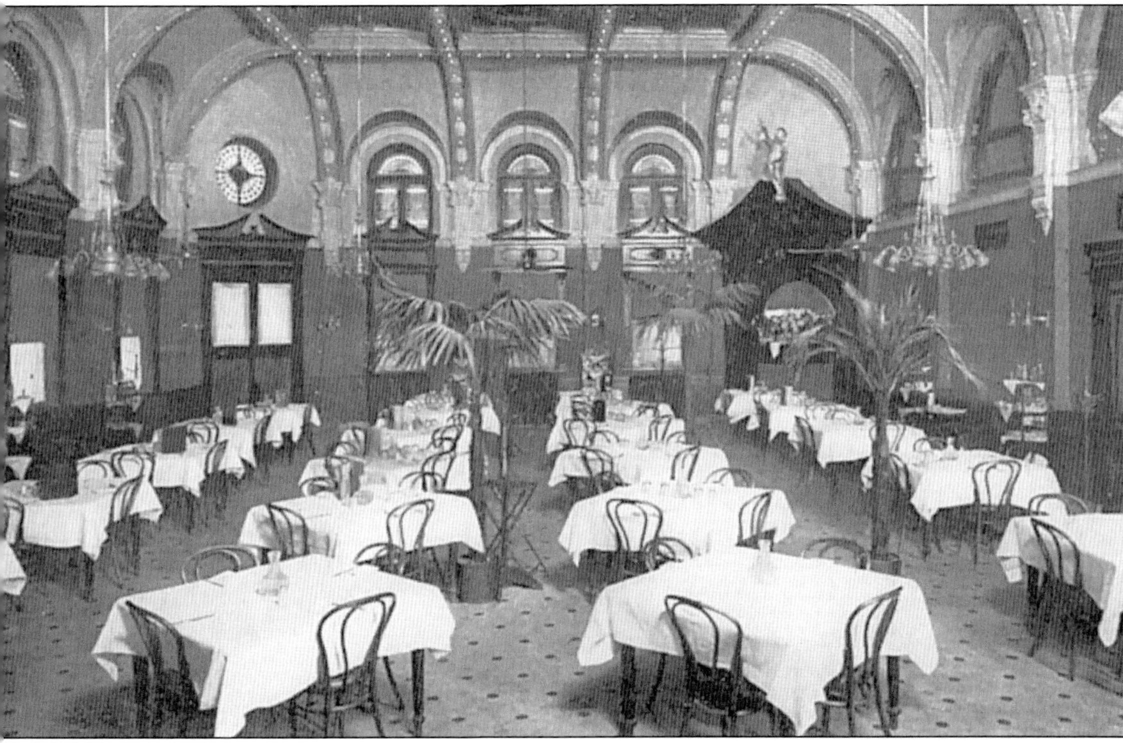

The Schlitz Cafe was a popular restaurant at the turn of the 20th century, but despite this, it closed a few years later. The building then became Saxe's Orpheum Theater. It retained its majestic interior, but was given a new façade.

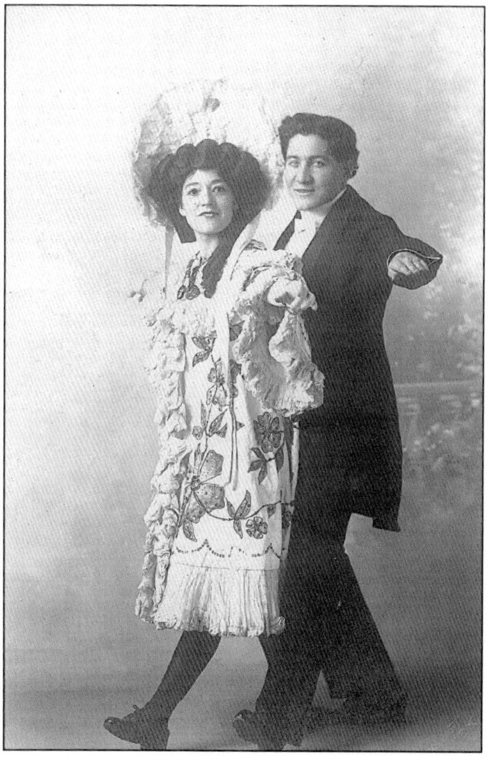

This vaudeville act, the Renos, was based in St. Joseph but traveled the country entertaining people. Mr. and Mrs. Denny Reno started as circus performers in the 1890s. In 1905, they chose St. Joseph as their home and built a house at 110 Sixth Avenue. In 1908, they switched to vaudeville and produced a musical comedy show that included acrobatics, music, and magic. They were still performing in 1960.

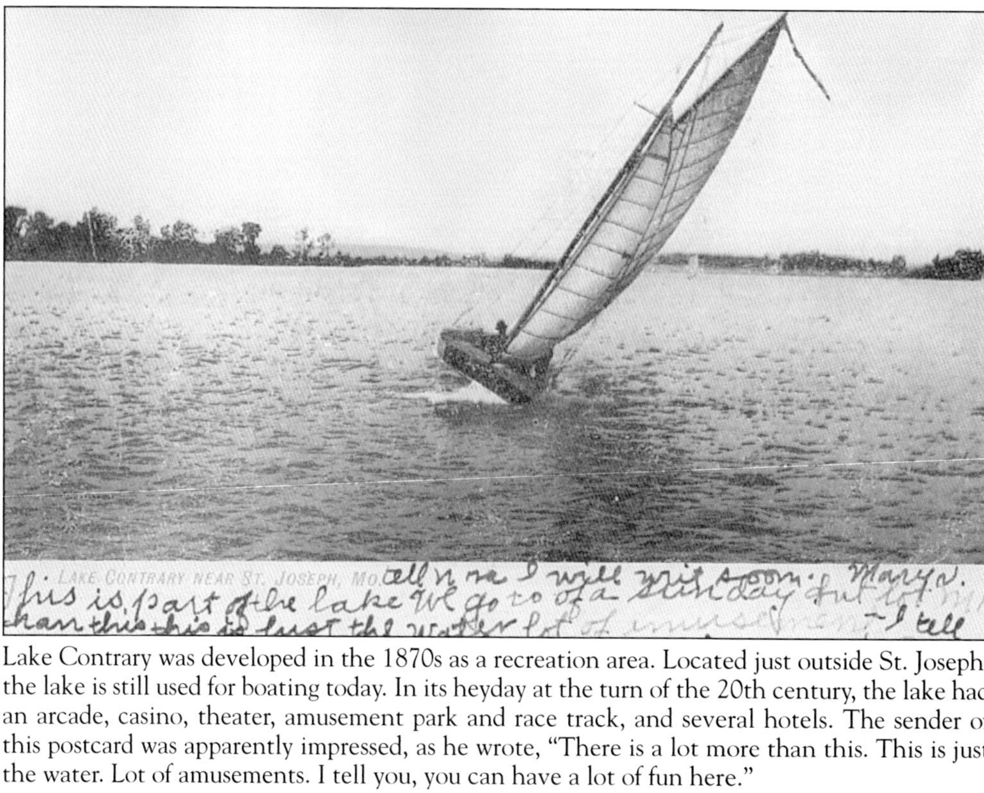

Lake Contrary was developed in the 1870s as a recreation area. Located just outside St. Joseph, the lake is still used for boating today. In its heyday at the turn of the 20th century, the lake had an arcade, casino, theater, amusement park and race track, and several hotels. The sender of this postcard was apparently impressed, as he wrote, "There is a lot more than this. This is just the water. Lot of amusements. I tell you, you can have a lot of fun here."

Yacht races were one of the highlights of Lake Contrary. The *Sylvia* was labeled the champion of the lake and holder of the Lake Manawa Challenge Cup. The boat was owned by the Van Brunts, brothers who owned St. Joseph Light & Power. Boats were shipped in by railroad cars for races, and a grandstand was constructed at the Lotus Club for viewers.

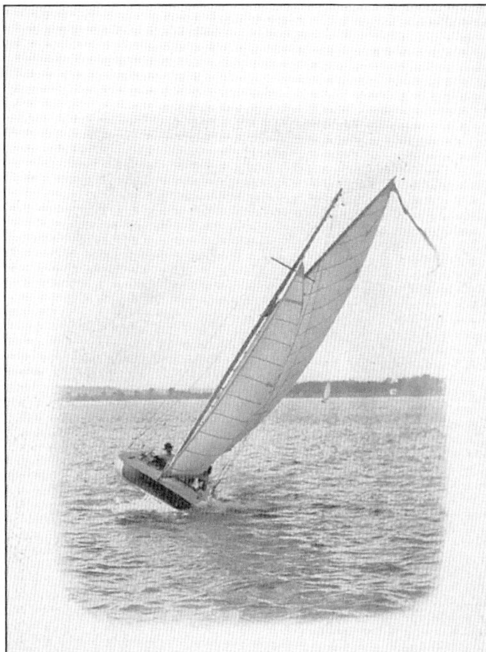

"Sylvia," Champion of Lake Contrary, St. Joseph, Mo., and holder of Lake Manawa Challenge Cup.

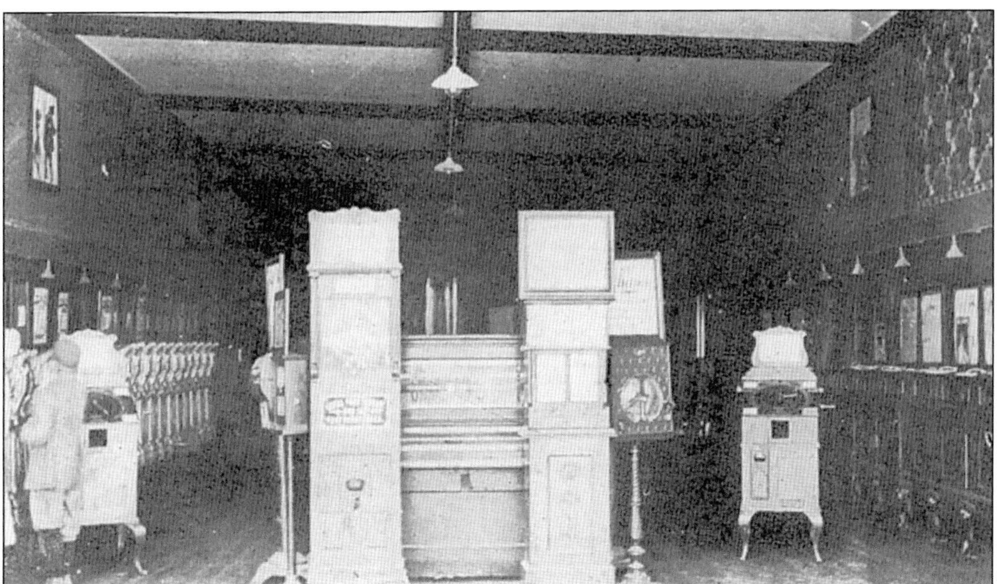

Mac's Arcade was one source of entertainment at the lake. It was a penny arcade when it was in operation. It was part of the amusement park and was probably built in 1910.

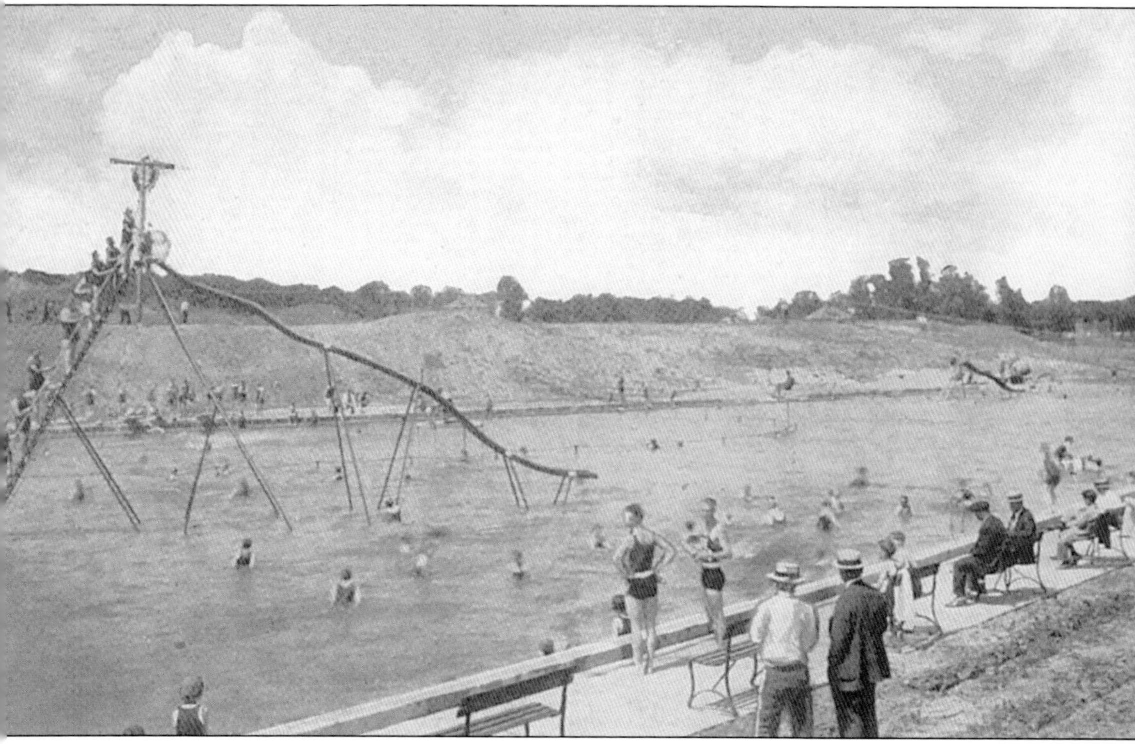

The municipal swimming pool boasted a water slide. It was one of several in the city. This one was constructed c. 1920. Waterslides have become popular in recent years, but as this card shows, it's just re-inventing what was a popular pastime for our grandparents.

Eight

KRUG PARK

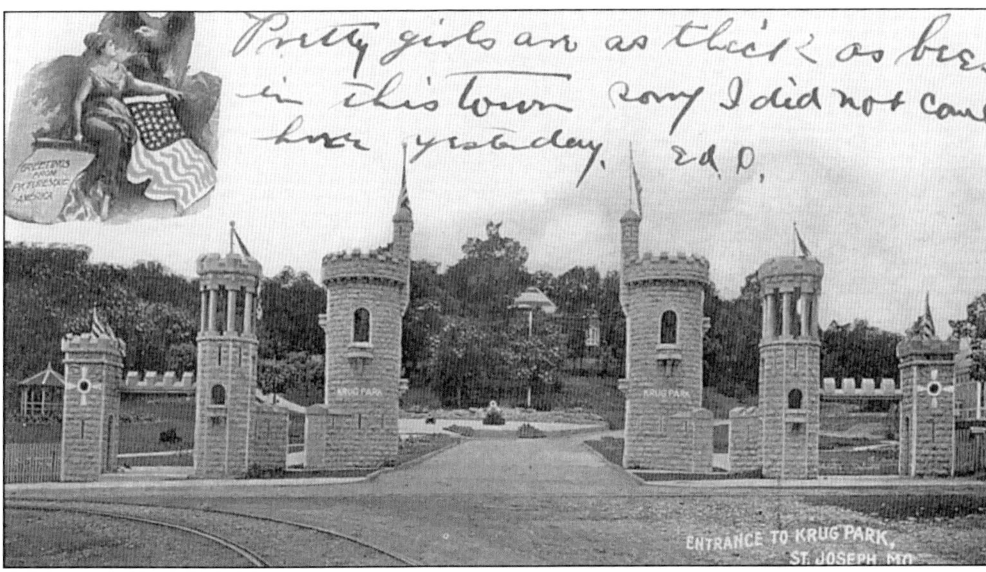

Named for Henry Krug Sr., owner of one of the first packing houses in St. Joseph, Krug Park was constructed because Mr. Krug did not want children going to the beer gardens along St. Joseph Avenue, near his home. The park's construction started in 1890 with 10 acres; one year later, it had doubled to 20 acres. Now, through the generosity of Krug heirs, the park is made up of 160 acres.

This view shows the turn-of-the-20th-century entrance to Krug Park. The towers were constructed in 1902 and were suggested by superintendent Rudolph Rau. It reminded him of the castles in Germany, his homeland. The entrance was financed by the St. Joseph Railway, Light, Heat and Power Company. The towers were the last Rau innovation to be removed when the park was renovated in 1936. The visitor to Krug Park who signed this postcard was impressed with more than the park. He wrote, "Pretty girls are as thick as bees in this town. Sorry I did not come here yesterday." It is signed Ed D.

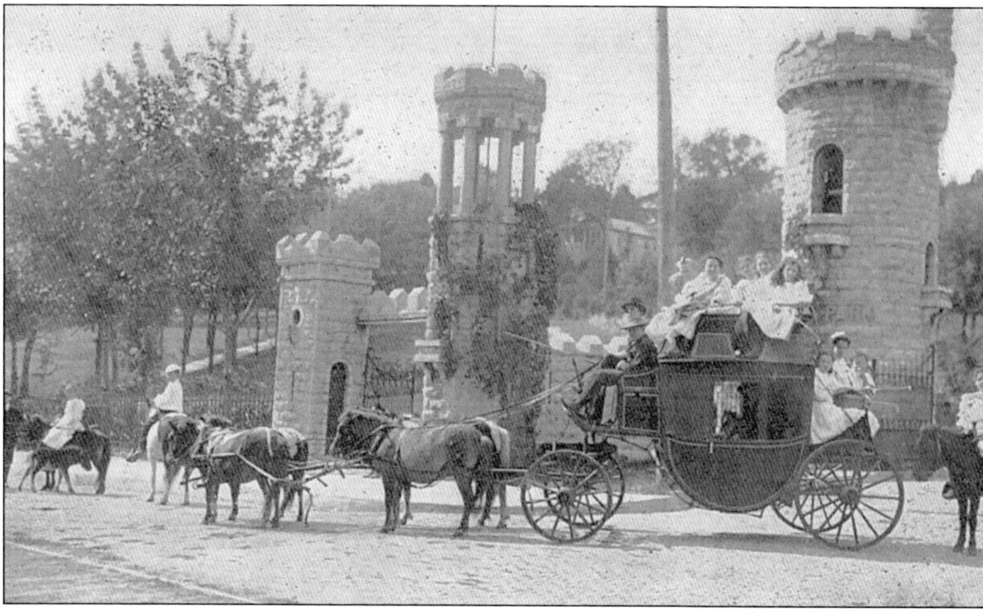

This stagecoach was taking these children on a leisurely ride through Krug Park. The ponies were kept on the Krug Mansion lawn.

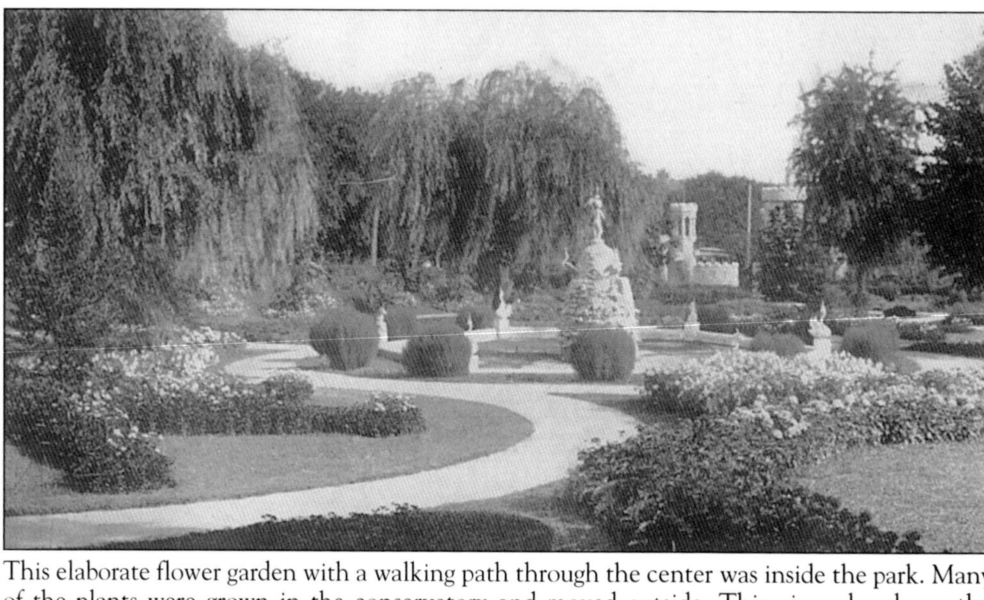

This elaborate flower garden with a walking path through the center was inside the park. Many of the plants were grown in the conservatory and moved outside. This view also shows the park's fountain in the center.

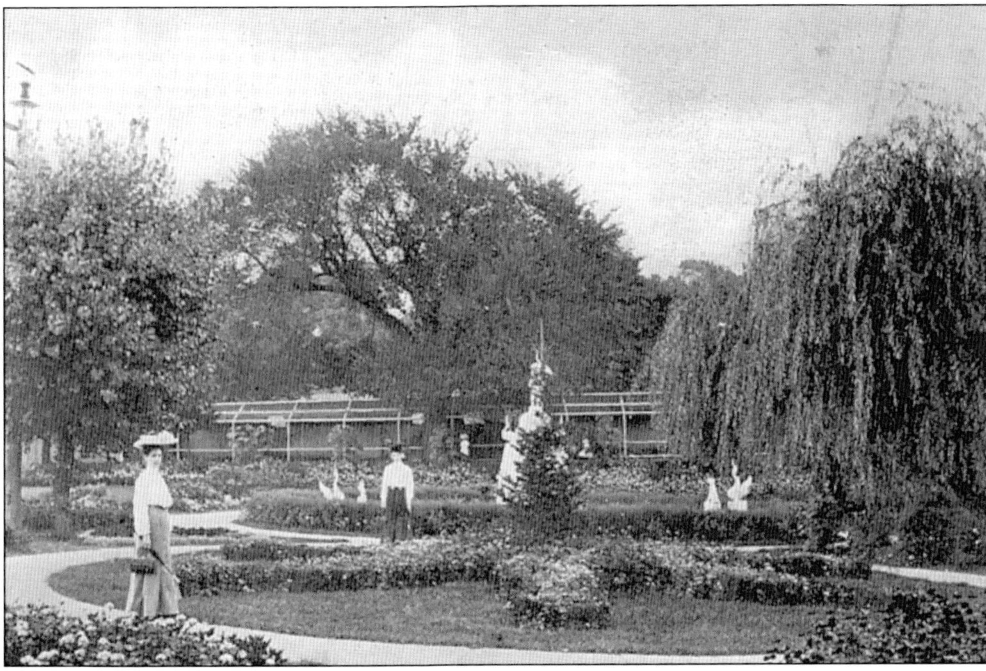

This is another photo of the flower garden, this time with visitors strolling through it.

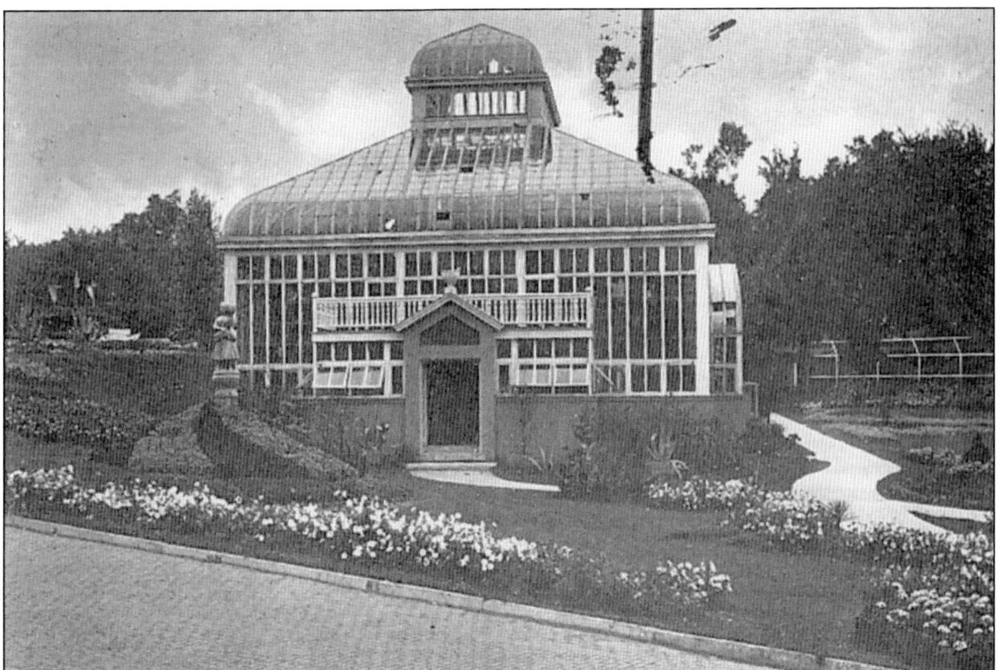

This conservatory at Krug Park was built in 1899 and cost $3,500. Measuring roughly 22 by 52 feet, it was used for growing flowers and such exotic plants as banana trees. The conservatory also hosted mum shows in which an orchestra would play on the balcony. It was torn down in 1924–25.

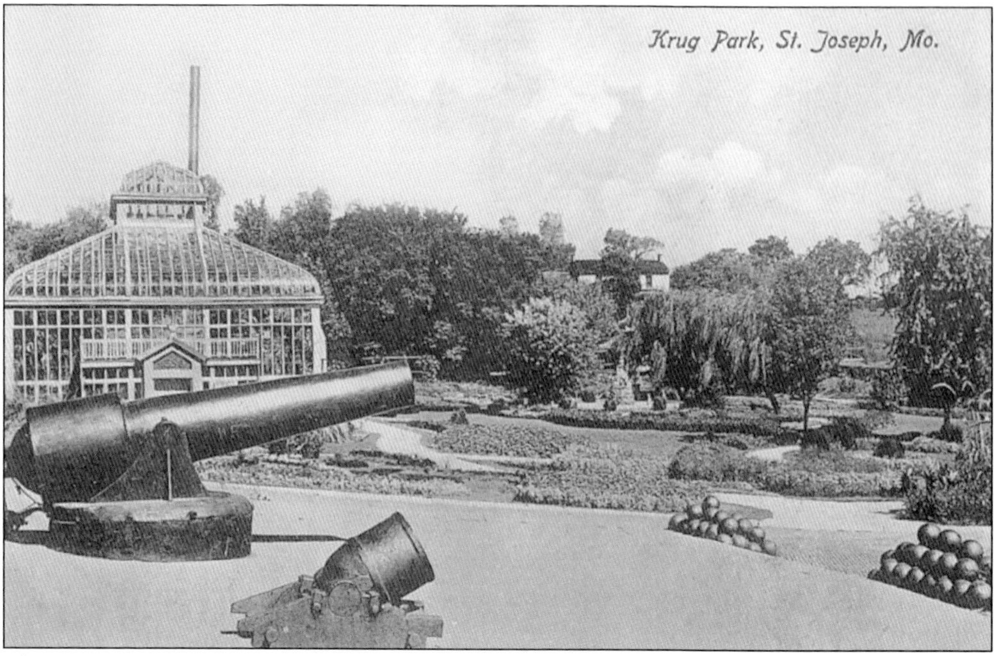

This cannon and cannonballs were located near the conservatory in 1908, when this picture was taken. They were in active use at Fort Barrancas, Florida, during the Spanish-American War. In the early 1920s, they were removed and placed in a junk pile for nearly two decades until they were donated to a World War II scrap-metal drive in the early 1940s.

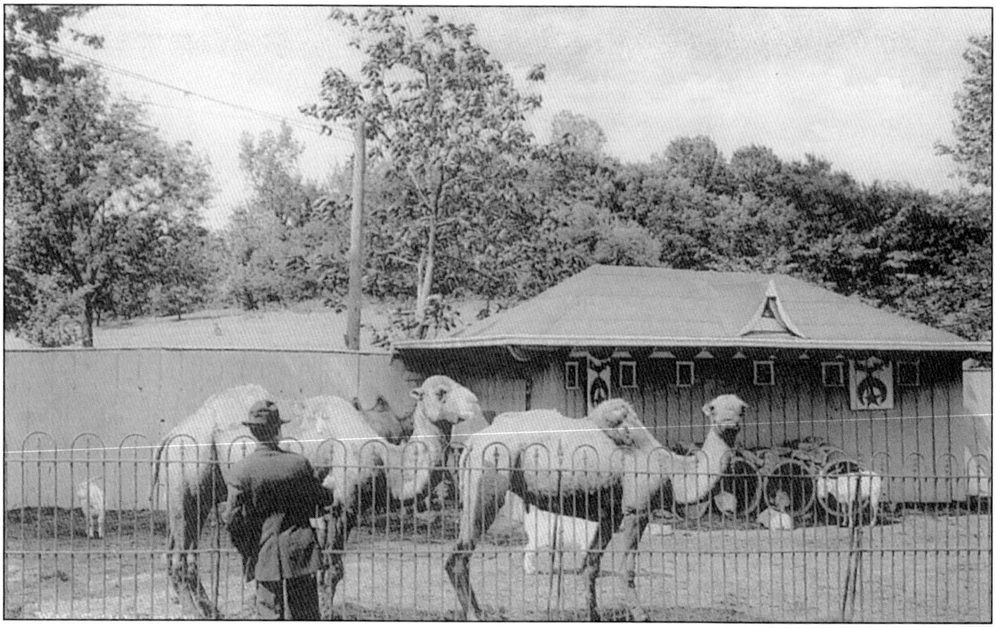

The Moila Shrine Temple kept its camels at Krug Park when they weren't on tour. Thiswas the beginning of the zoo at Krug Park that was developed by Rudolph Rau. The menagerie had bears, monkeys, and camels. They were named Pet and Moila. Pet was named for former St. Joseph Mayor A.P. "Pet" Clayton. Alligators, wolves, foxes, and goats were also kept in the park.

Nine

FRIENDS AND FAMILY

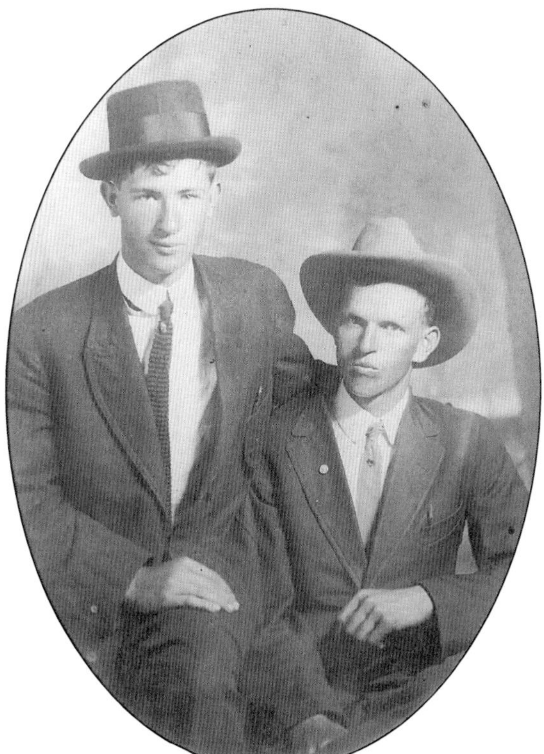

Just as we might have a family portrait made into a Christmas card, the generations before us had their pictures made into postcards, which they sent to friends and family. Portrait studios not only took the photos but also produced postcards, an efficient method for those wishing to make a picture into a postcard. This postcard is identified only as "Mr. Dempsey Babb and his friend." The portrait was taken at the Majestic Studio.

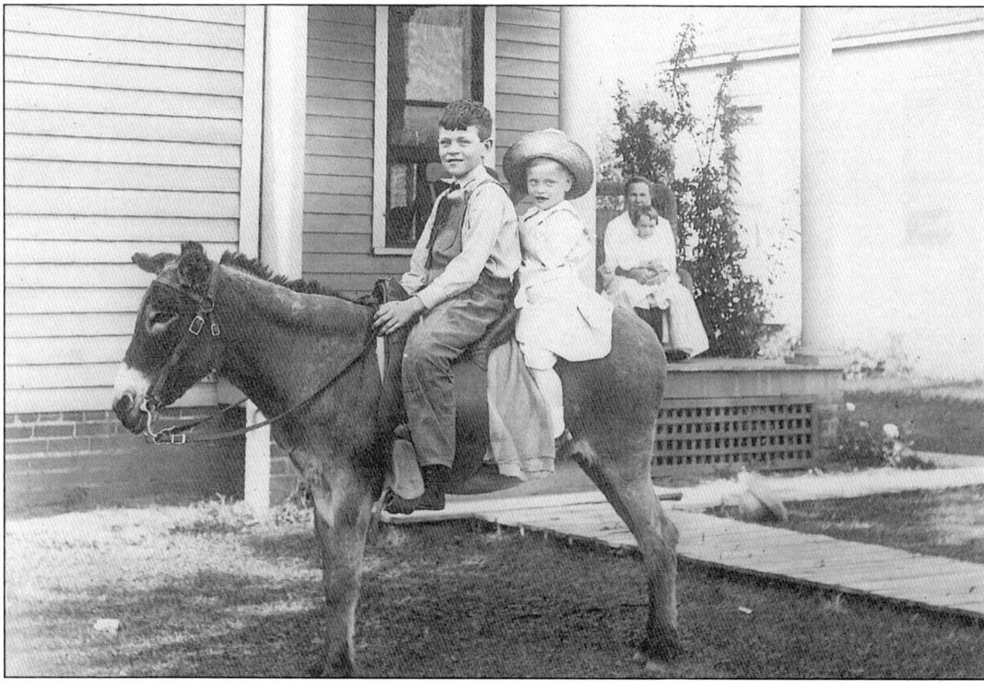

Elbert and Hugh Gaunt were visiting their grandparents at 217 Virginia Street when they posed for this portrait on a Missouri mule. A third child sits in Margaret Arnold's lap on the porch. A professional photographer probably took the shot and put the number 68 on the ground to identify the picture.

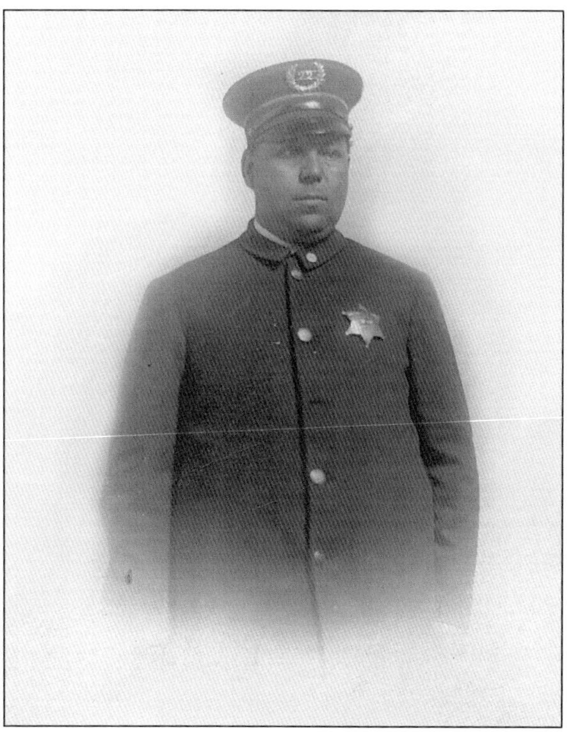

Shown here is an unidentified St. Joseph police officer, badge No. 22, who was photographed at the Empress Studio, *c.* 1920. The studio was located at 117 N. Fifth Street.

The people in this portrait, exhibiting varying degrees of fascination with the camera, are also unidentified. The photo was taken at Blarlay, 116 S. Eighth Street, c. 1910.

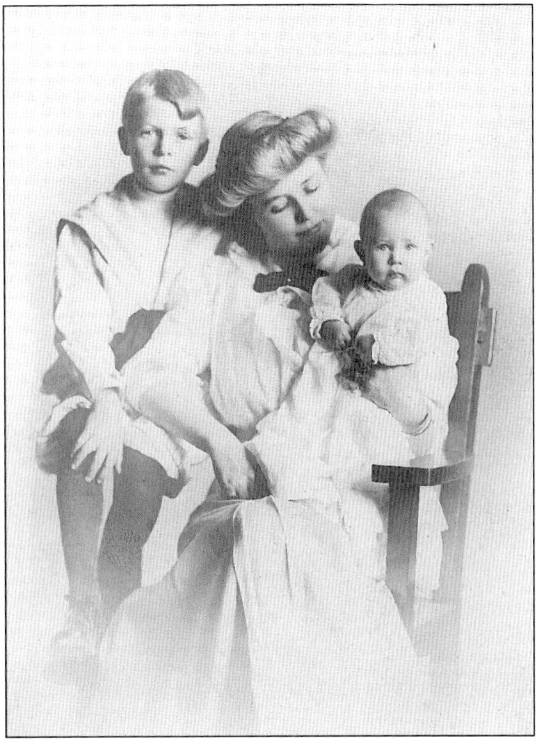

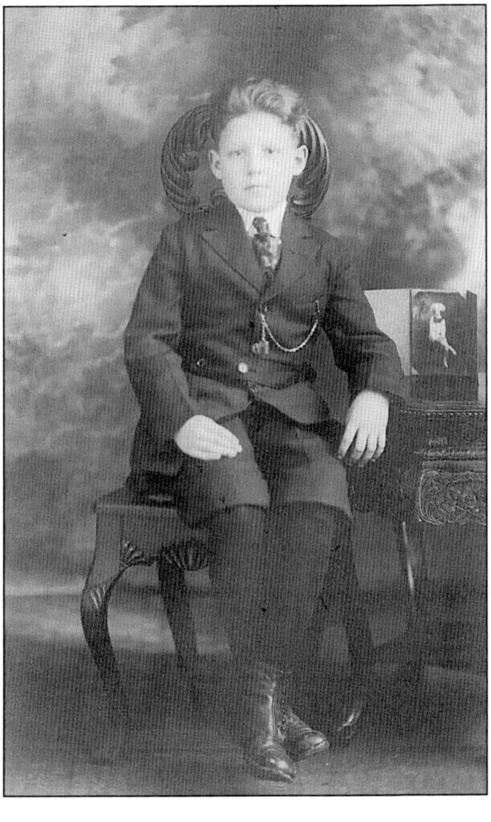

This distinguished portrait of an unidentified boy was taken at the Bloomer Studio, located at 706 1/2 Felix Street.

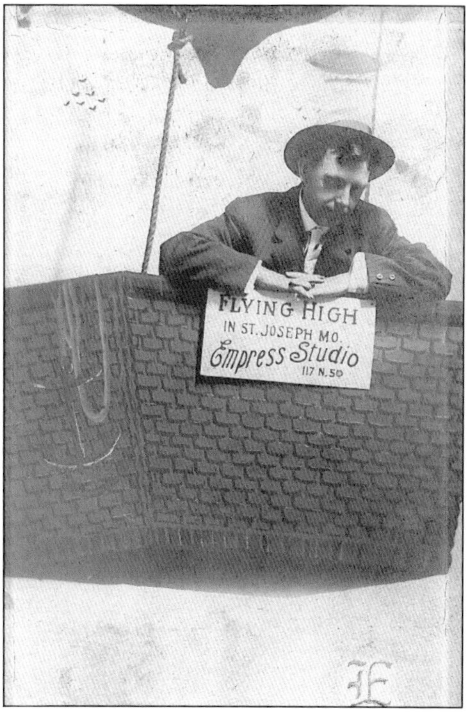

Taking a portrait of a person in a balloon was a technique employed often by photographers. On the back of this postcard, the sender writes, "This is the fellow. Please telephone as soon as you get this card and say how you like the looks. If I don't look good to you, I may be afraid to come." It is signed "H," with a phone number included.

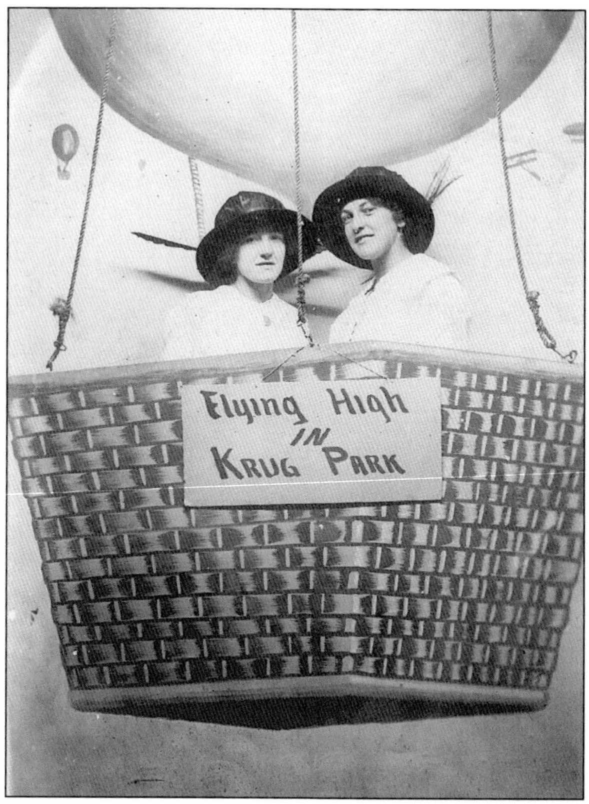

This photographer's set placed these young women in Krug Park, though they were really only in a studio. The women are unidentified.

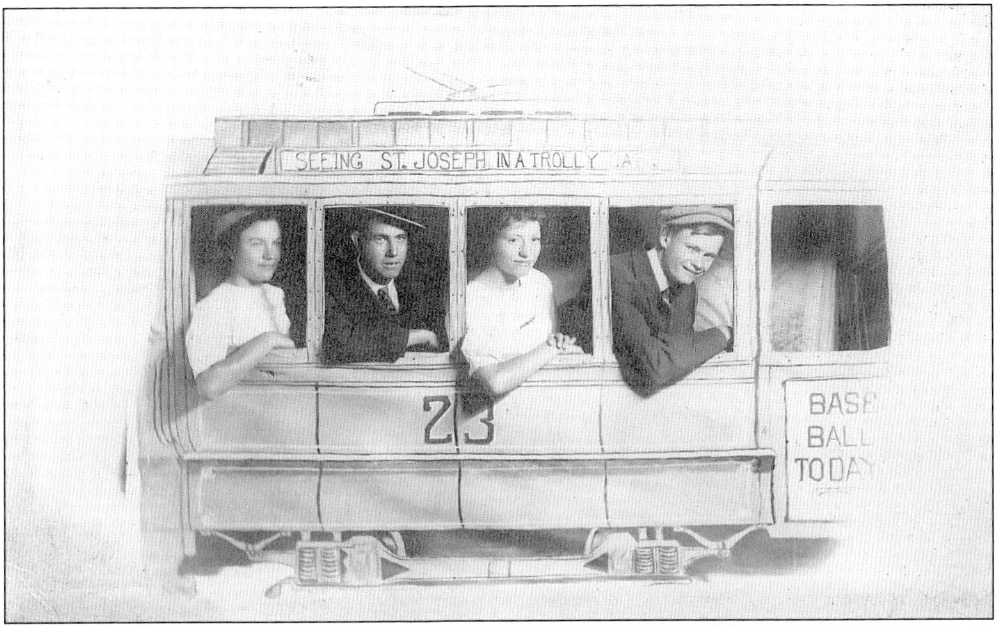

These four young people posed in a photographer's set that was shaped like a miniature St. Joseph trolley car. Note the sign at the front that says "Baseball today." The photo was taken c. 1919.

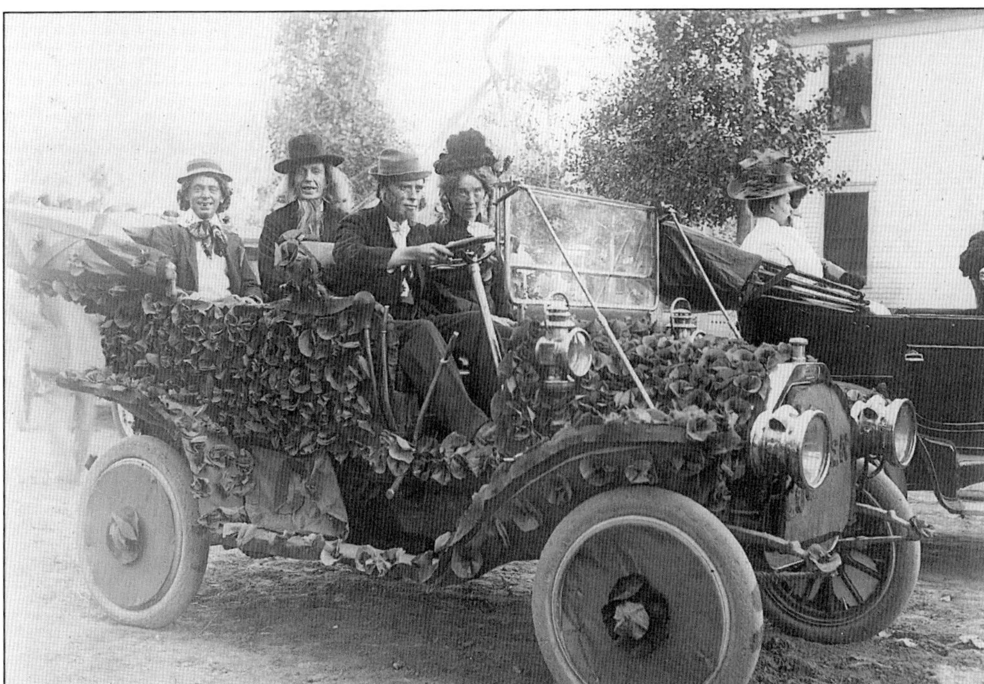

Though it may look more like they are dressed for Halloween, these people have decorated their car and dressed up for a parade. Several of the car's occupants have blackened their teeth and are wearing wigs. The photo was taken c. 1920.

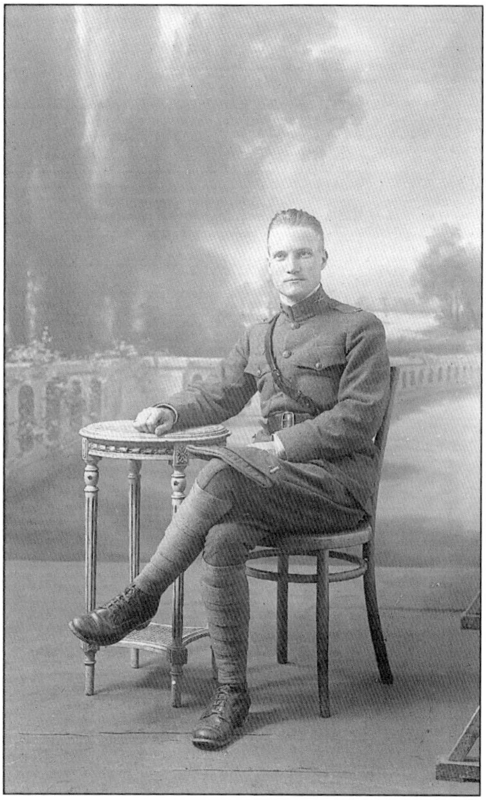

This is a photo of Bartlett Boder in his World War I uniform. He held the rank of lieutenant. For many years, he was president of the St. Joseph Historical Society.

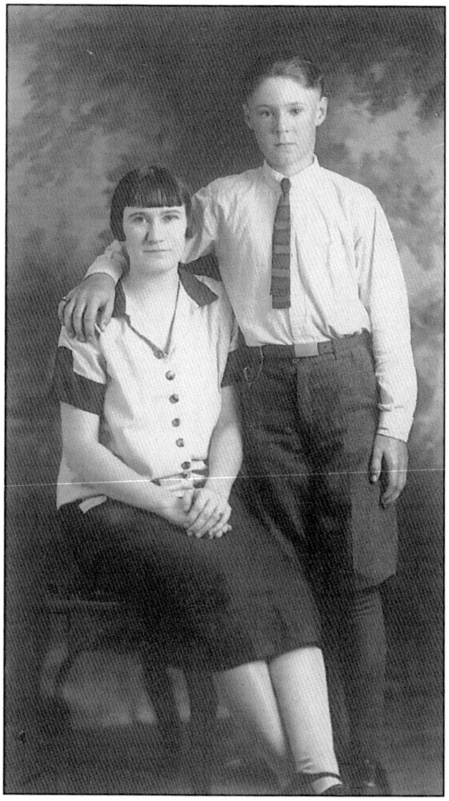

No identifications are written on the back of this postcard other than the description that it is a mother and her 11-year-old son. The photo was taken at the Bloomers Studio, located at 706 1/2 Felix Street.

This woman dressed in her finest clothes to have her photo taken at the Trumpter Studio, 320 Edmond Street. The photo was taken in the 1920s.

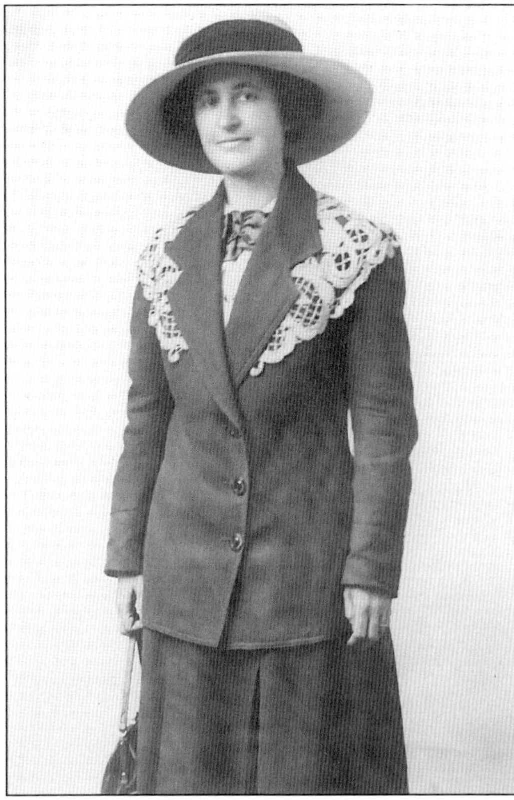

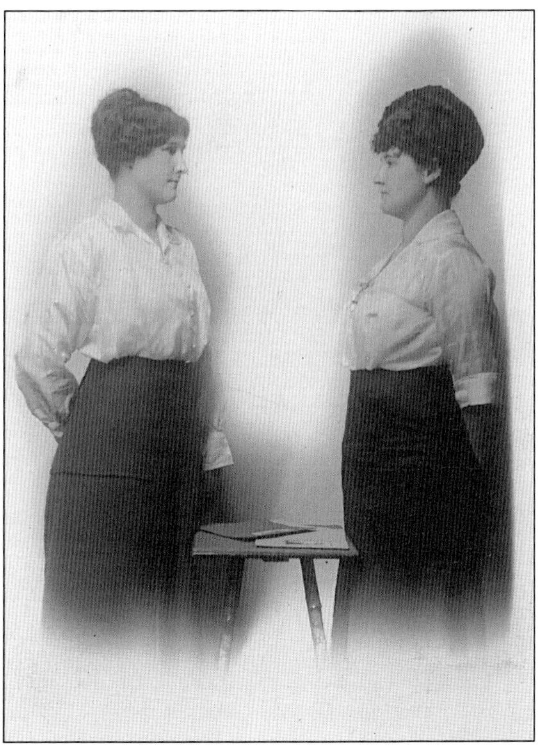

These two women look like sisters, but no identification was written on the card. The photograph was taken at the Eastern Photo Post Card Studio at 513 Edmond Street.

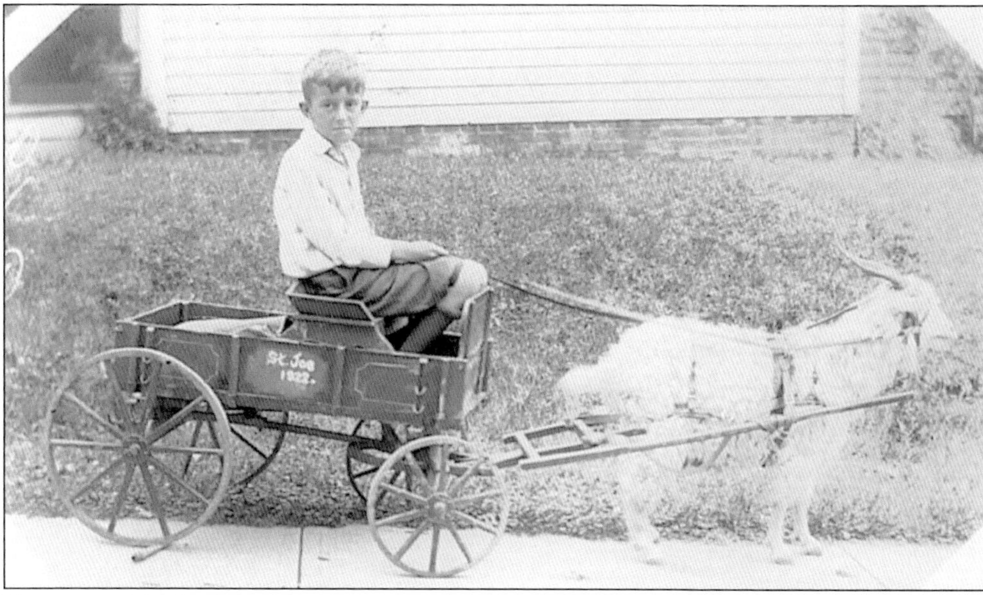

Nine-year-old John David Miller is pictured here, riding in a goat car near the intersection of Twenty-ninth and Francis Streets. The photo was taken during the summer of 1922. This postcard is actually a photograph of another postcard in an album, as evidenced by the white mounts at each corner.

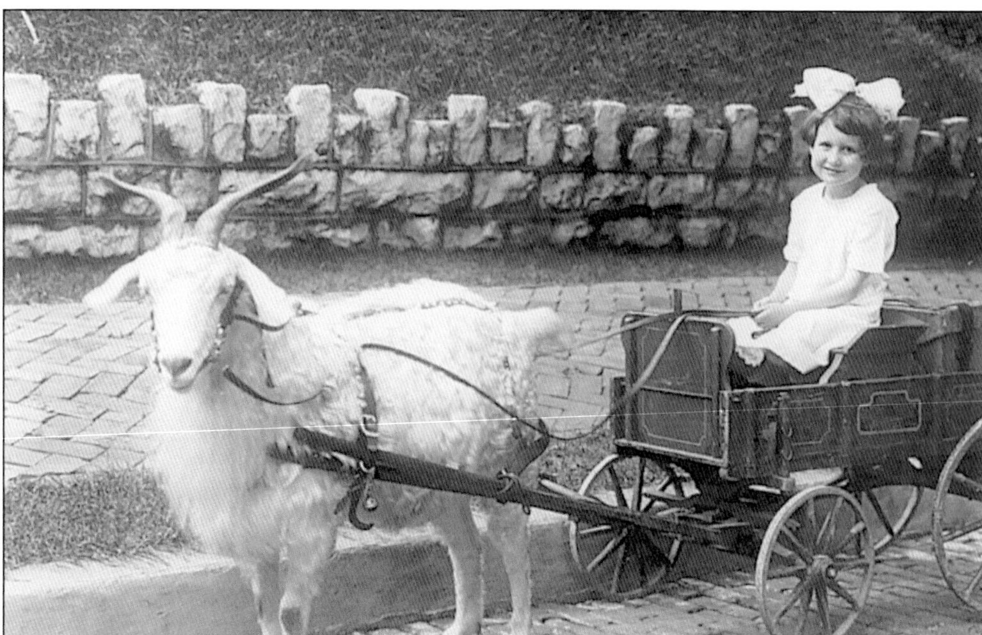

Nine-year-old Sally Miller sits in front of the Miller home at 1106 Ridenbaugh Street. This is the same goat cart pictured in the photograph at the top of the page, only five years earlier.

Ten

HOUSES

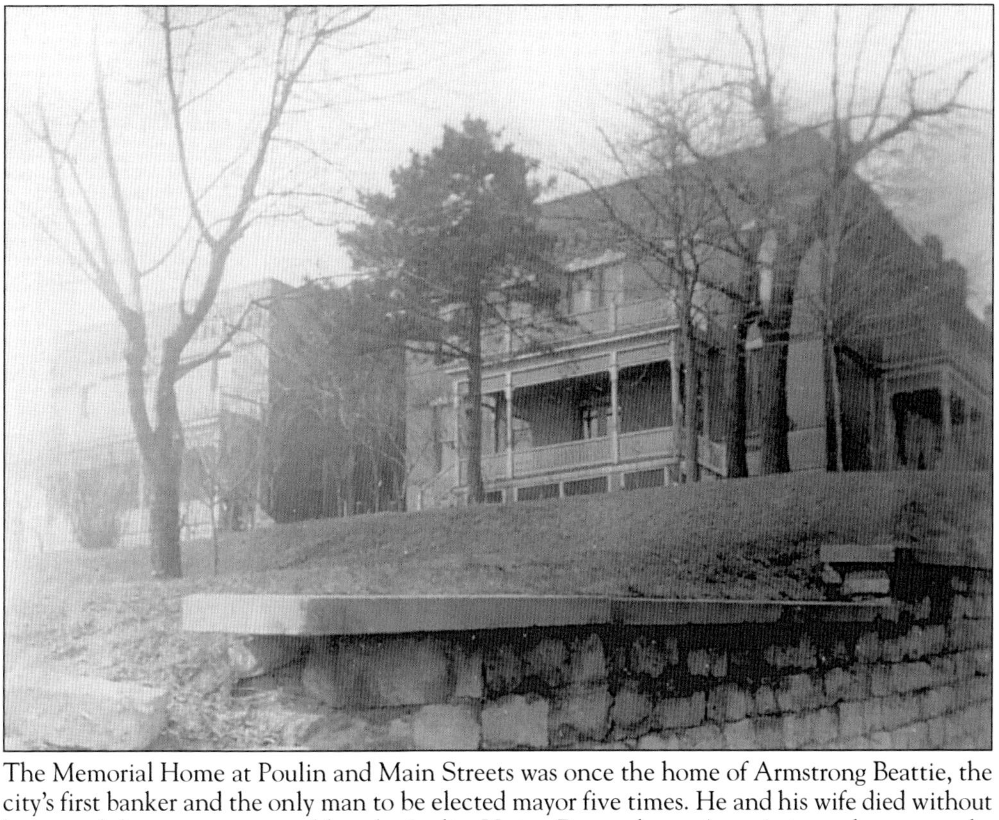

The Memorial Home at Poulin and Main Streets was once the home of Armstrong Beattie, the city's first banker and the only man to be elected mayor five times. He and his wife died without heirs, and the property was sold to the Ladies Union Benevolence Association, who operated a home for elderly women. The building was expanded in 1895 with additional funding from the Hoagland family, and it still stands.

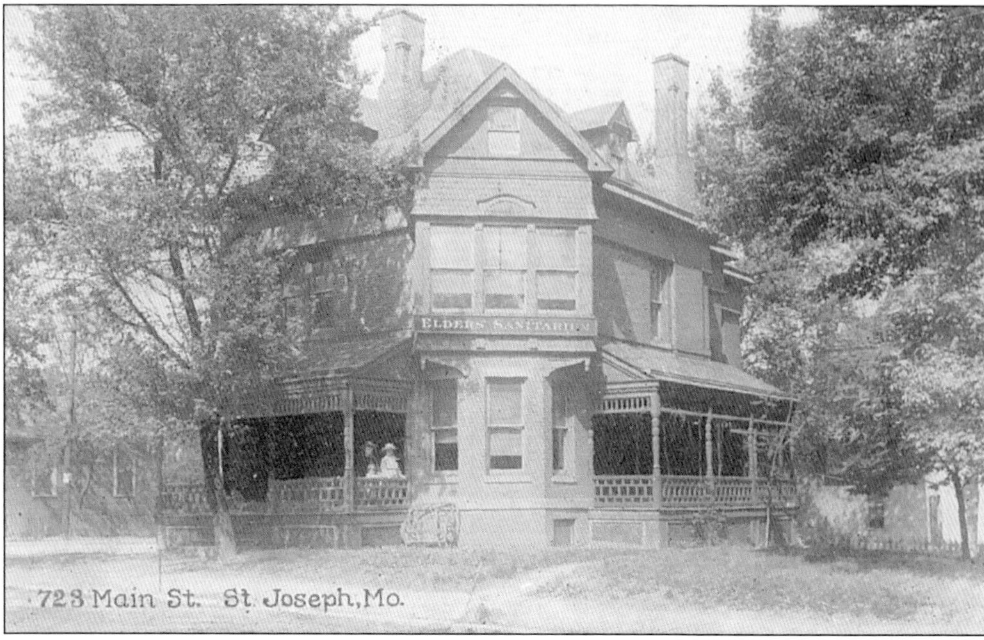

The "Elders Sanitarium" was located at 723 Main Street. It no longer exists, and no information on it could be obtained by the authors.

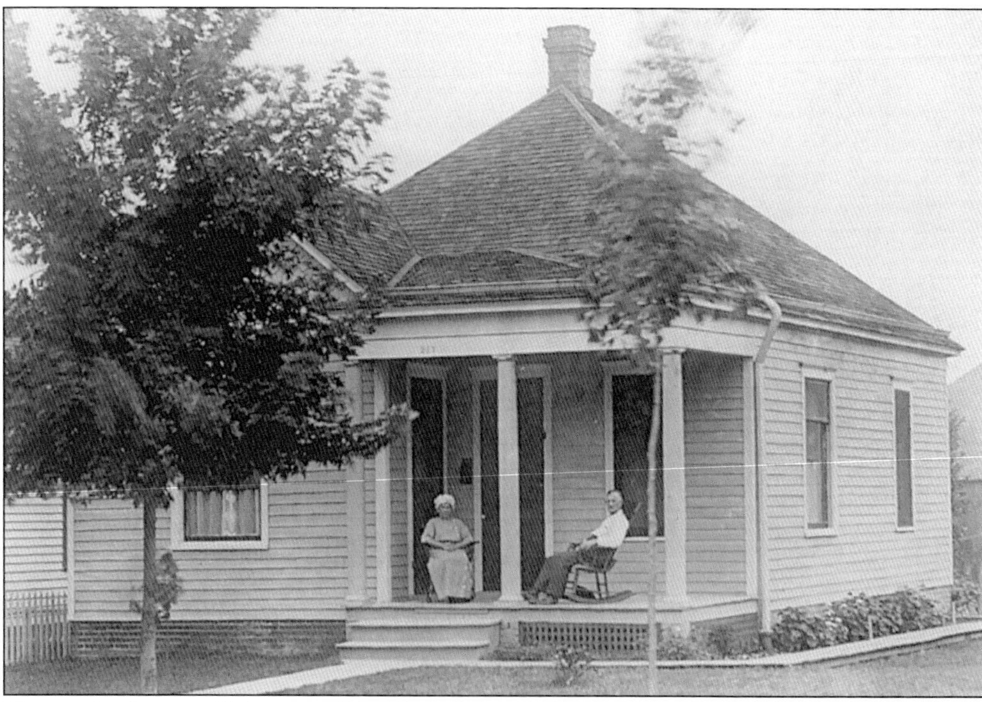

This is the home of Margaret Arnold, 217 Virginia Street, as it appeared *c.* 1915. On the right side of the house, a barn is visible in the distance. The house still stands without major alterations. The barn is gone, and it now stands in a neighborhood in south St. Joseph.

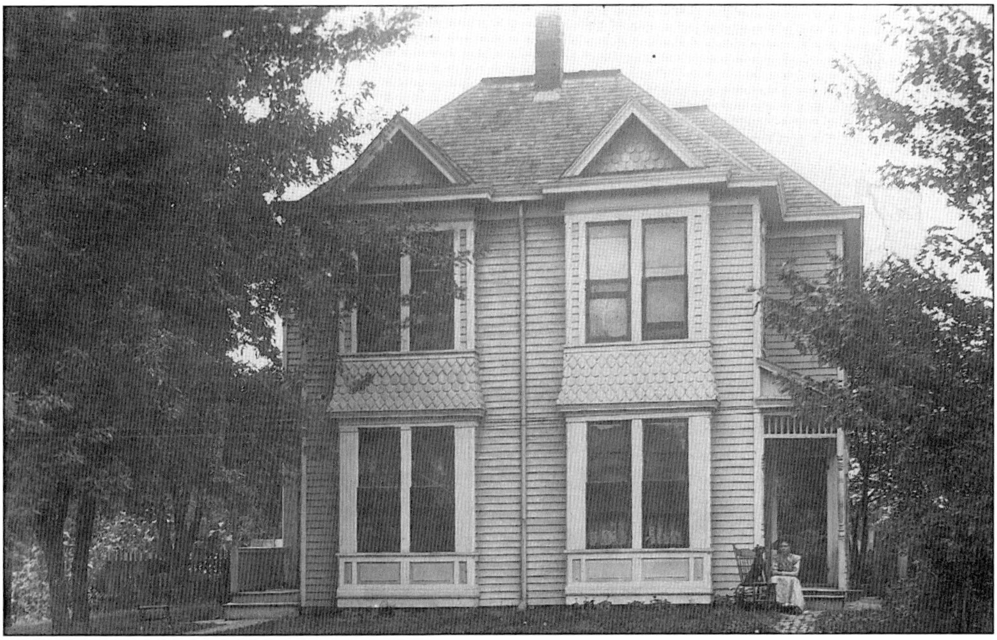

Building permit records indicate that this home at 922–24 S. Fourteenth Street was built in 1892 for Harry Holley. Mrs. J.H. Tracy is pictured sitting in the front with her dog Teddy in the chair. The picture was taken *c.* 1909. The house is still standing and has been recently restored. The duplex was a popular housing type favored by St. Joseph builders in the late 19th and early 20th centuries. The design for this duplex is found in numerous locations throughout the city.

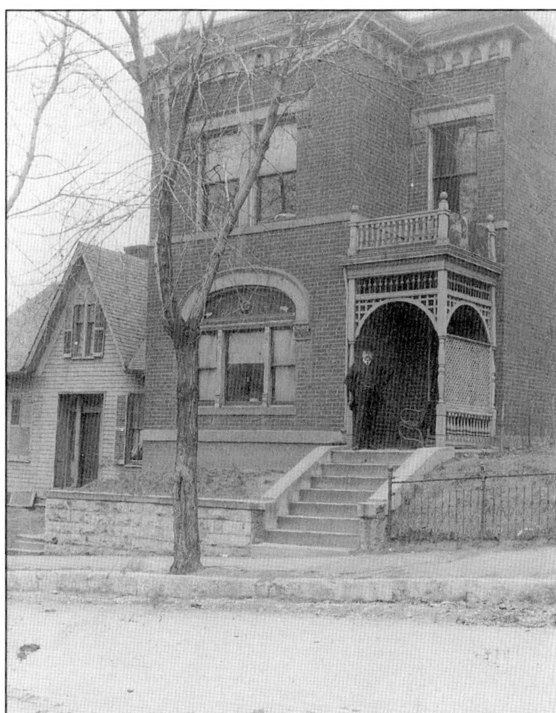

This is the J.B. Feyen residence at 917 Angelique Street. The owner is standing on the porch of the late Victorian home. The house was demolished in 1935, according to building permit records. The small Gothic Revival home to its left is still standing.

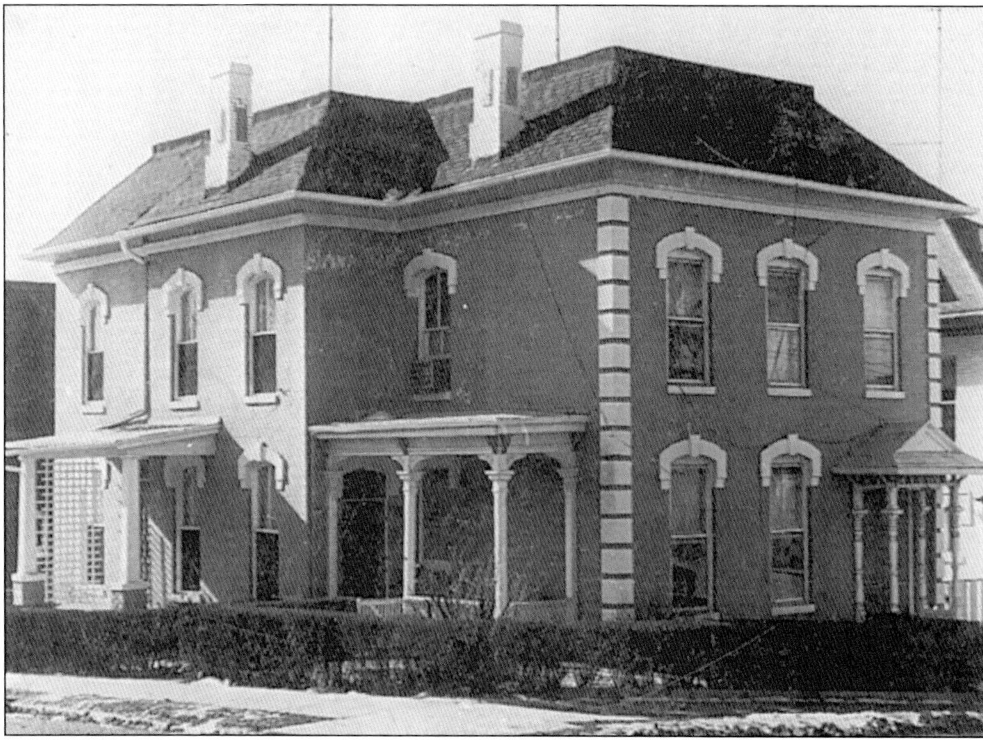

The Bernard Patton house was apparently known as the Cameron house at the time this postcard was produced, is pictured in a perfect state of restoration. It was built in 1866 for its owner, Patton, who was a brick and stone mason responsible for the masonry on the Buchanan County Courthouse. The courthouse was damaged by fire in 1885, and Patton was contracted to supervised the restoration. He was also the brickmason for the St. Joseph Cathedral.

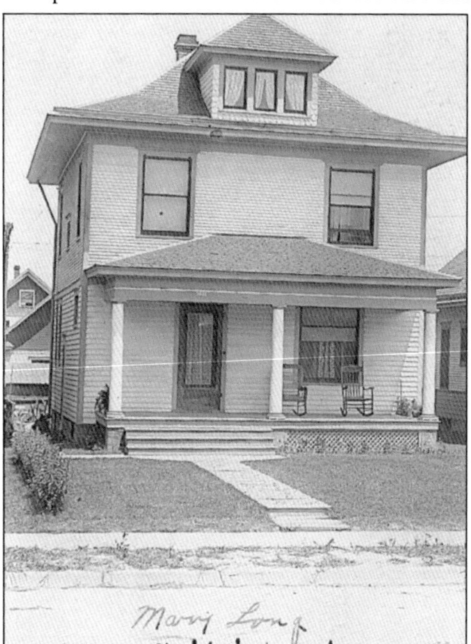

This is the Mary Long residence at 2611 Sacramento Street. The Munger Real Estate and Investment Company built this home on speculation in 1909 at a cost of $3,100. The home is still intact, with only minor changes, including the replacement of dormer windows with louvres.

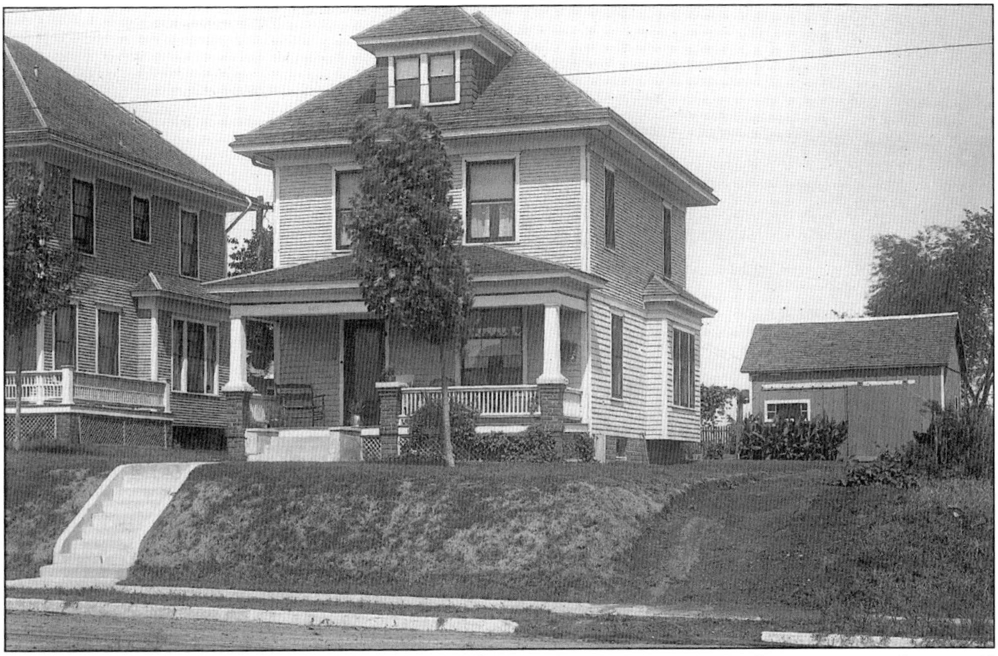

The C.F. Emanual house, located at 3013 Sylvanie Street, was once a foursquare with a small barn in the rear. Though the house still stands, the barn in back is gone, and a large addition has been made to the back of the house. The porch posts were replaced and other minor changes, including the addition of asbestos siding, were made.

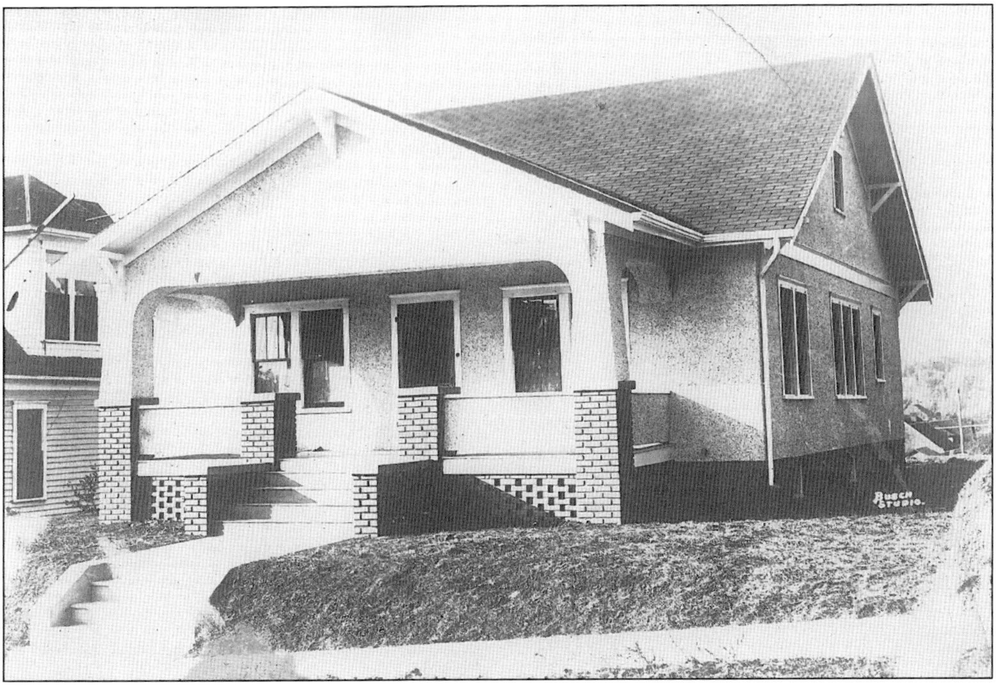

This photograph was taken by the Busch Studio. The house is located at 2841 Sylvanie Street. Interestingly, the house's stucco was replaced with wood siding soon after it was built. The porch remains the same, and the house is well maintained.

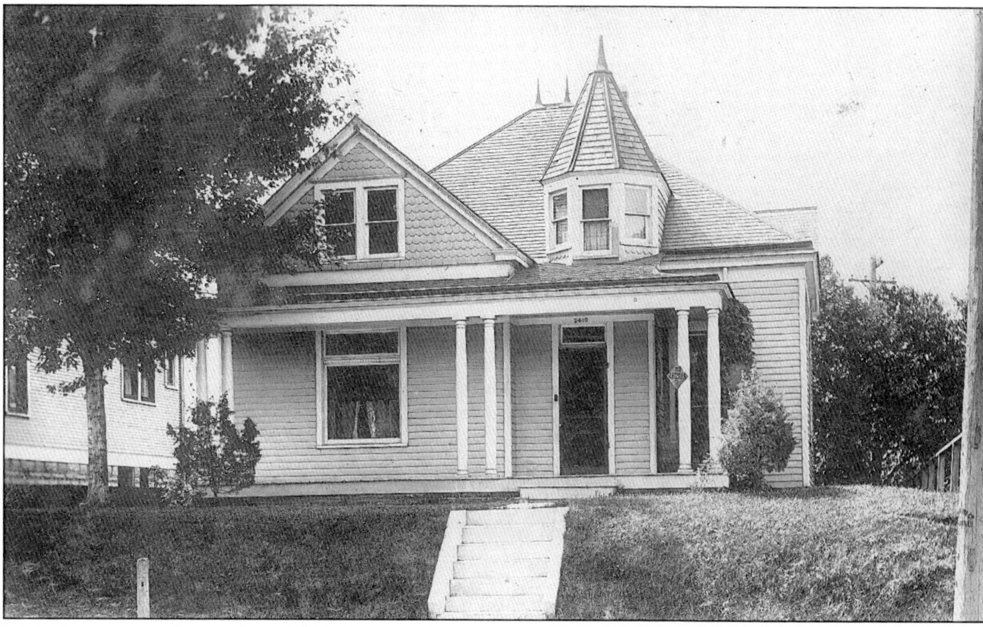

This house was located at 2410 Faraon Street in 1909; it was most likely constructed in 1898 and first occupied by Charles E. Thornton, a cashier for the Union Printing Company. The value of the residence was listed as $1,000. Notice the small Artesian Ice sign to the right of the front door. Artesian is a local company, still in existence today, which delivered ice to homes. The signs were posted so the ice company would know how much ice a family wanted. Today, this house is gone, and a bungalow from the 1920s has replaced it.

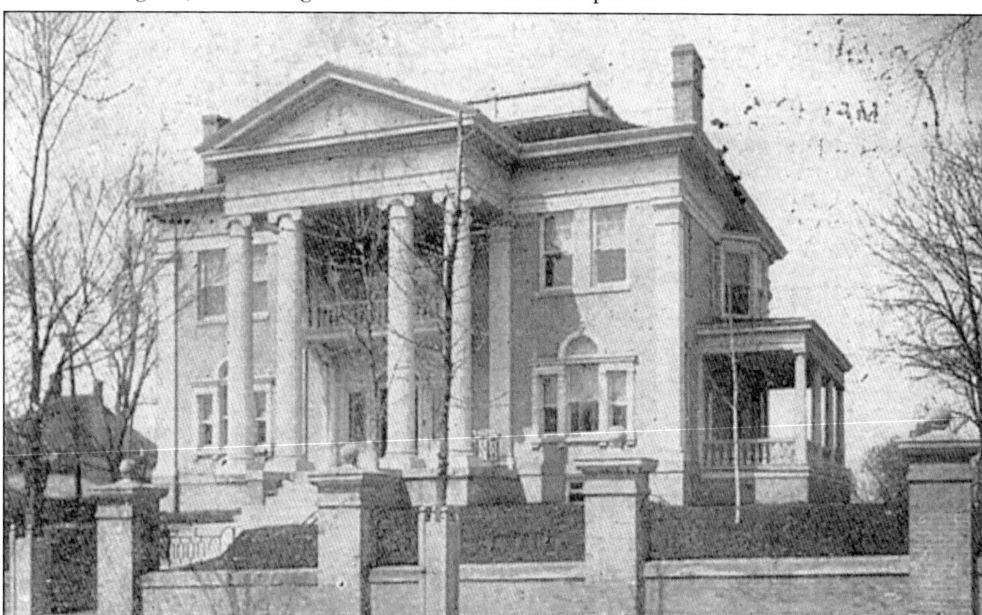

A photo of the David L. Bartlett Jr. house at 1923 Clay Street was used as an advertisement by the St. Joseph Railway, Light and Power Company. The house, built *c.* 1900, belonged to Barlett, a partner in the Bartlett Brothers Real Estate and Investment Company. It remains largely unaltered.

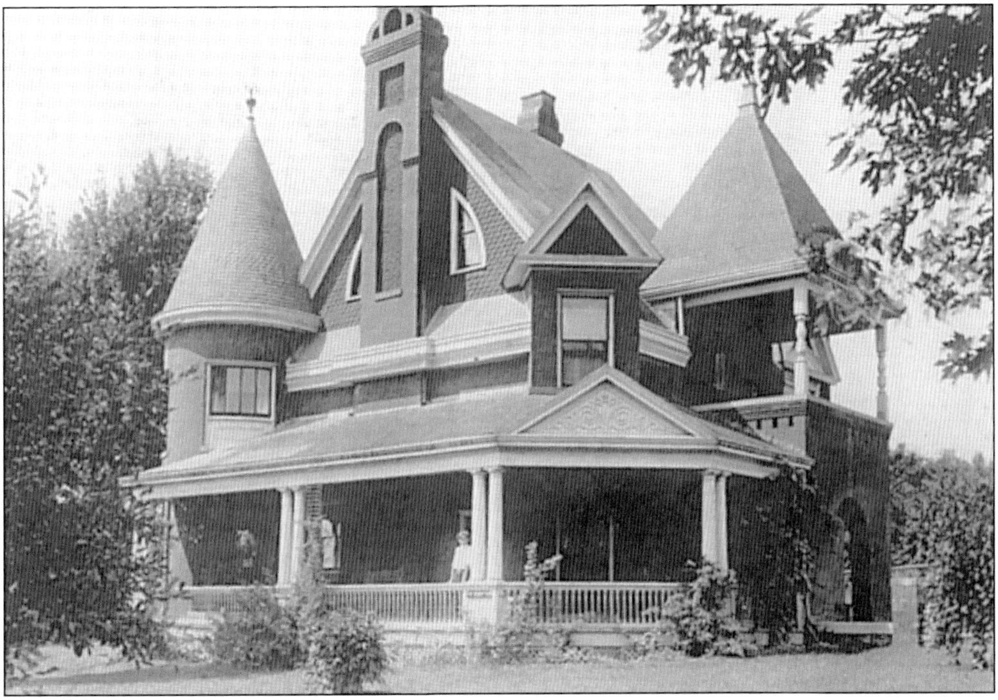

Thompson's Sanitarium and Rest House was located at 2202 Goff Avenue. This facility treated mental and nervous disorders. At the time it was built in the late 1880s, the house was located in a section of the city that was fairly isolated. The building still stands but has been altered. Among the changes are the closing in of the front porch, the removal of the conical roof from the turret, the addition of a dormer to the back, and alterations to the small side porch. Building permits indicate the house was altered in the 1920s by a Dr. Thompson, who was presumably the owner.

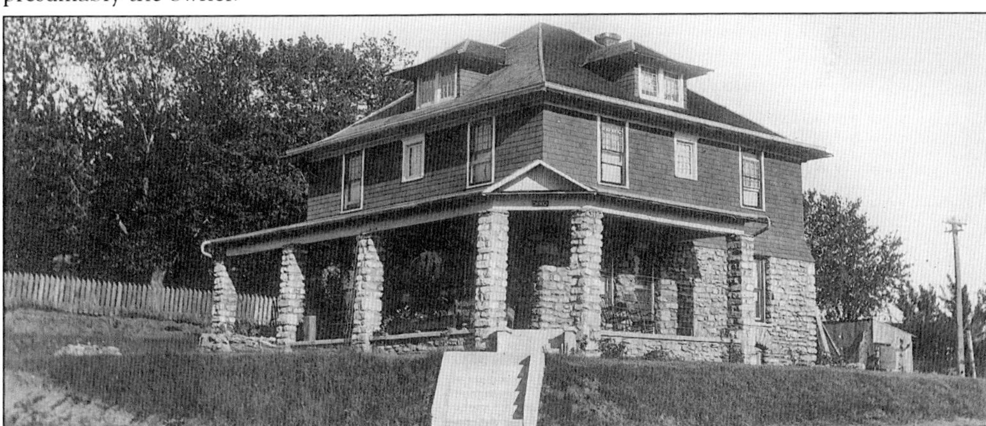

The Schuler residence at 3002 Francis Street was a foursquare with an unusual corner entrance. Building permits indicate a 1910 construction date for a cost of $3,000. The first occupant of the house was Henry Schuler, a credit manager for the Townsend and Wyatt Drygoods Company. The senders wrote to friends in Chicago that they were having "the time of their lives" at the home and said it was "way up high on a hill." The house still stands with only minor alterations, which include the addition of asbestos siding to the top half. A rock wall and rock newel posts were added to the street-level stairs in 1925.

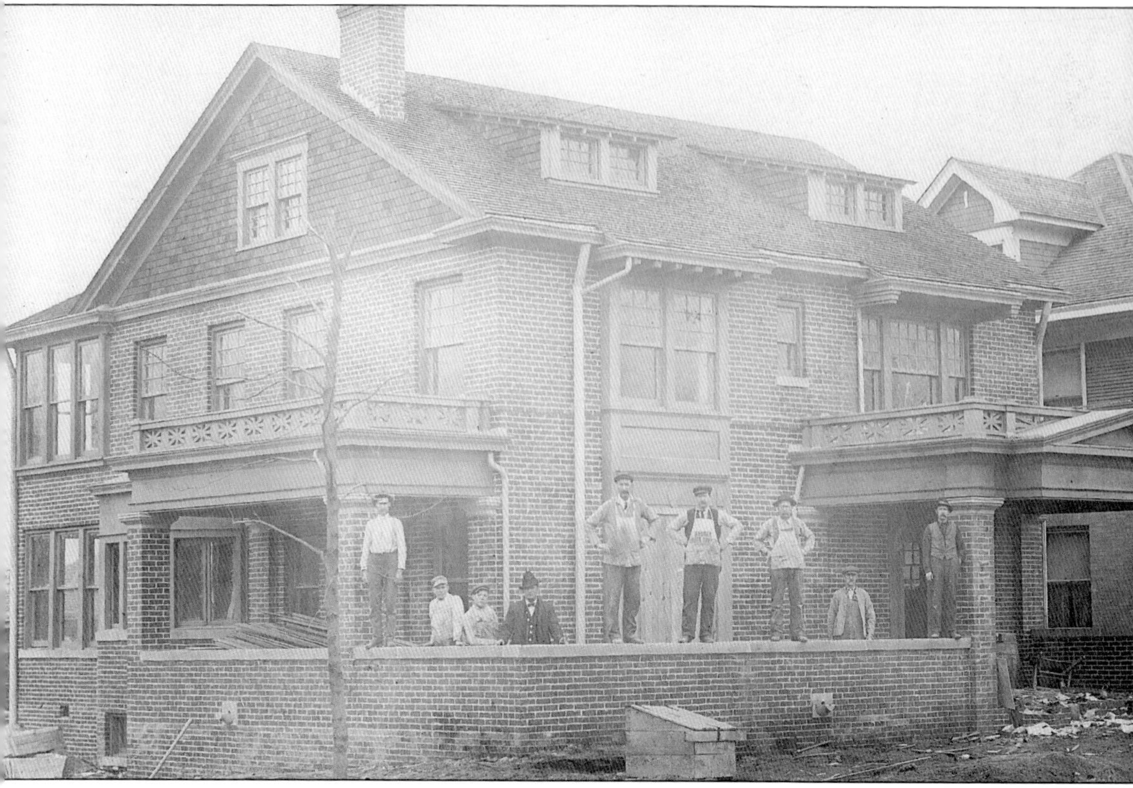

This house was built on speculation for an investment company in 1912. Its first owner was a German immigrant named Hugo Miller who became president of the Combe Printing Co. shortly after buying the house. The current owners are restoring the home.

Eleven

Clubs and Meeting Houses

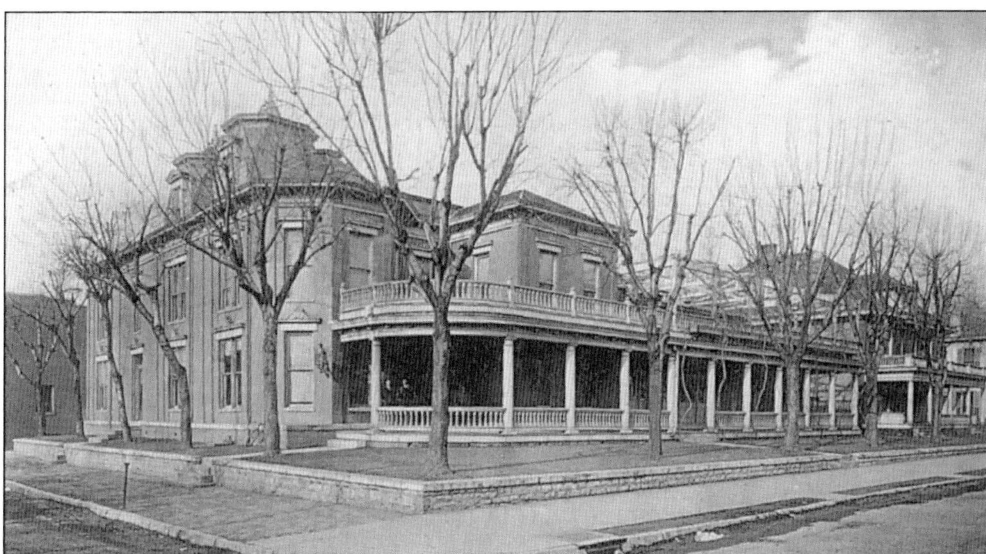

The Benton Club at Seventh and Faraon Streets is the oldest-surviving private club in the city, having been established in 1887. Winslow Judson and W.D.B. Motter, attorneys who formed the firm of Judson and Motter, are credited with starting the club by sending out 125 invitations to socially prominent St. Joseph residents, asking them to join a new social club. They formed a corporation, and 41 stockholders gave $500 each to start the club. They then purchased the property on which their club now stands.

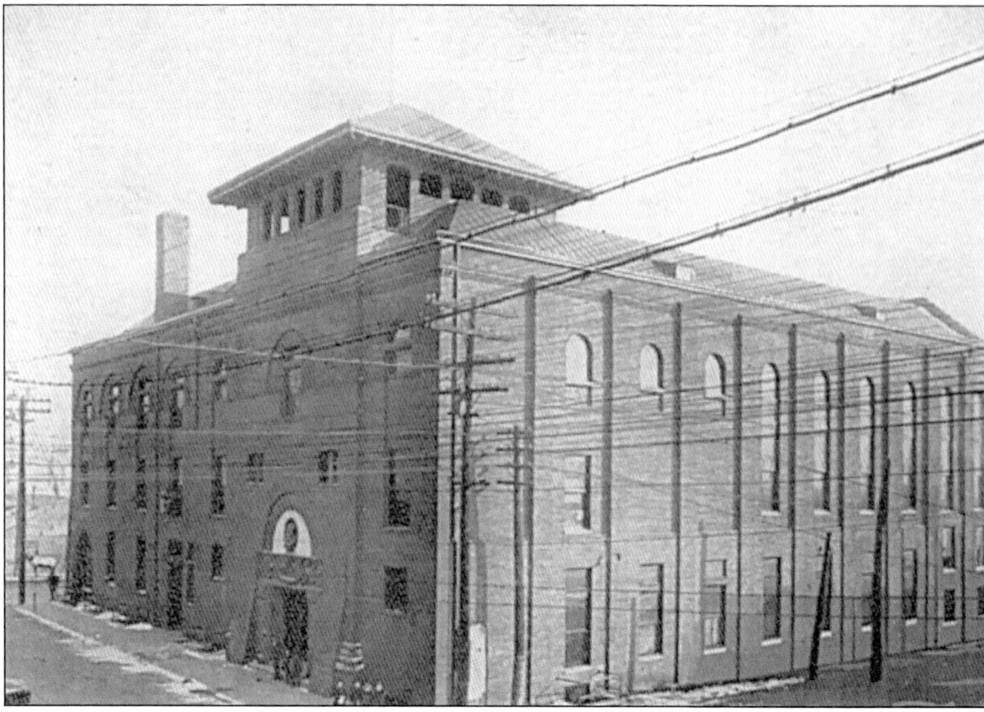

Turner Hall was located between Sixth and Seventh Streets. It was also known as the Turner Dramatic Society, a group with German origins. Turnerverein, commonly called the Turners, was a nationwide society founded by German Americans in 1848 to promote healthy minds and bodies. The St. Joseph chapter was organized in 1855. It had several buildings. The one pictured here was built in the summer of 1890 at a cost of $50,000.

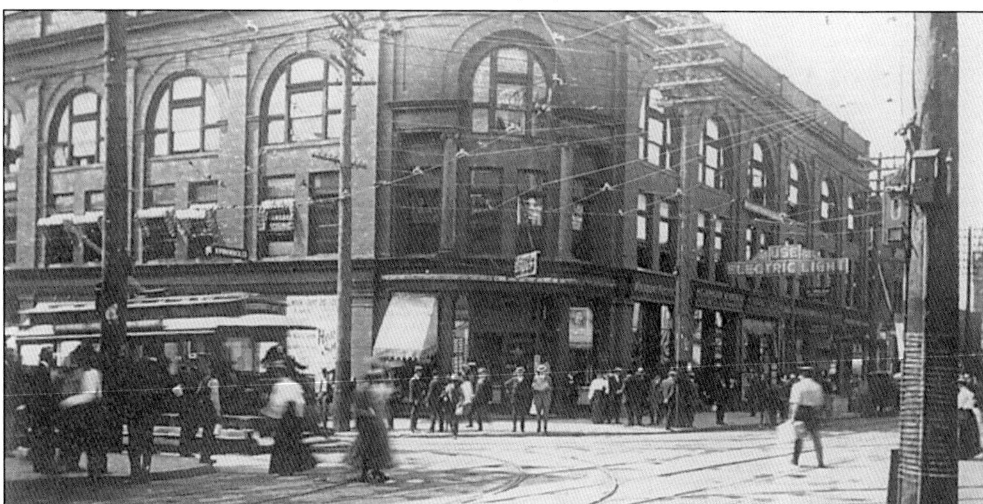

The Masonic Temple once stood at Fifth and Edmond Streets. The signs to the right of the building advertise electric lighting. The first lodge was chartered on May 28, 1859. At one time, there were 12 separate Masonic organizations in St. Joseph. Perhaps the most famous is the Moila Temple, organized December 17, 1887; it was famous for its small group of camels, which toured the U.S. and were housed at Krug Park.

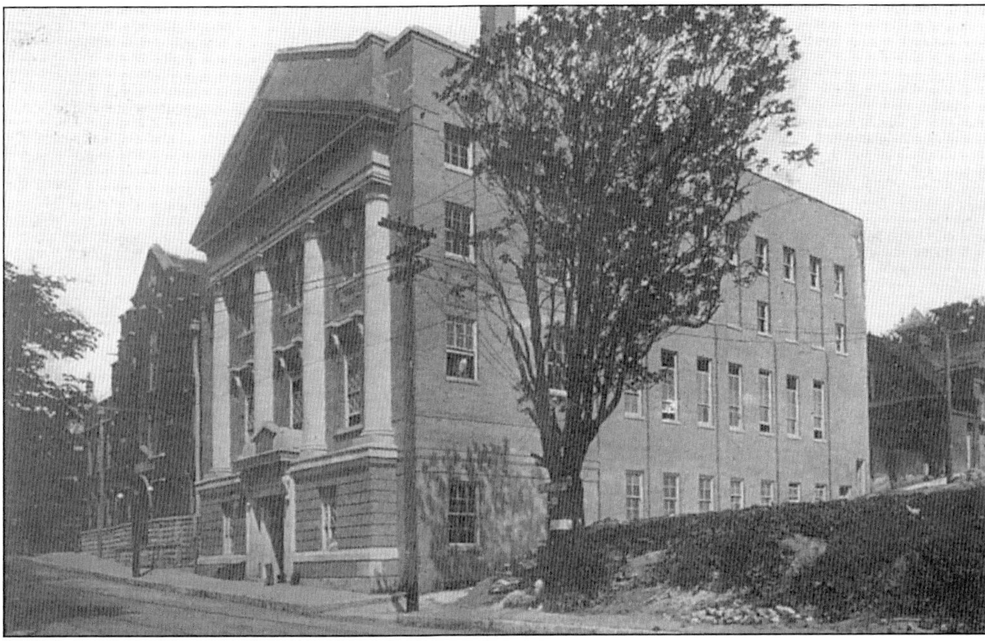

The building shown above, the later Masonic Temple at Sixth and Robidoux, is still standing. It was built side-by-side with the Scottish Rite Cathedral, shown below, between 1905 and 1908. The cathedral was replaced in the 1970s.

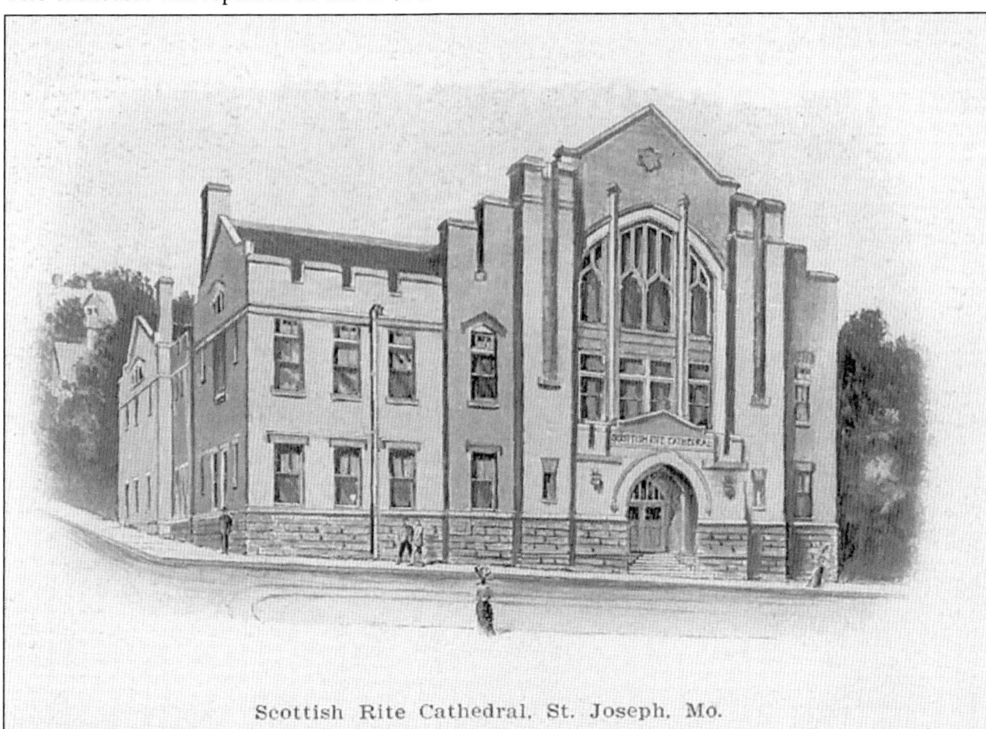

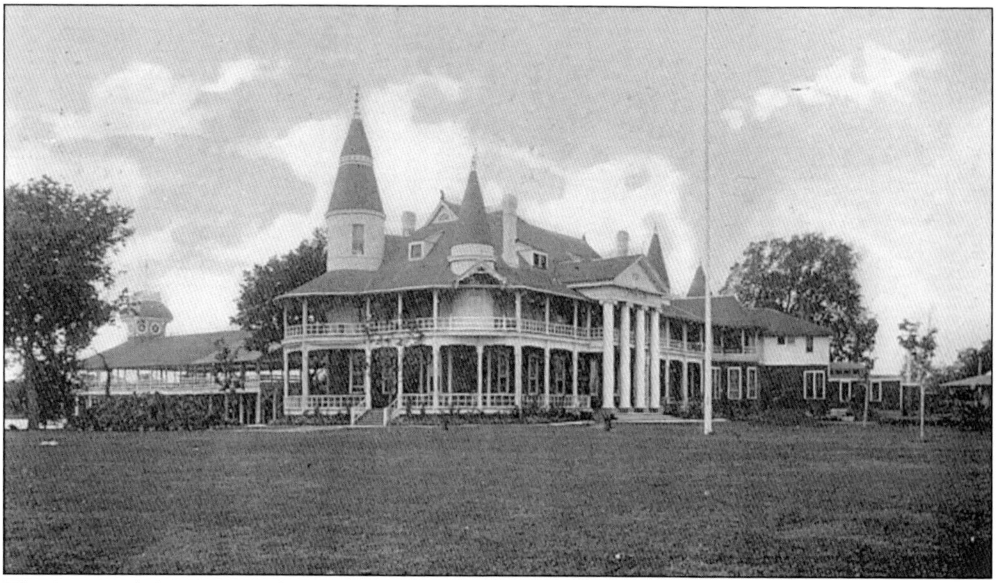

The Lotus Club was one of Lake Contrary's most notable buildings. It was built in the 1880s by the St. Joseph Boating Association as a private men's club for $50,000. In 1900, the St. Joseph Railway, Light and Power Company bought it, changed the name, and turned it into a hotel. In its heyday, it had a dance floor built over the lake, tennis courts, and hotel-hosted regattas. It burned in 1924 and was never rebuilt.

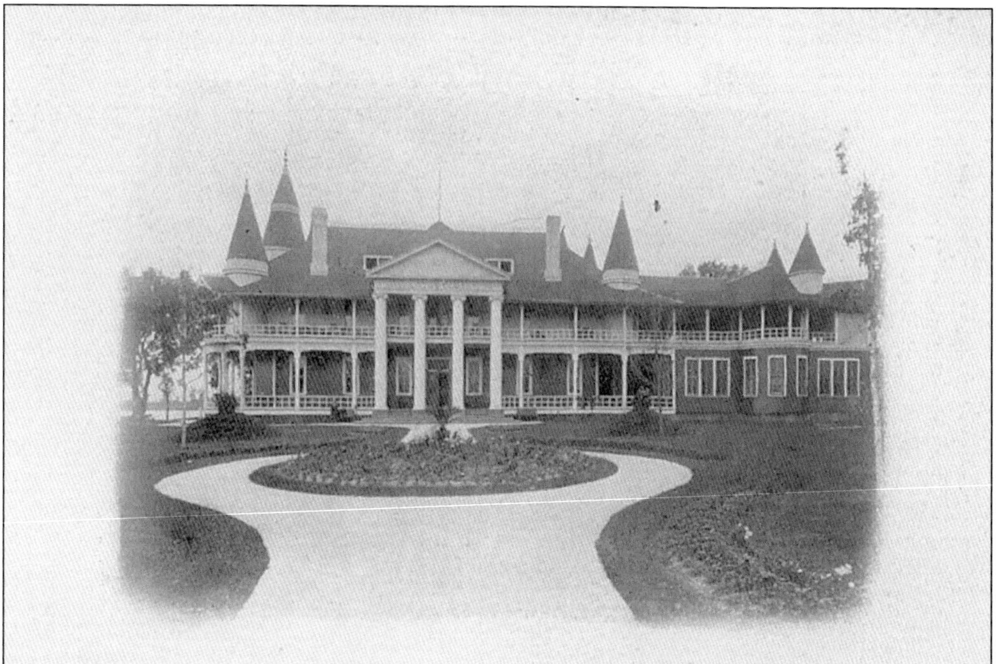

Lotus Club, Lake Contrary, St. Joseph, Mo.

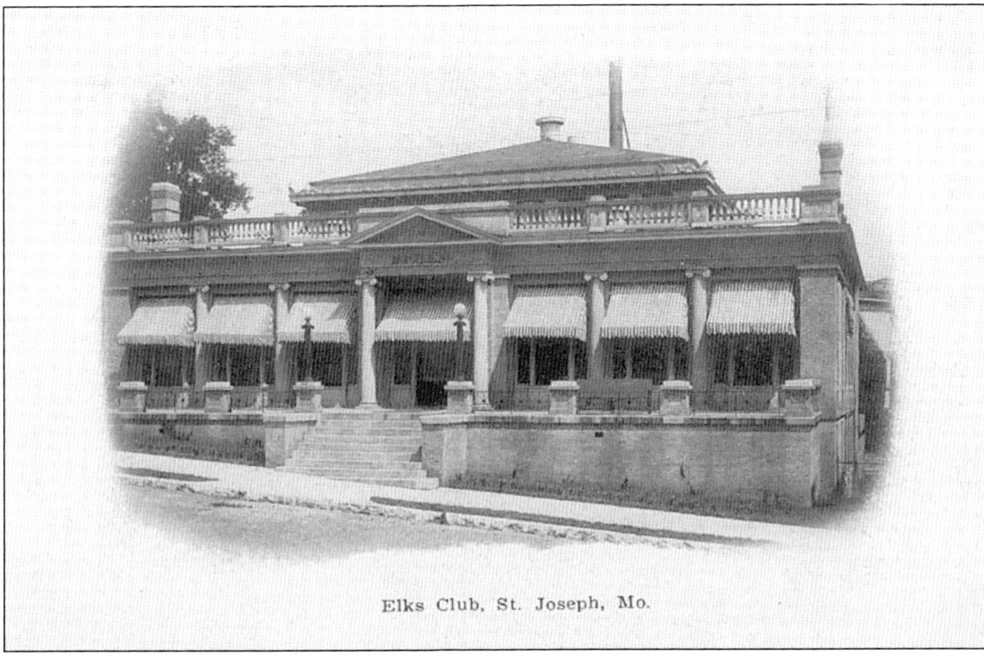

The Elks Club building was originally built as a forerunner to the local chamber of commerce. It was later sold to the Elks.

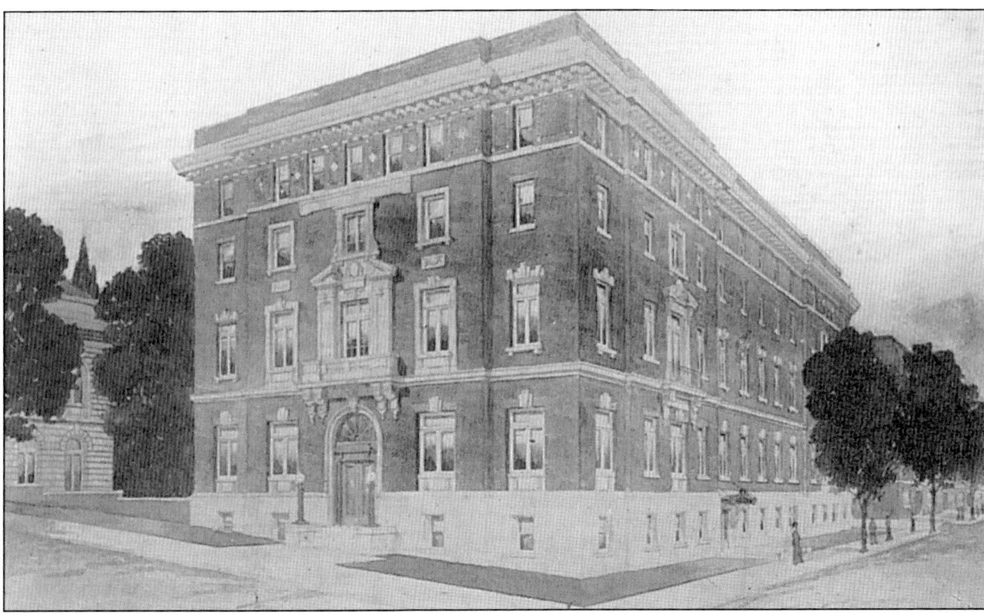

The YMCA at the corner of Tenth and Faraon has since been demolished. The postcard is addressed to an inmate in the Buchanan County jail. The addressee writes, "I thought I would be able to see you but they won't allow visitors until Wednesday. I got those pictures from Kansas. Please don't worry." It is signed Lola.

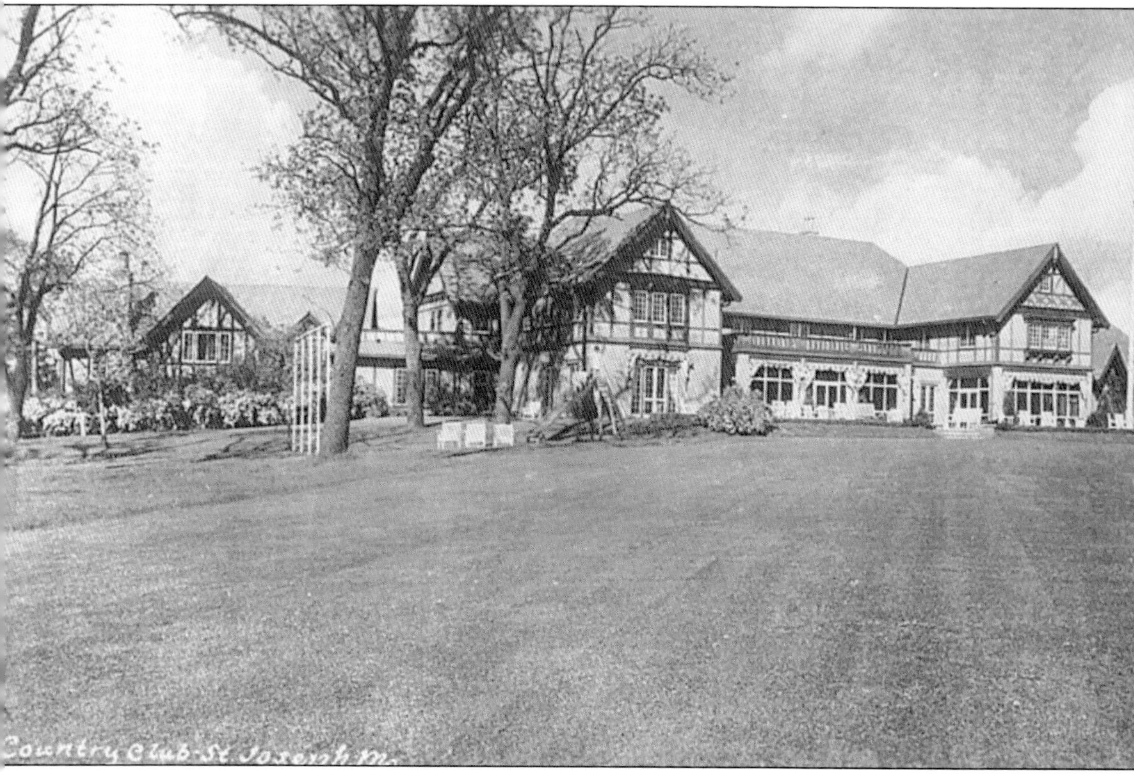

The St. Joseph Country Club is still in use today. It is located north of St. Joseph, in Andrew County. It was designed in 1911 by architect Walter Boschen in the Tudor Revival style.

Twelve

SCHOOLS

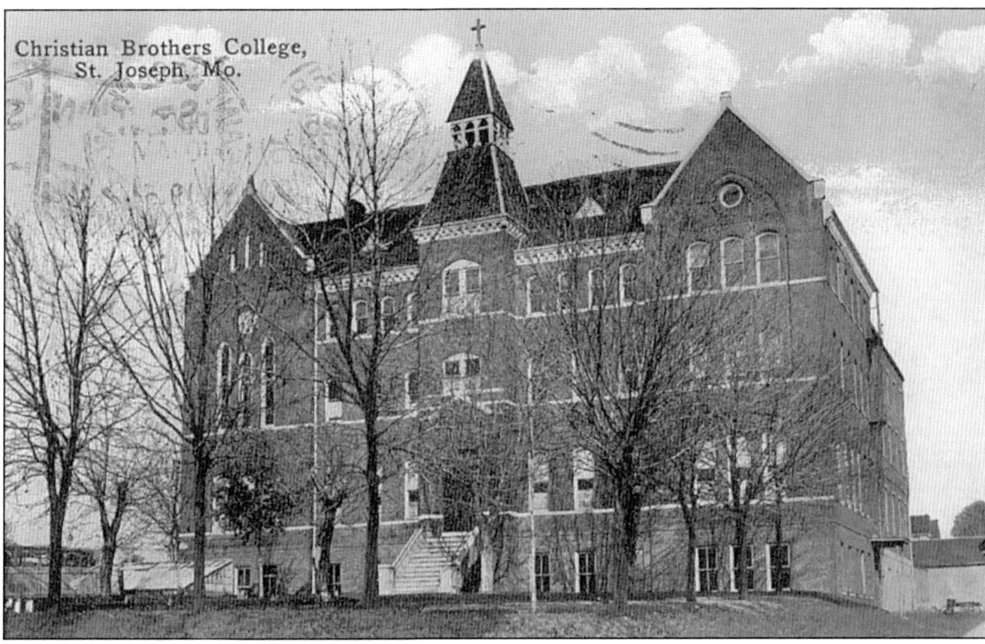

St. Joseph's first schools were private academies, which were later replaced with religious schools catering either to boys or girls. The first public schools were erected in 1860, when residents got a charter from the Missouri General Assembly to form a local school board and build schools for each of three wards. Each of the buildings were brick, two stories high, and seated 100 to 120 students. The city's first school for black children was opened in 1867. The city opened the first high school for blacks in 1885, adding another three years later.

Built in 1850 but first used as a school in 1867, Christian Brothers College was located at the corner of Thirteenth and Henry Streets in what is now the Cathedral Hill neighborhood. Catholic boys of high school age usually attended the school. The building was demolished in the 1920s and the land was donated to the city of St. Joseph. It was developed into College Hill Park in 1928.

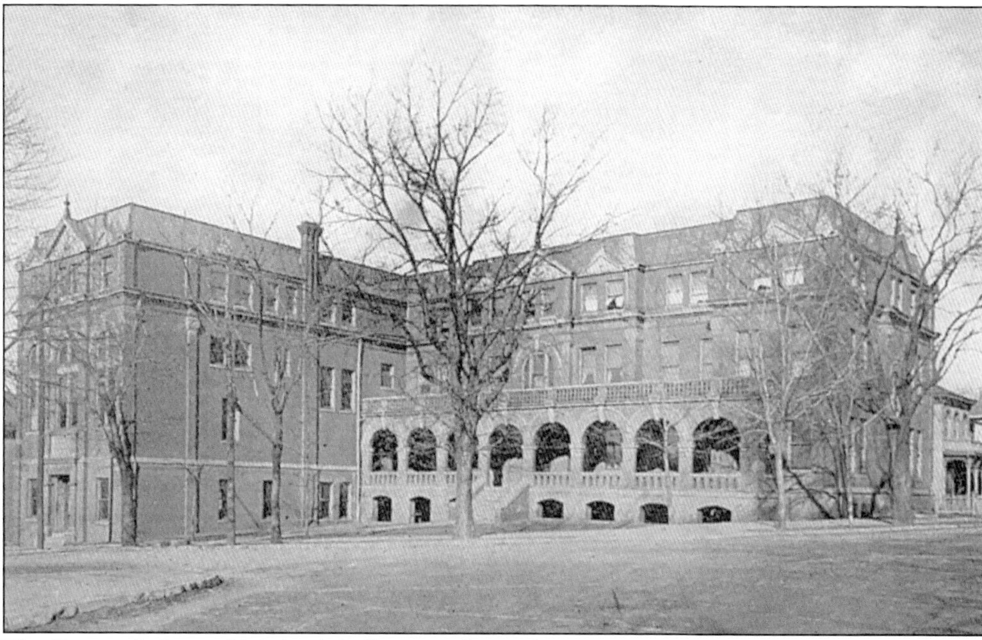

The Ensworth Central Medical College was located at Seventh and Jules Streets. Ensworth was named in honor of Samuel Ensworth, who gave $100,000 to start the school. The Ensworth Deaconess Hospital was erected in 1888 and was the amalgamation of the St. Joseph Hospital Medical College and the College of Physicians and Surgeons. Perhaps its most locally famous faculty member was Dr. Jacob Geiger, who taught and practiced here.

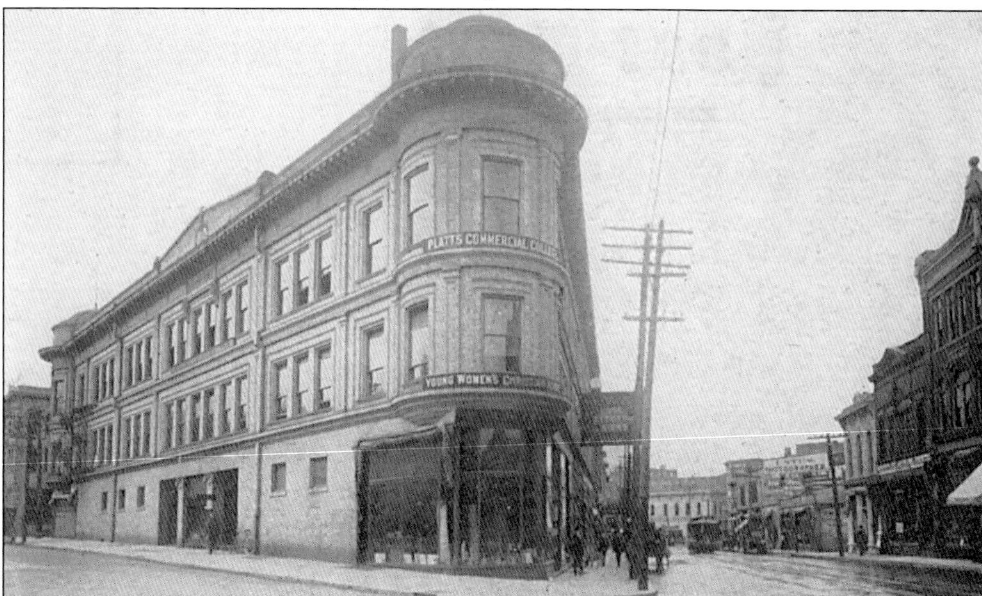

Platt's Commercial College was in this building at Ninth Street and Frederick Avenue. It was founded by the Platt family in 1879, continuing under a variety of names including Platt Junior College, Northwest Community College, and the Platt College of Commerce. The college filed for bankruptcy in 1995 and Vatterott College took over its programs. The building pictured here was destroyed during urban renewal.

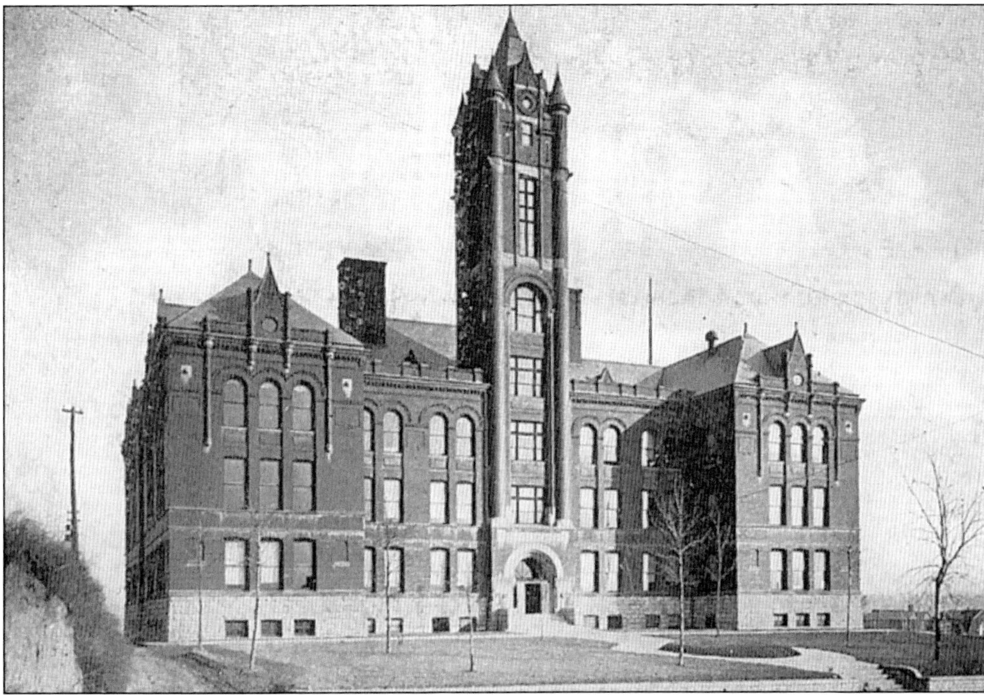

Central High School was known as the New High School for several years. It was built in 1895 on what was called Carpenter's Hill, it was first occupied in 1896. The building was located just northwest of Everett School on Thirteenth Street. This was the city's second high school building until Benton High School was built in 1907. The new Central High School stands at Twenty-sixth and Edmond Streets and is still in use today.

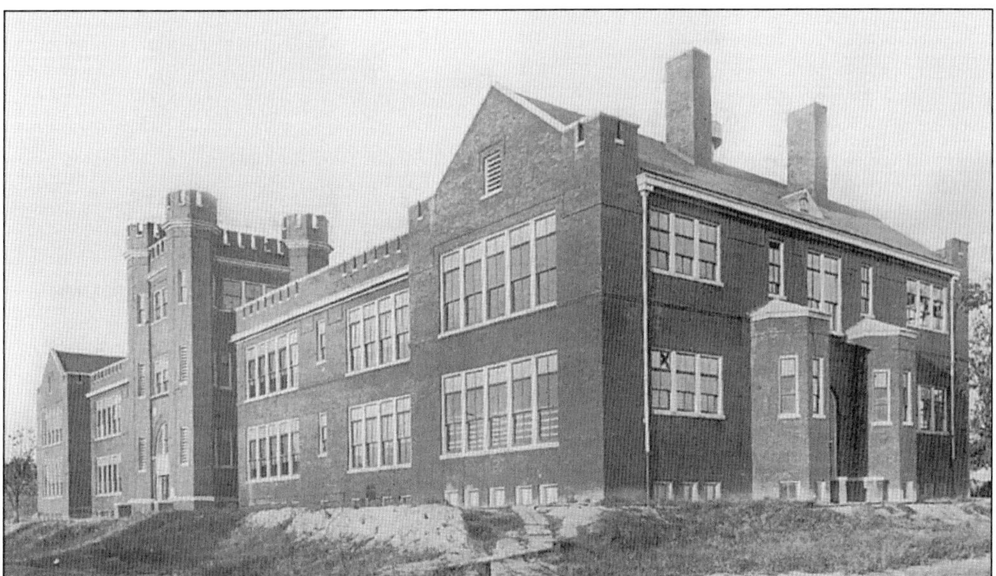

This earlier version of Benton High School, completed in 1907 to serve St. Joseph's south side, is no longer in use. The building cost $91,000 to build. A more modern school replaced it in the 1940s. This image was used as an advertisement for the Hirsch Brothers Dry Goods Co.

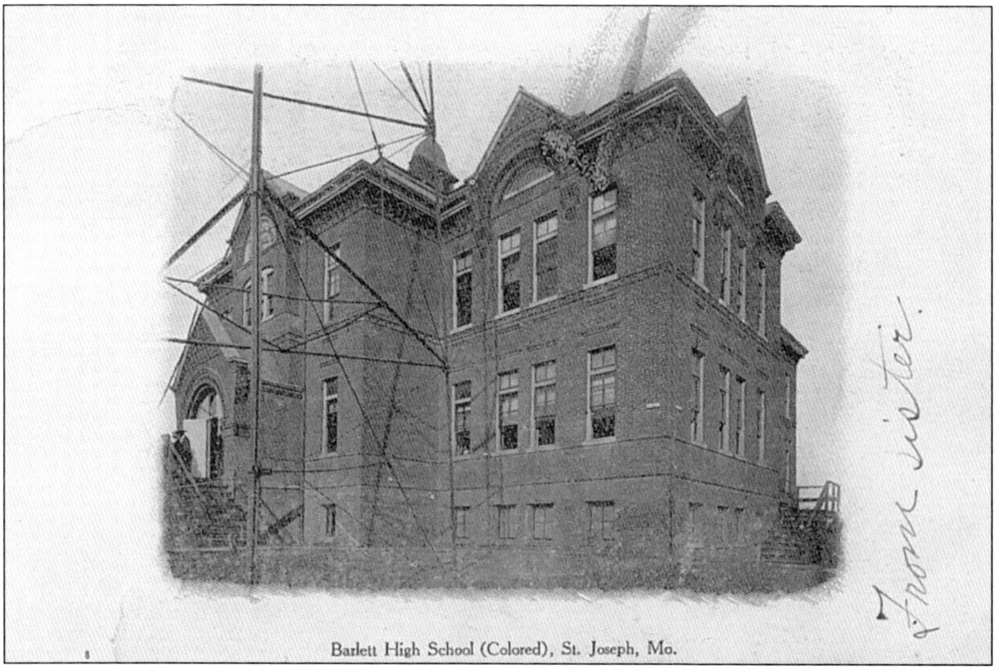

The Colored High School, built in 1888 for $17,500, served the black population of St. Joseph. It encompassed primary, junior high, and high school grades, and served children living south of Frederick Avenue. The building was located at the northeast corner of Angelique and Eighteenth Streets. A 1923 survey recommended expansion of the site and school. The building no longer stands.

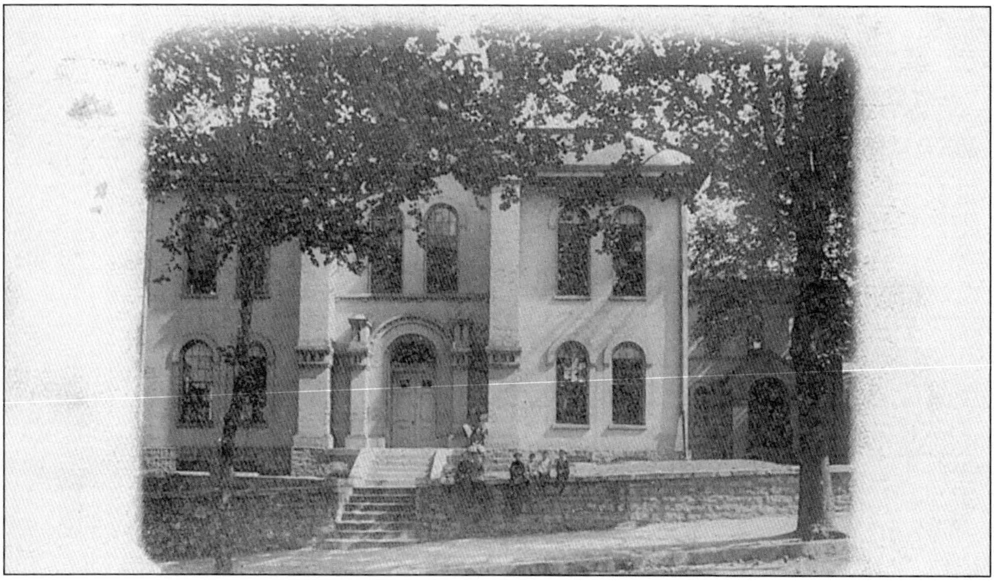

The German-English School, located on the southeast corner of Tenth and Felix Streets, was originally constructed as a private school in 1868. It was formed for the purpose of perpetuating the German language among immigrants' children. In 1872, the school was purchased by the city on the condition that the school continue to teach German and English in equal proportions.

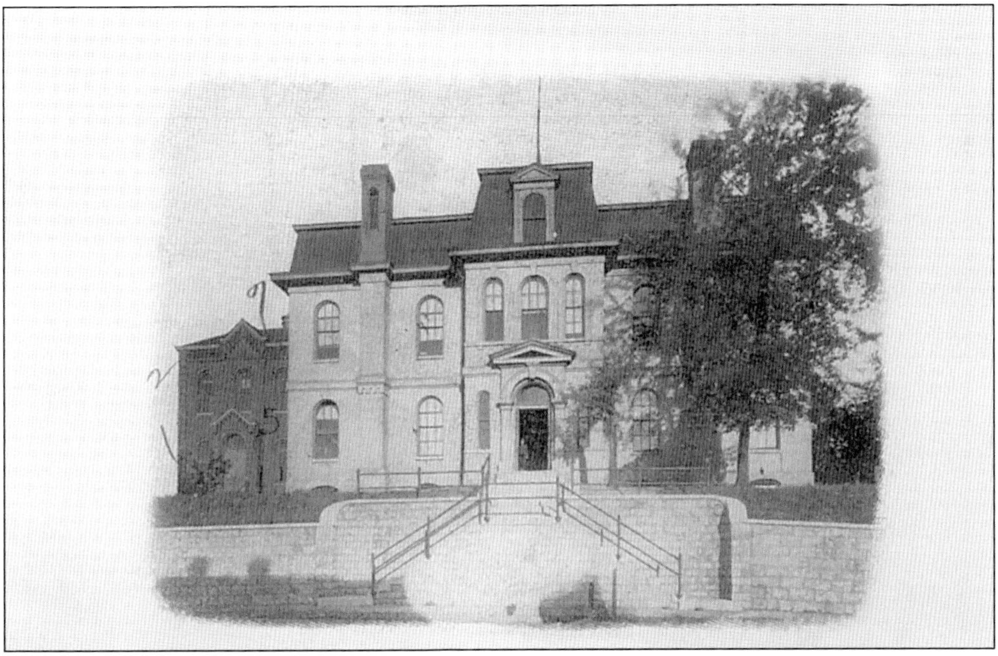

Washington School sat on the hill at Fifth and Poulin Streets. It was built in 1869 at a cost of about $11,500.

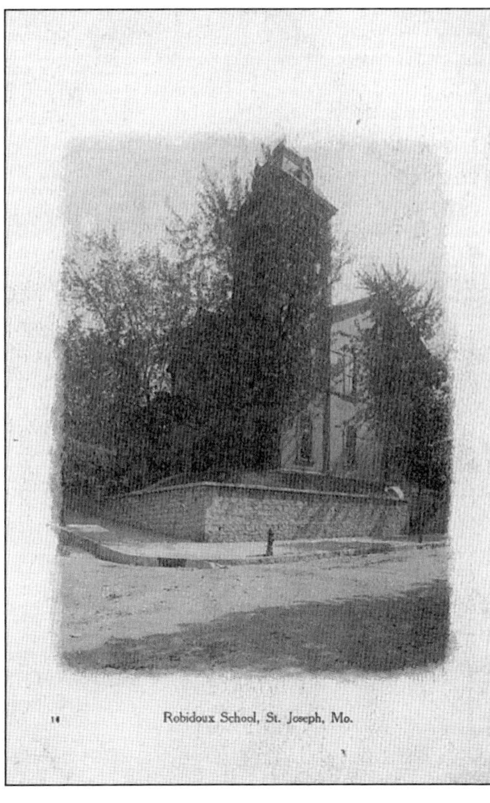

This version of Robidoux School was built at Tenth and Edmond Streets. The school had been the site of the city's high school until the building was damaged by fire in 1889. It was rebuilt and enlarged. Six years later, it was remodeled to accommodate an elementary school and board of education offices, and its name was changed to Robidoux School. It was eventually torn down and another Robidoux School was built. That building now houses apartments.

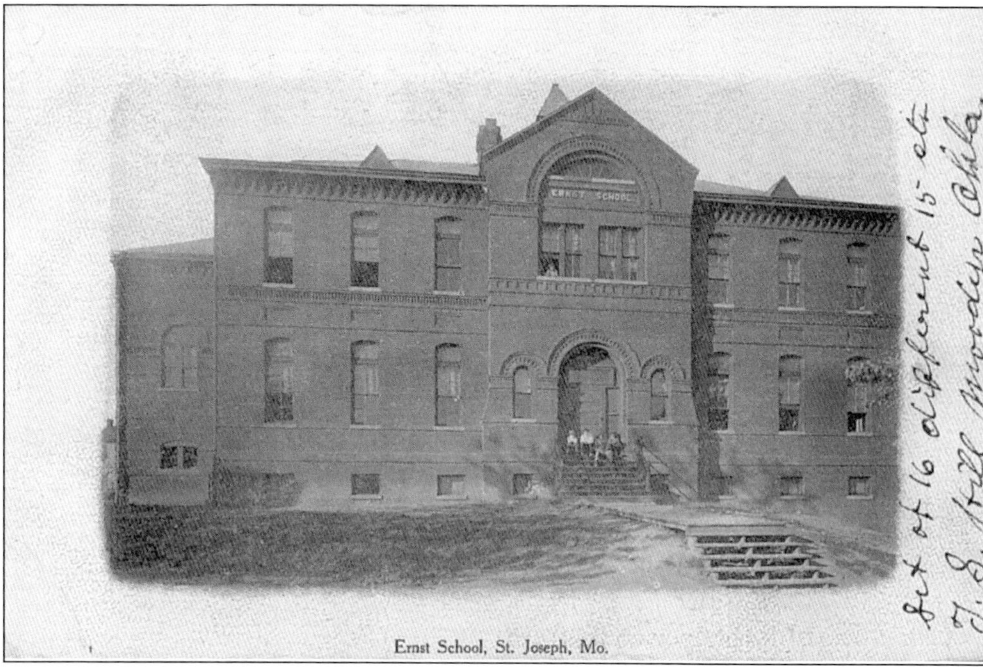

Ernst School, built in 1891, was located on St. Joseph and Fifth Avenues in what was known as "Walker's Addition." It was replaced by Lindbergh School.

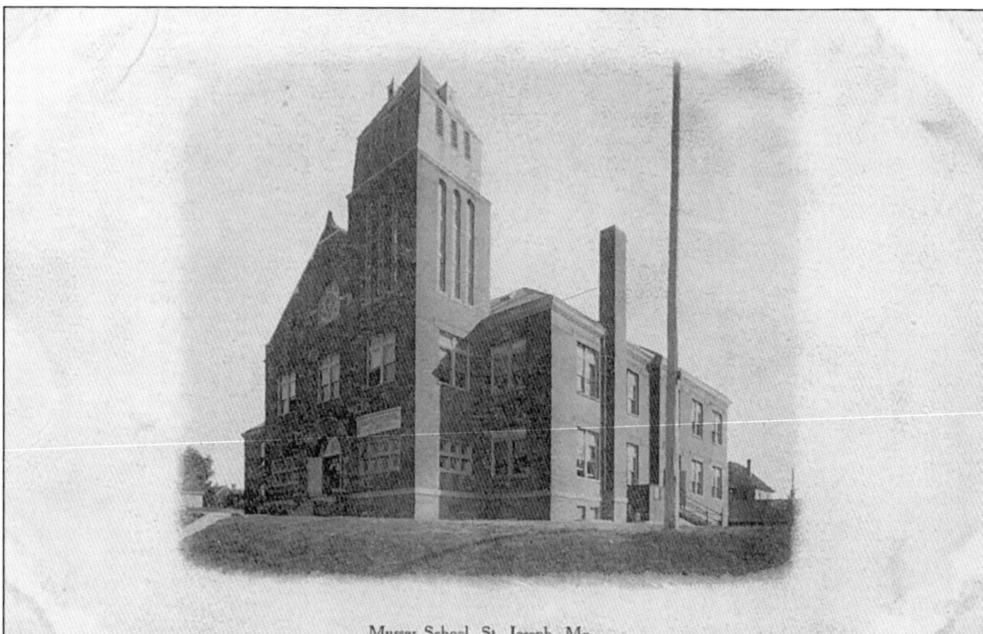

Musser School was located at Twenty-fourth and Olive Streets. This card was one of several printed with an advertisement for the Independent Messenger Company on the back. The building no longer stands.

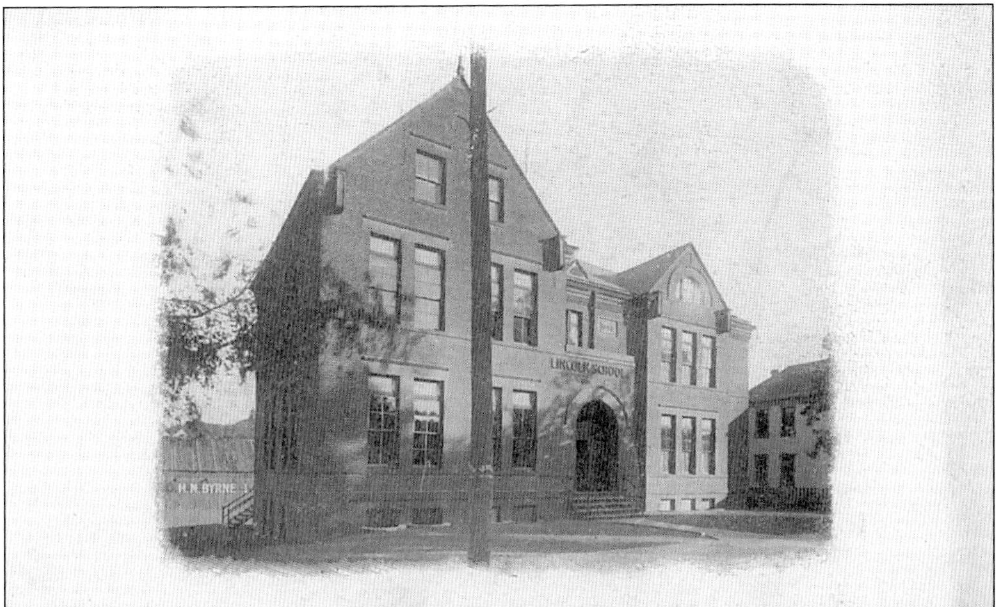

Lincoln School (Colored), St. Joseph, Mo.

St. Joseph's north end elementary school for blacks was named for Abraham Lincoln. It was built in 1894 for $10,600. The school was located at St. Joseph Avenue and Pendelton Street. In the 1923 survey of schools, the authors said the building had few merits.

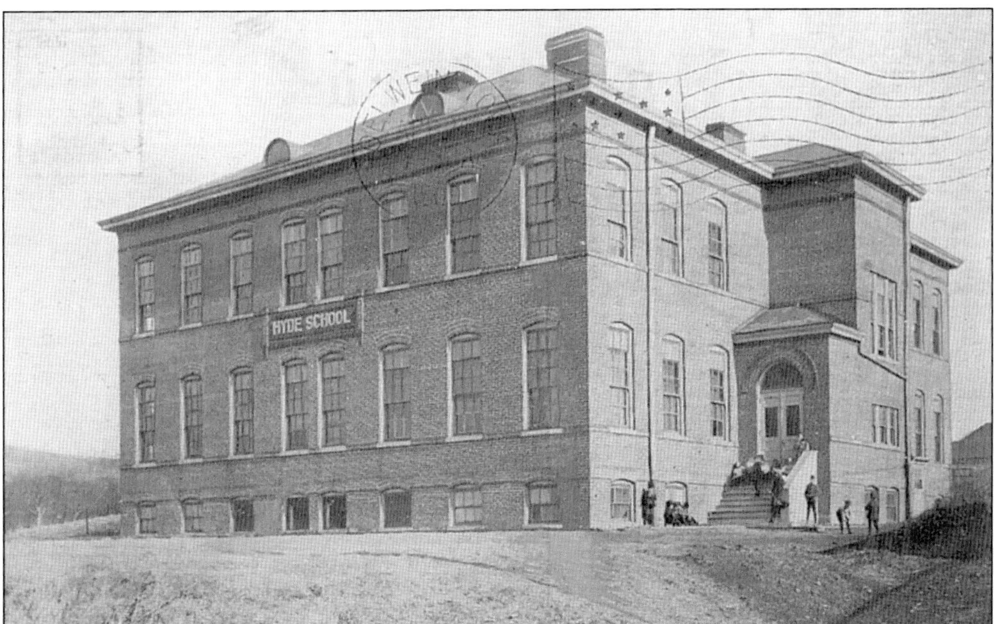

Hyde School, built in 1901 at a cost of $17,000, was located at 509 Thompson Street. It was replaced by a later version of the school. It no longer stands.

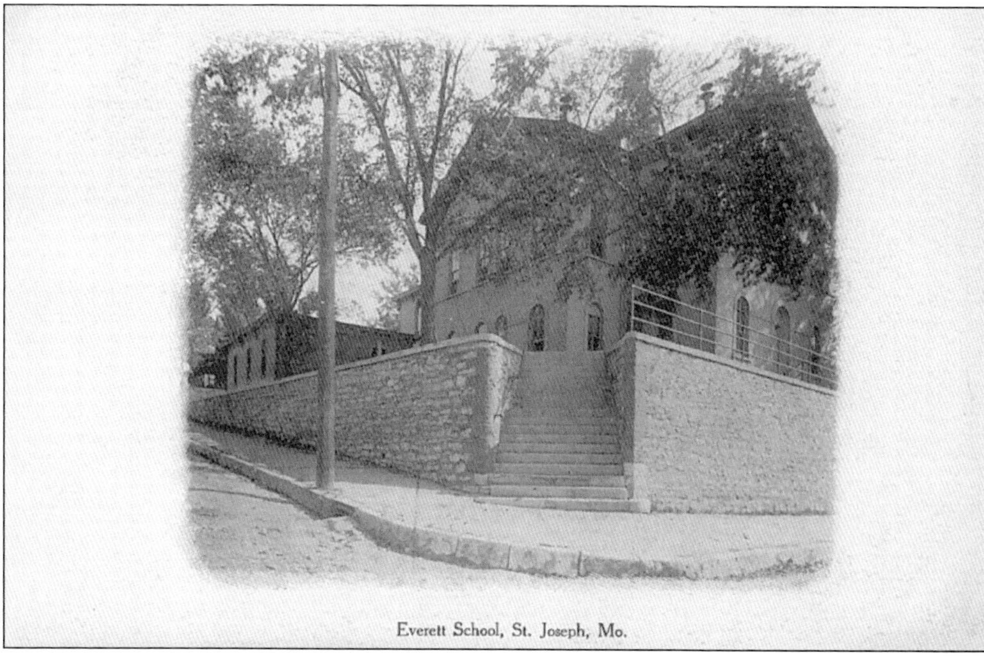

This earlier version of Everett School, located at Twelfth and Olive Streets, was built in 1866 and enlarged in 1872. It was later demolished to make way for a more modern school.

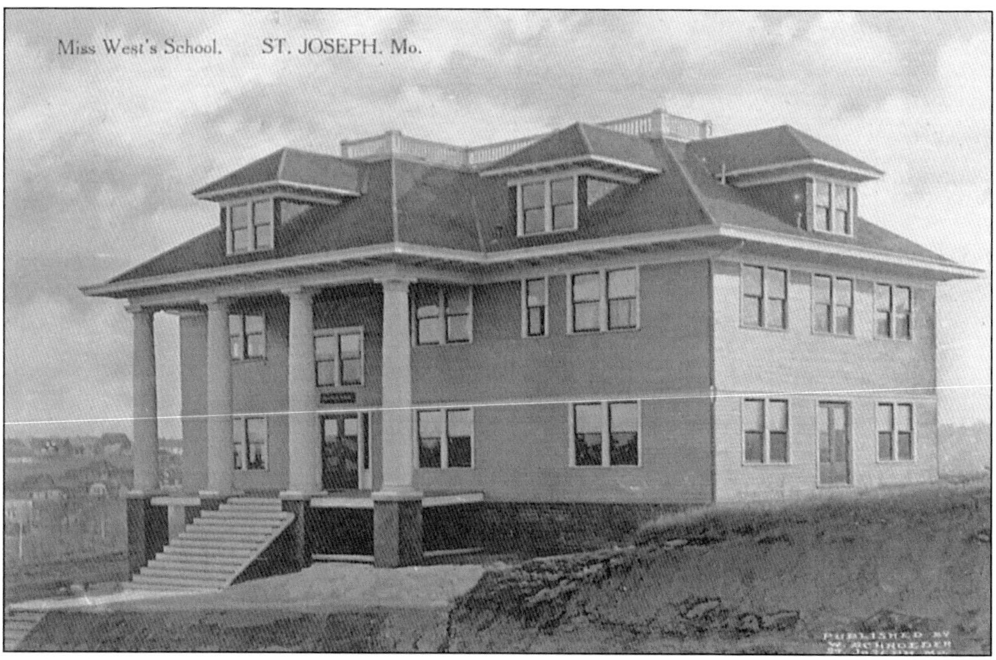

Little is known about Miss West's School, a private academy. It existed sometime around 1910, when this image was photographed, but no records of the school could be found.

Thirteen

CHURCHES AND CEMETERIES

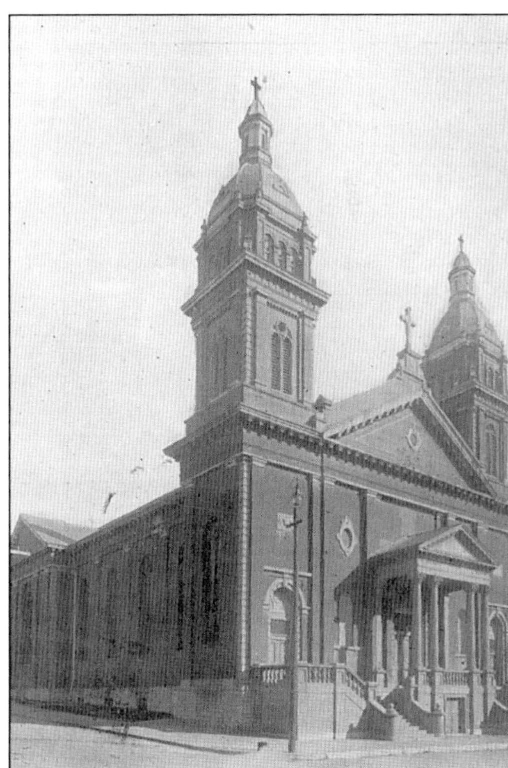

In St. Joseph's infancy, religious services were held in homes or schoolhouses. The first Protestant church was built in 1844, and various congregations began to establish themselves after this. Fr. Thomas Scanlan was the first Catholic priest in St. Joseph, arriving in 1845. Jews were first organized in 1849, erecting their first synagogue at Sixth and Jules Streets a decade later.

The first Mass was celebrated in St. Joseph Cathedral on March 17, 1871, making it St. Joseph's oldest church building. This view shows the towers, pediment, and stairs that were added in a 1900 renovation, features that were later removed in a 1950s remodeling. After a 1956 merging of the Kansas City and St. Joseph dioceses, both cities were allowed to keep their cathedral designations. The St. Joseph Cathedral is now known as the co-cathedral.

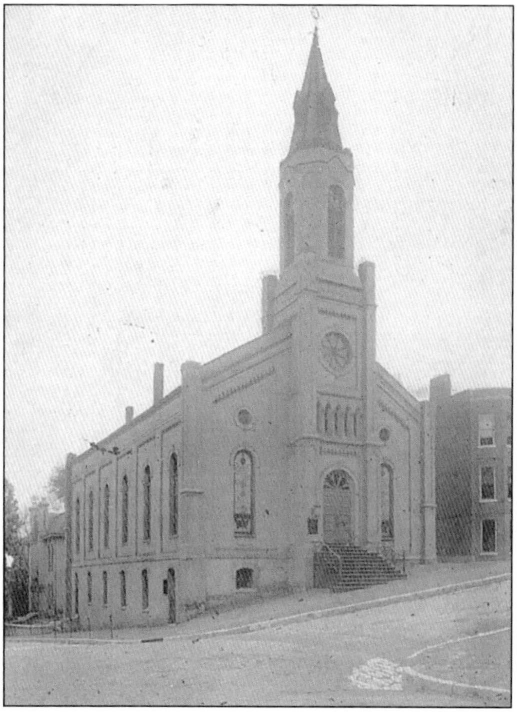

First Christian Church is shown here at its original location, at Tenth and Edmond Streets. The congregation built a new building in 1917 at Tenth and Faraon Streets and eventually sold the old church to the St. Joseph Junior College, but without the top half of the steeple. As part of the college, it came to be called the Grotto because of the school's kitchen and social area in the basement. The sanctuary was used for administrative offices and art classes. The building was torn down when Missouri Western State College, the junior college's predecessor, moved to its new campus.

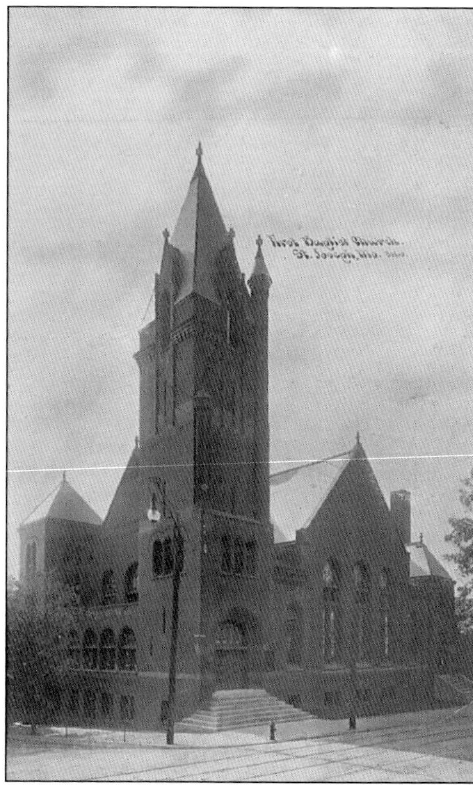

Built between 1895 and 1899 and designed by the architectural firm of Eckel and Mann, First Baptist Church was constructed in the Romanesque Revival style. This is a view of First Baptist Church before exterior changes modified the wing left of the tower in the 1930s. It still stands at the corner of Thirteenth and Francis Streets and is used by its original congregation. The congregation first organized in 1845.

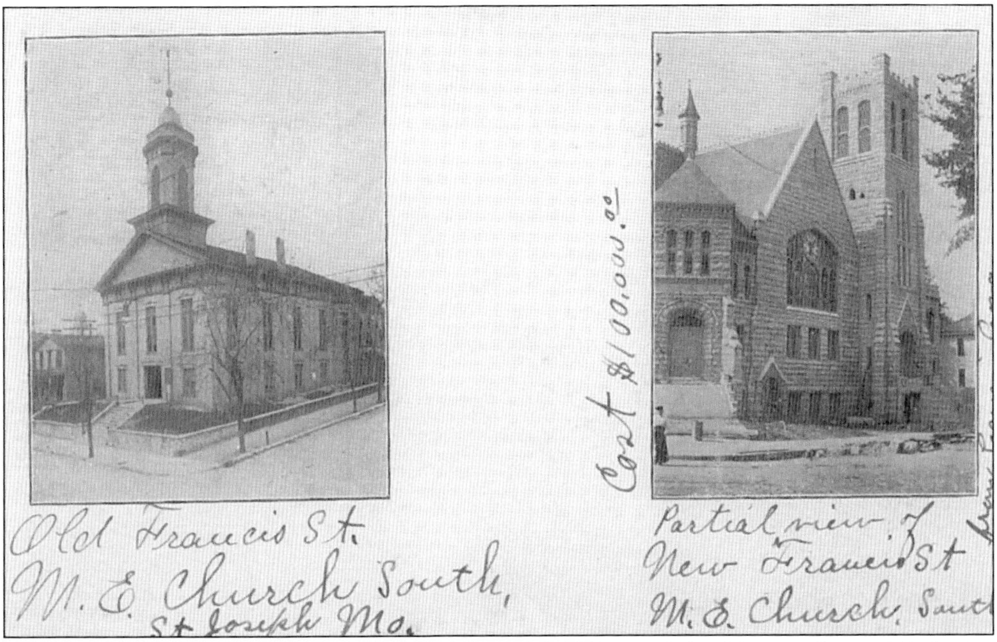

This dual view postcard shows the old and new buildings of the Francis Street Methodist Episcopal Church. The first view is of the old church at Seventh and Francis Streets, built *c.* 1855. The newer Francis Street church, constructed in 1905, is located at Twelfth and Francis Streets. The old church was torn down. The new church is called the Francis Street United Methodist Church following the decision of First United Methodist and Francis Street to merge. A note on the card indicates that the newer church cost $100,000.

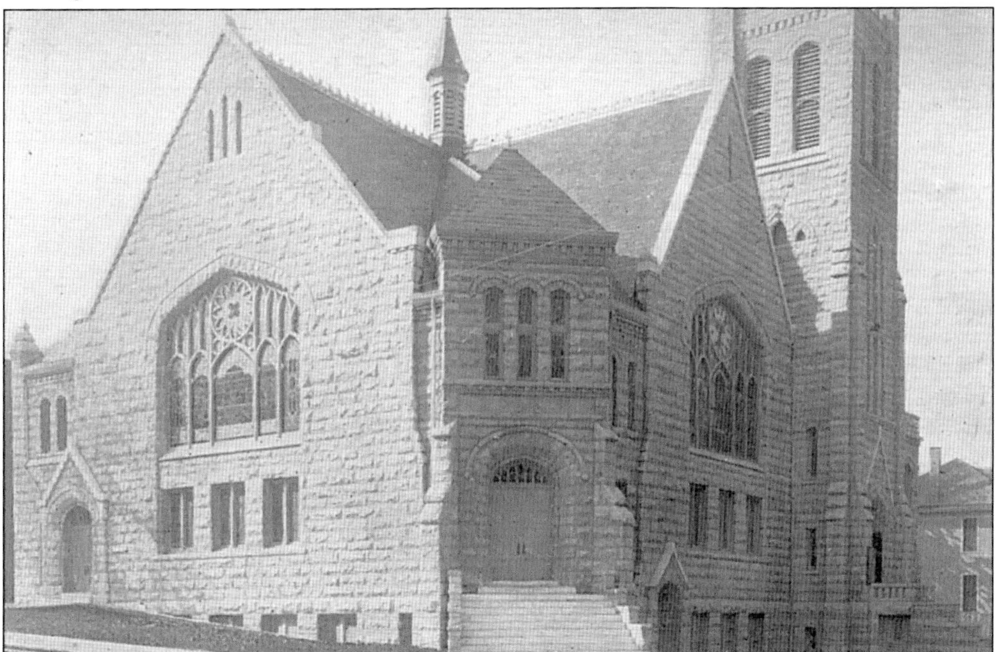

This is another view of the Francis Street M.E. Church. The church is now called the Francis Street United Methodist Church. It is constructed of Indiana limestone.

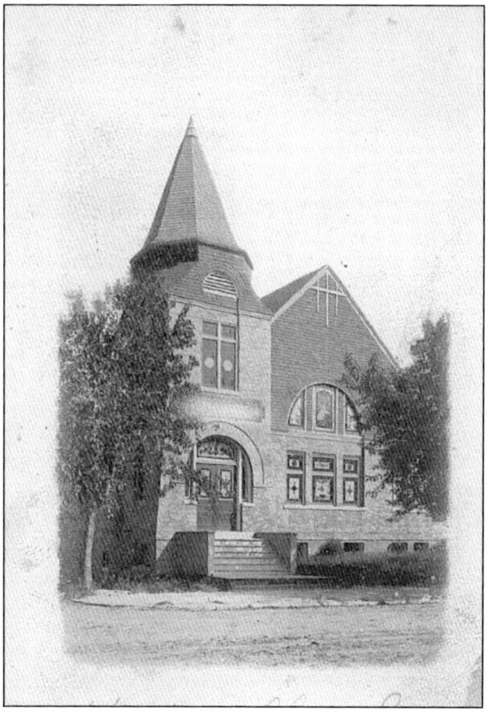

Woodson Chapel at 2525 St. Joseph Avenue was originally affiliated with the Christian church. It was built in 1906. This photo is from *c.* 1915. The building still stands but is missing most of its tower.

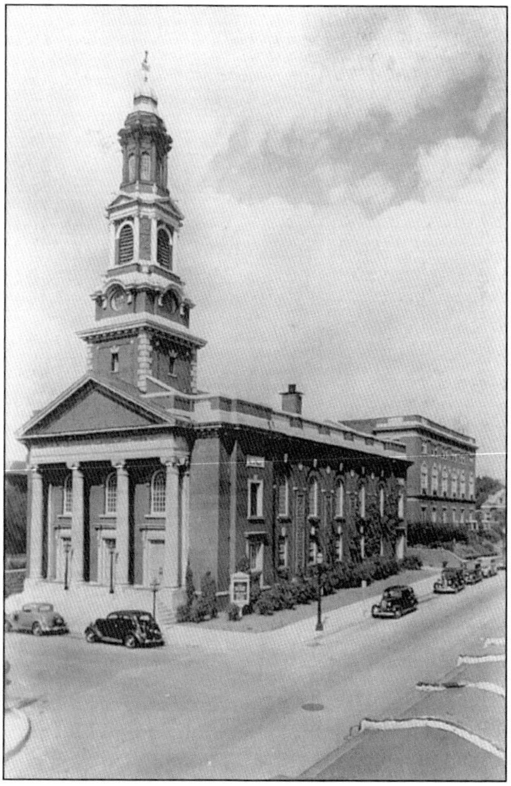

First Presbyterian Church was built in 1909, designed by the architectural firm belonging to Edmond Eckel. Located at the corner of Seventh and Jules Streets, the building was inspired by the Georgian architectural style popular in Great Britain and New England in the 18th century. The building's classical features were borrowed from Baroque and Italian Renaissance architectural styles. The first congregation was organized in 1854, and the first church on this site was dedicated in 1872. It was razed in 1908.

The interior of First Presbyterian Church largely remains unaltered from this image. Reminiscent of London churches created by architect Sir Christopher Wren, the interior exhibits rich classical detailing, including fluted Corinthian columns supporting the nave and a complex vaulted ceiling.

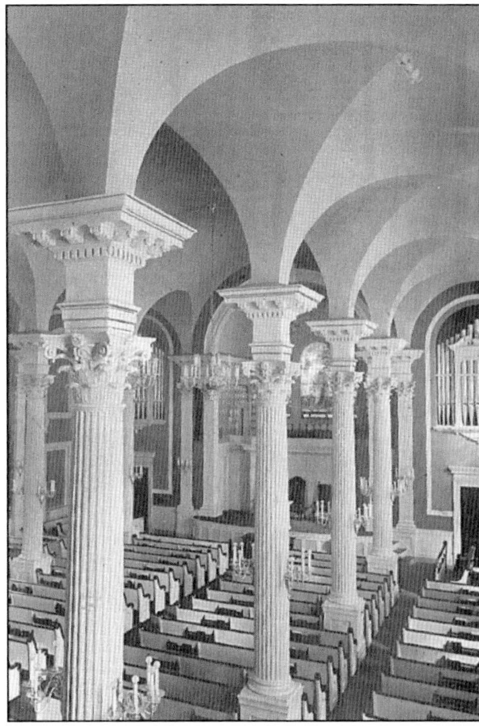

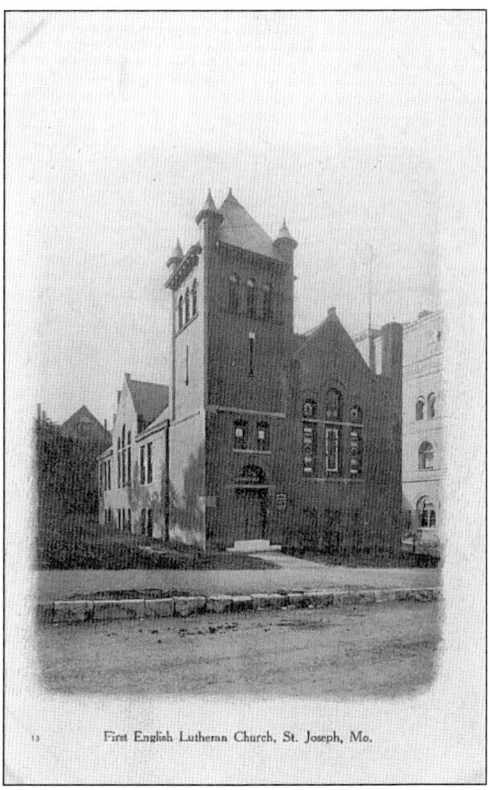

13 First English Lutheran Church, St. Joseph, Mo.

First Lutheran Church was founded in 1894. The building shown here, which was located at Eighth and Edmond Streets but is no longer standing, was the first of two buildings for the church. The congregation continues as the only evangelical Lutheran church in St. Joseph.

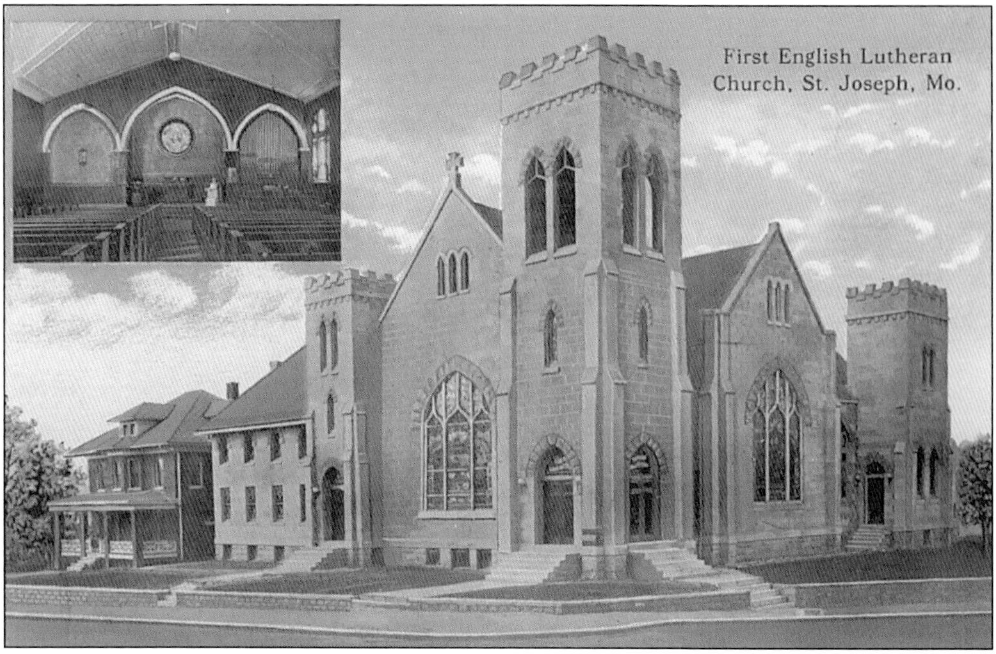

This newer First Lutheran Church was built at Tenth and Edmond Streets. It is still used by the congregation today.

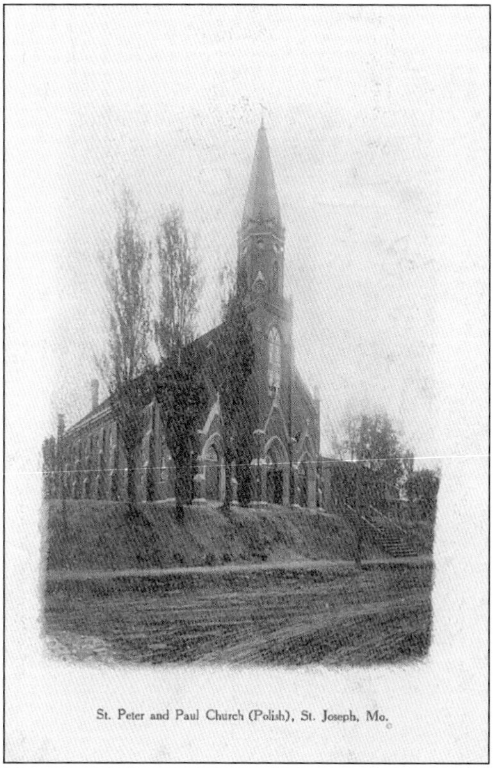

Sts. Peter and Paul Church was organized as a Polish Catholic congregation, a spin-off of Immaculate Conception Church, in 1883. The newly formed congregation purchased the former home of Gov. Willard P. Hall at Twentieth and Messanie Streets and converted it to a church. By 1903, the group began construction on this church. In 1977, due to a dwindling congregation, the church was closed and reunited with the congregation of Immaculate Conception. The building still stands.

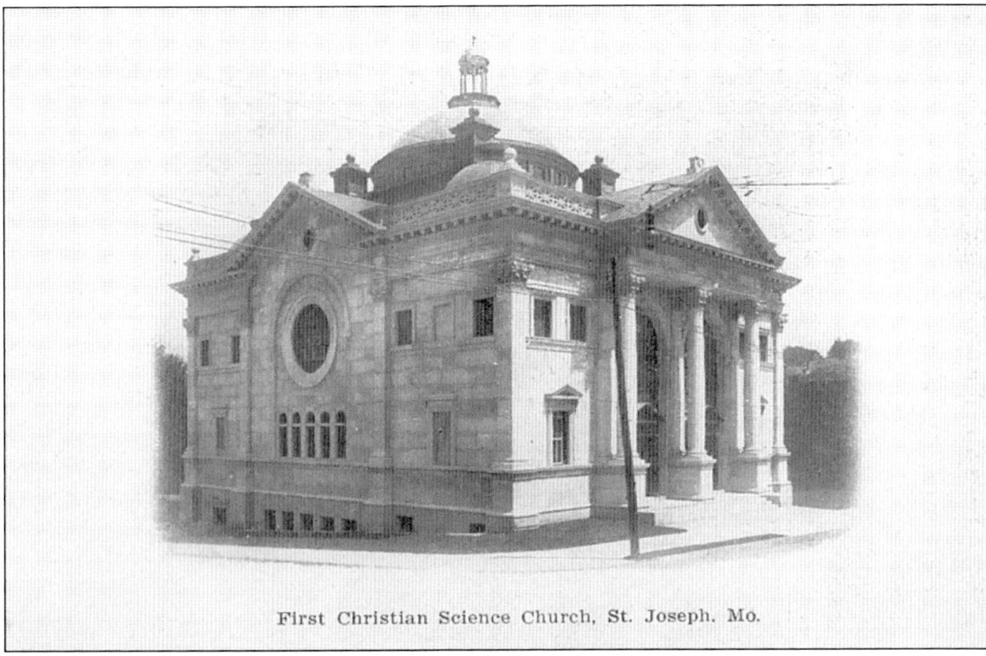

First Christian Scientist Church was dedicated in 1905. It was designed by R.F. Comstock of New York and reflects the emerging Beaux Arts style of the time. The congregation of this church, having decreased in recent years, is marketing the building.

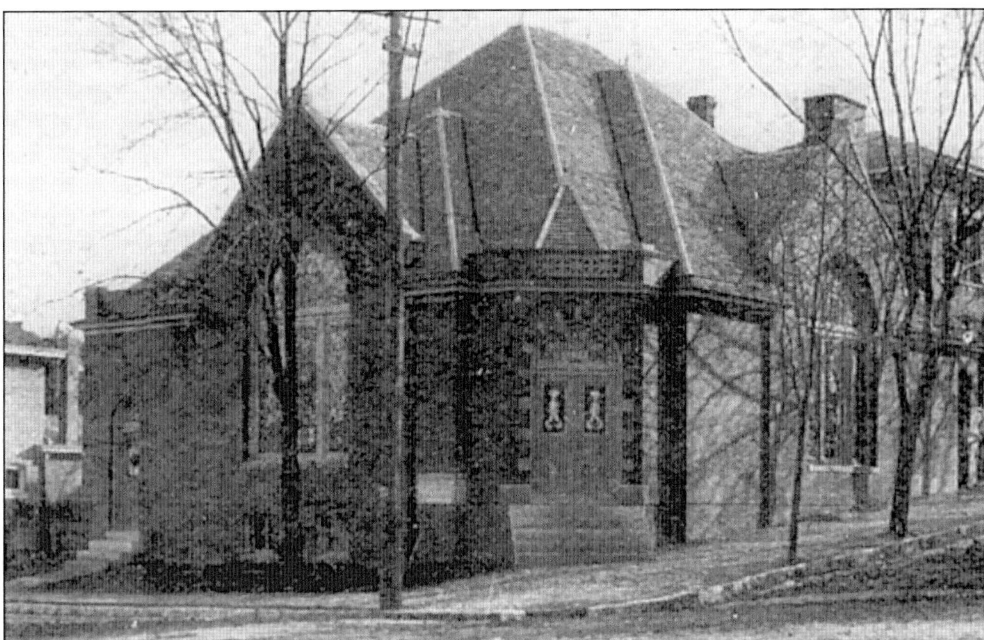

The First United Presbyterian Church at Twelfth and Felix Streets is now used as a Unity church. It was designed in the Beaux Arts style like First Church of Christ Scientist across the street. Originally built as a Presbyterian church, it later became a synagogue. In 1936, it became a Unity church.

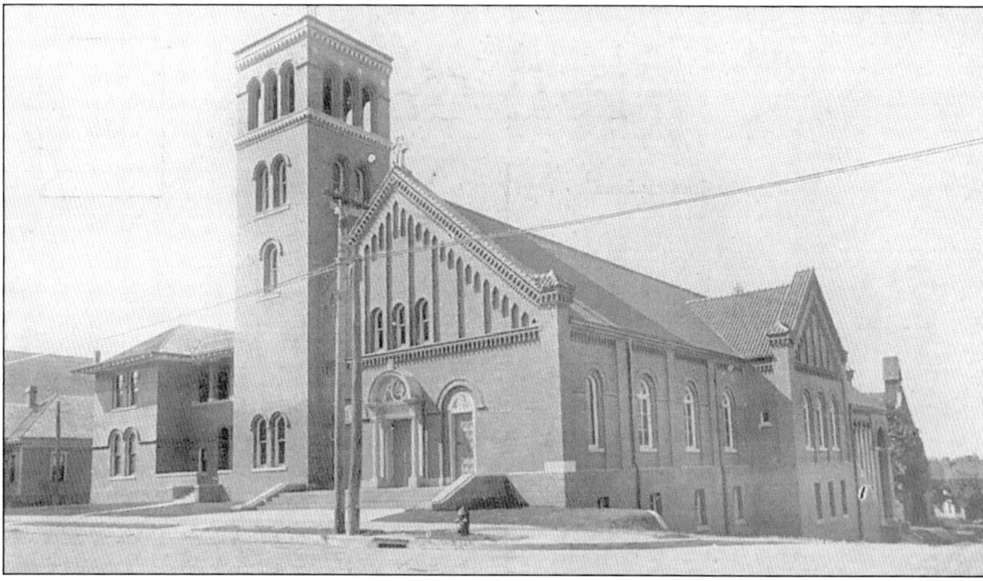

Serving St. Joseph's south side, St. James Catholic Church and parochial residence is still used by the Catholic Church. It is located at King Hill and Michigan Avenues. The church was built in 1912 and was designed by Edmond Eckel.

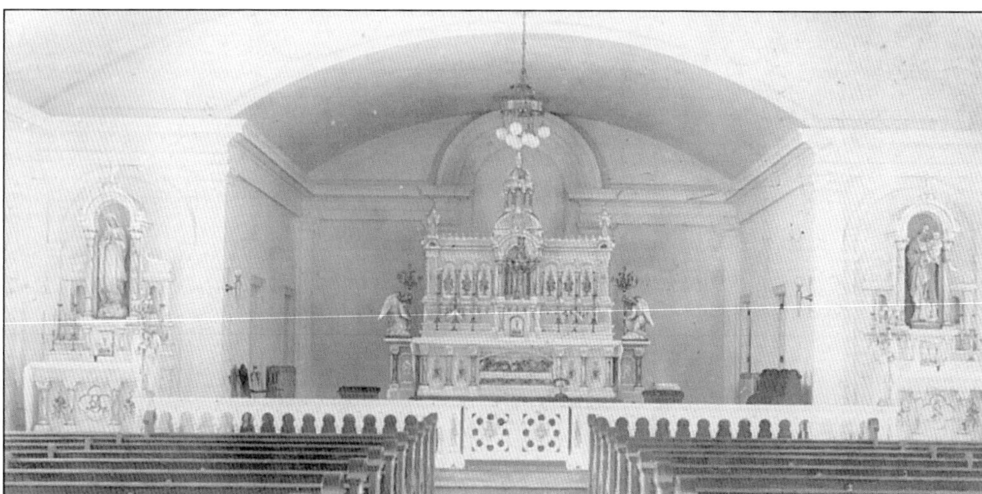

This interior view of St. James shows that the church has been altered considerably since the photograph was taken. The main and side altars and communion rail have all been removed. The arches and pilasters on the altar walls remain, although the central arch is obscured by a modern partition wall.

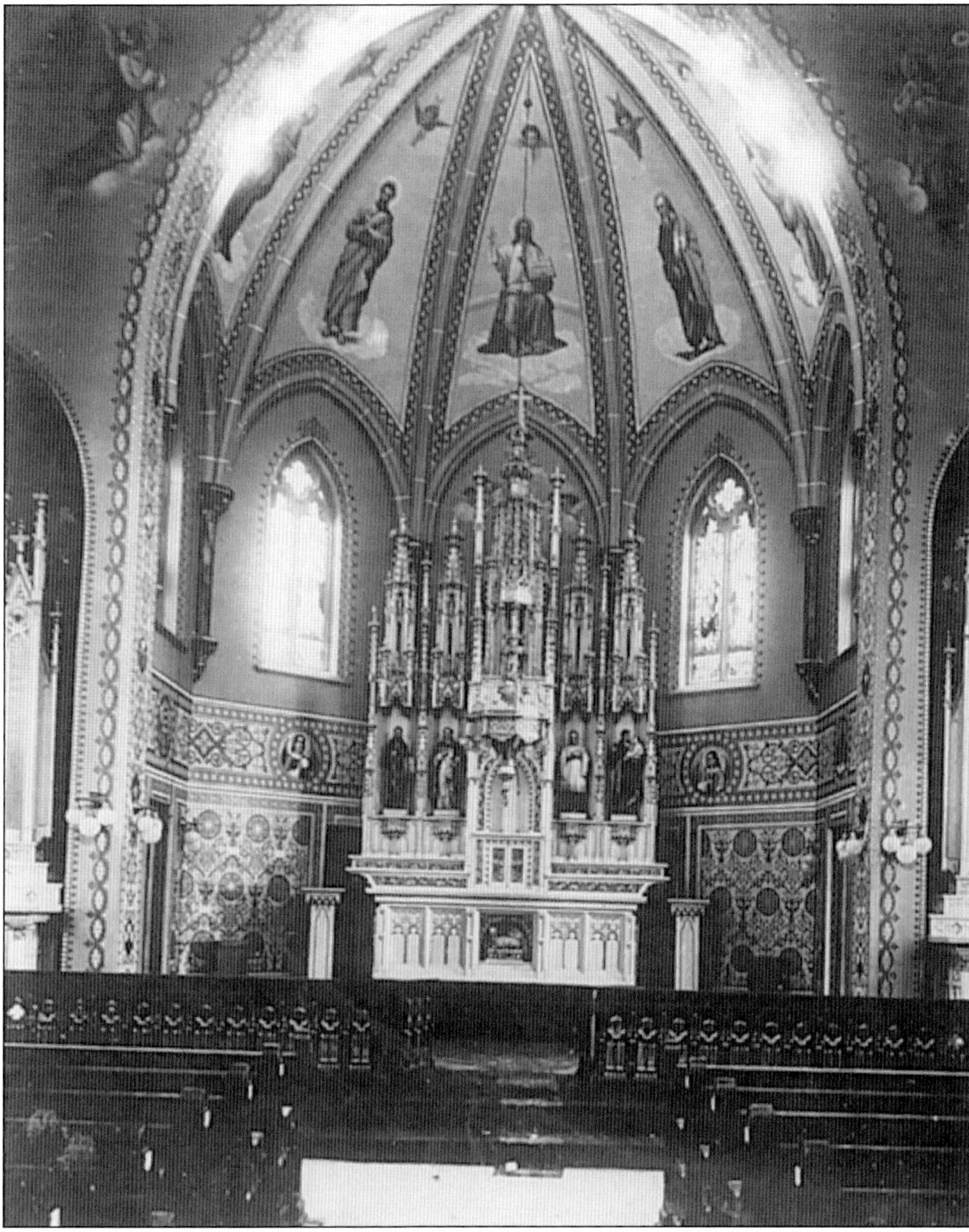

The Church of the Immaculate Conception was erected in 1908 after two previous buildings across the street were destroyed by fire and a tornado. The church houses stained-glass windows from Austria that tell the story of Mary's life. When Sts. Peter and Paul Church was closed in 1977, it merged with Immaculate Conception and the church changed its name to Queen of the Apostles. In June 1992, the diocese closed Queen of the Apostles. Local residents saved the building from demolition and turned it into a museum called Twin Spires Religious Museum.

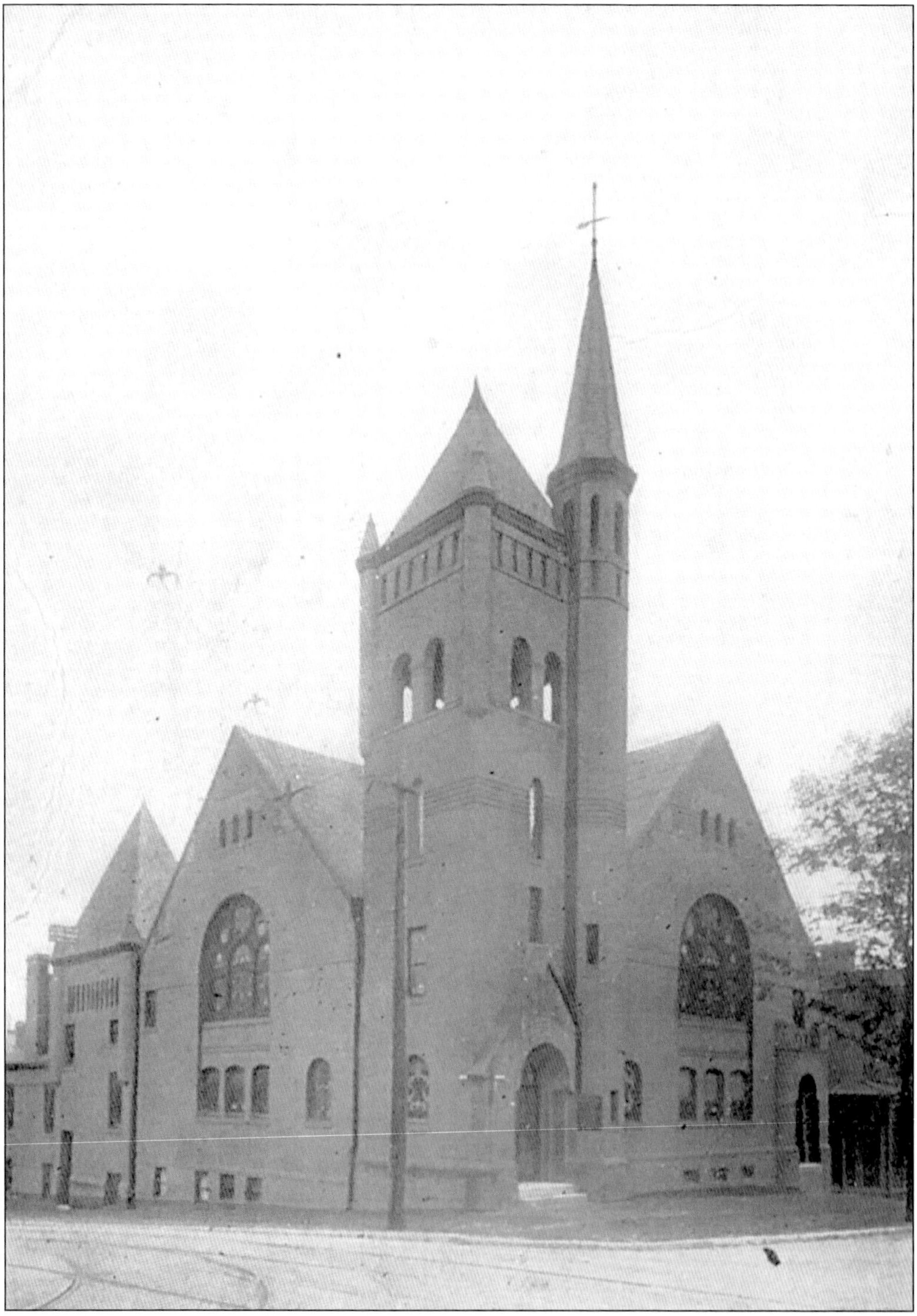

First Congregational Church at Thirteenth and Jules Streets eventually dissolved its membership. The building was donated to First Baptist Church, which later sold the building. It was designed by the firm of Eckel and Mann and constructed in 1890. The church was the first of the Chateauesque/Romanesque style in St. Joseph. The building is now Calvary Chapel.

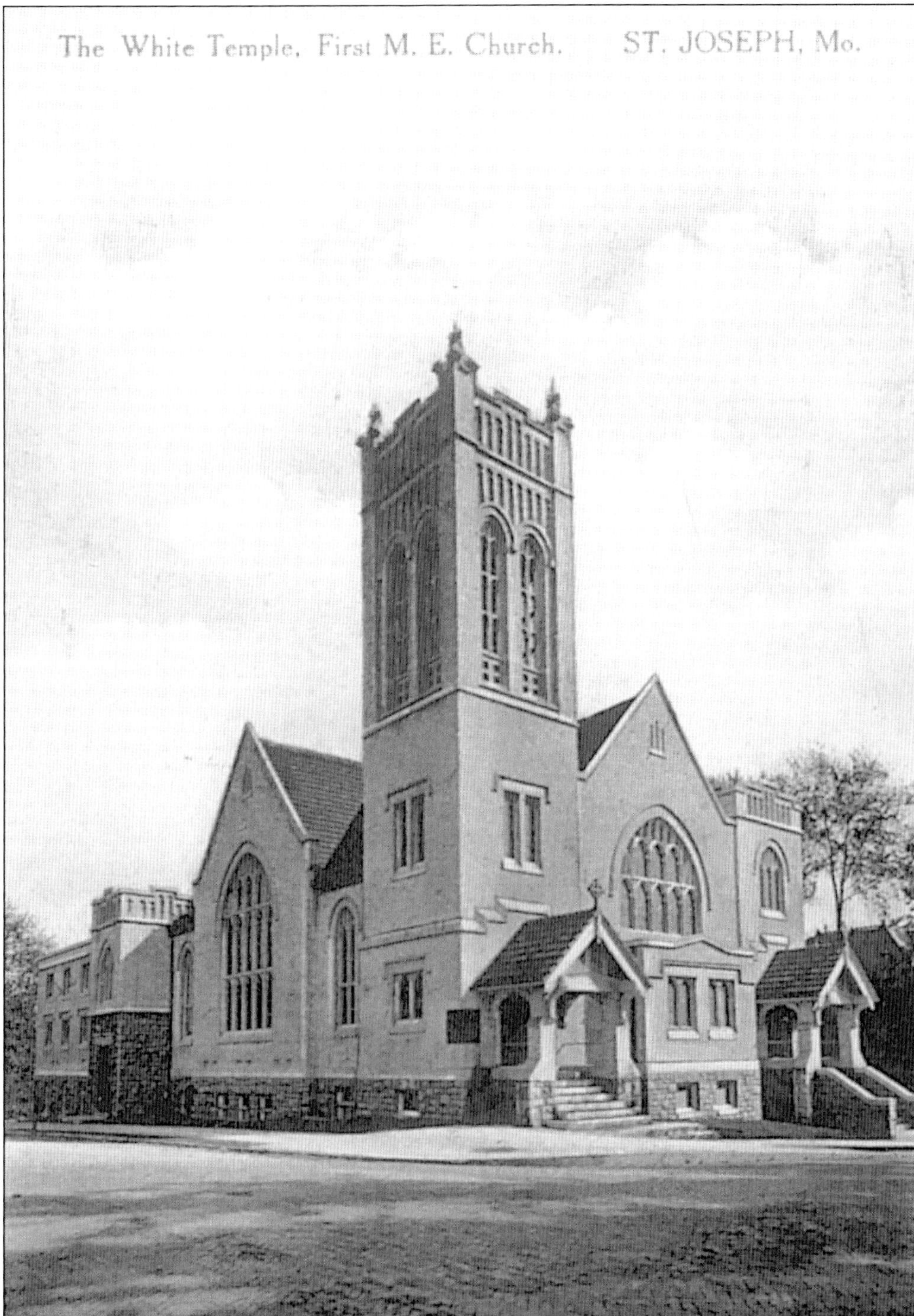

Built in 1909, the First Methodist Episcopal Church was known as the White Temple. It is located at Eighth and Faraon Streets and is used by another group. Eventually, the congregation joined with the Francis Street United Methodist Church.

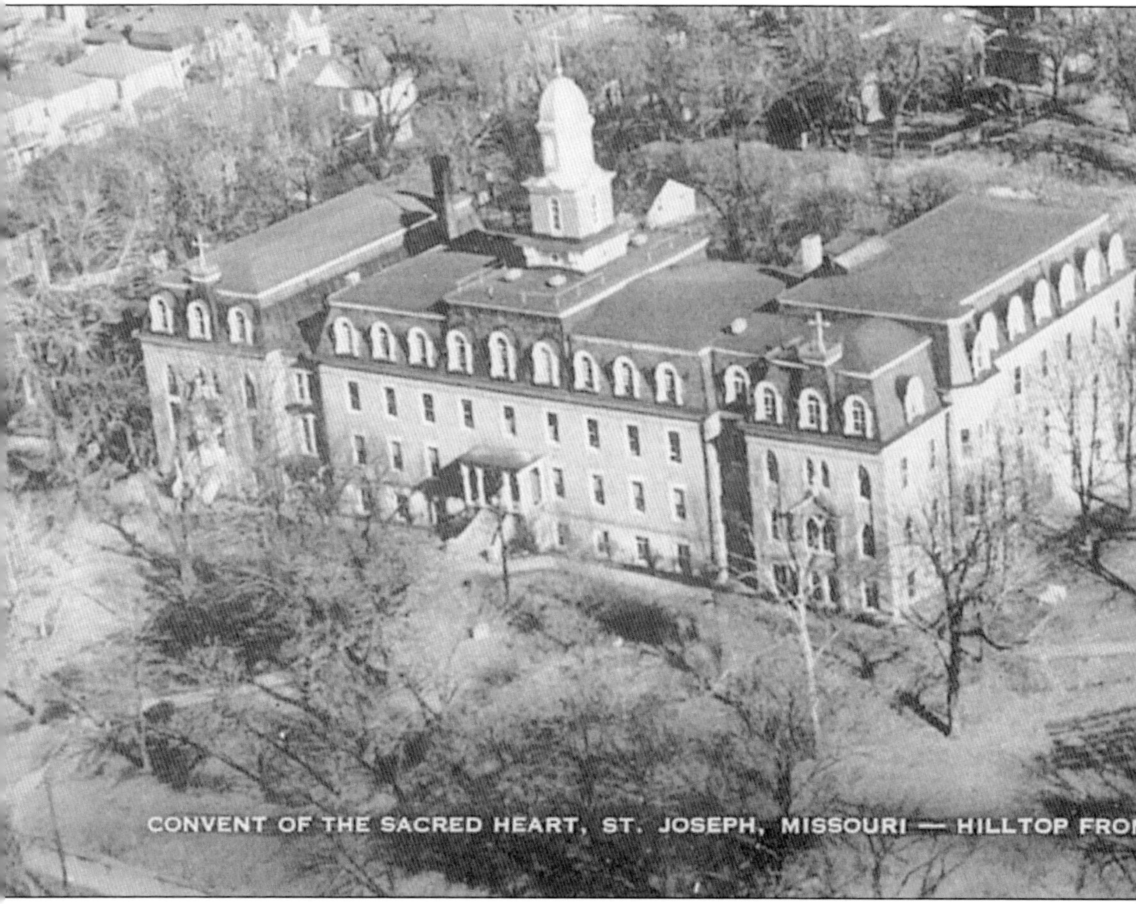

This aerial view of the Convent of the Sacred Heart shows the massive building and its surroundings. The Order of the Sacred Heart established a convent here at the urging of Catholic missionary Fr. Thomas Scanlan, the first priest in St. Joseph, in 1853. The religious order established one of the first parochial schools to educate young women in St. Joseph just a month after they arrived in 1853. Construction was started on their new building in 1856, on the southwest corner of their property at Twelfth and Angelique. When the convent closed in the 1960s, an effort was made to make it part of the nearby St. Joseph Museum. When that effort failed, the property was sold, the convent demolished, and Oak Ridge Apartments were constructed.

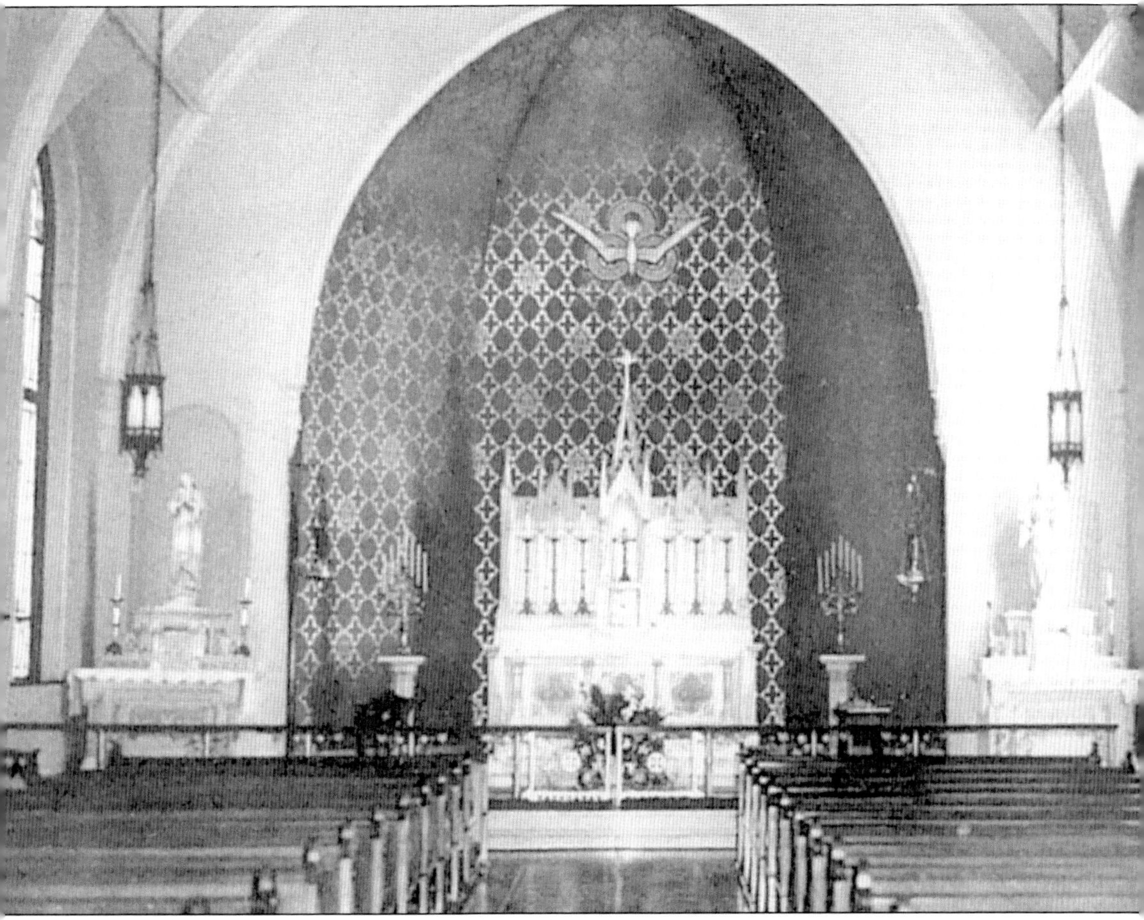

This photo shows the interior of the chapel inside the Convent of the Sacred Heart. Elements of the chapel have been incorporated into the St. Joseph Co-Cathedral.

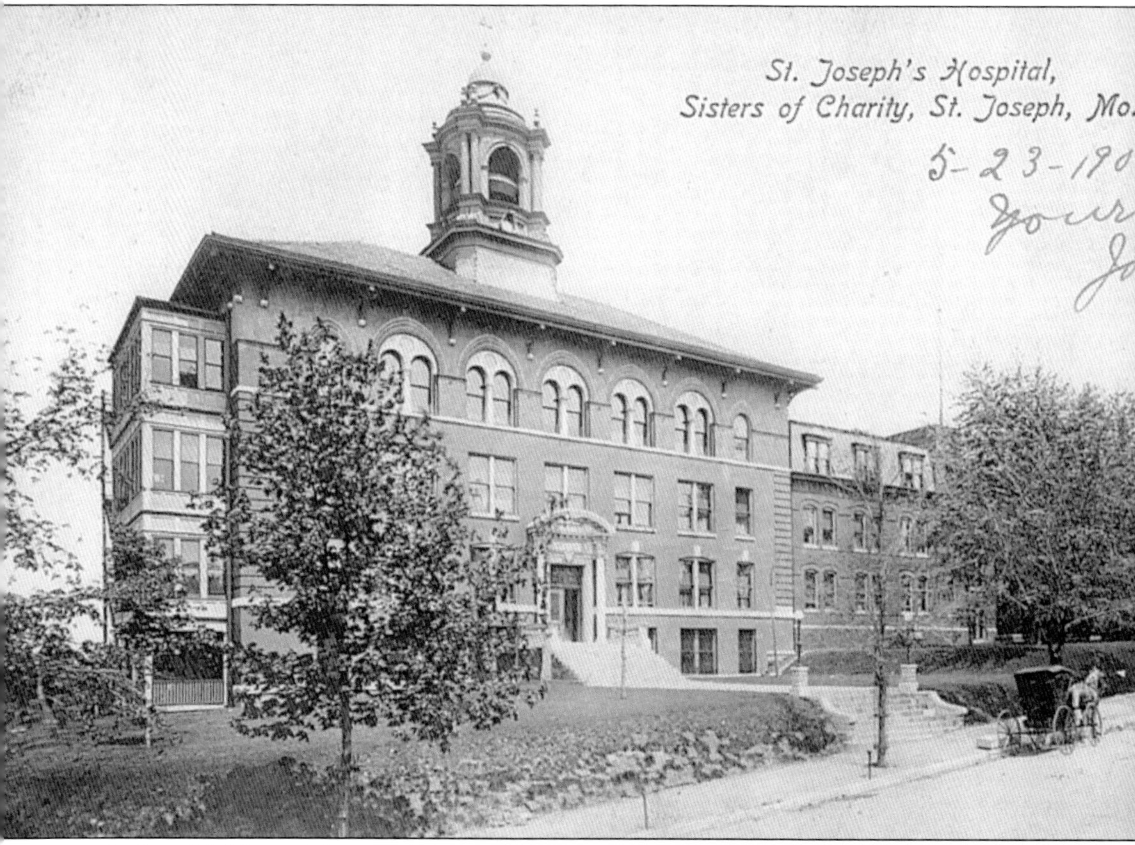

St. Joseph's Hospital became known as Sister's Hospital for the Sisters of Charity, who ran it. It was located at Tenth and Powell Streets. It was one of three Catholic institutions in the Cathedral Hill neighborhood. The hospital was merged with Heartland Health System and closed in 1980. The building was torn down in 1994 and the site is now a park.

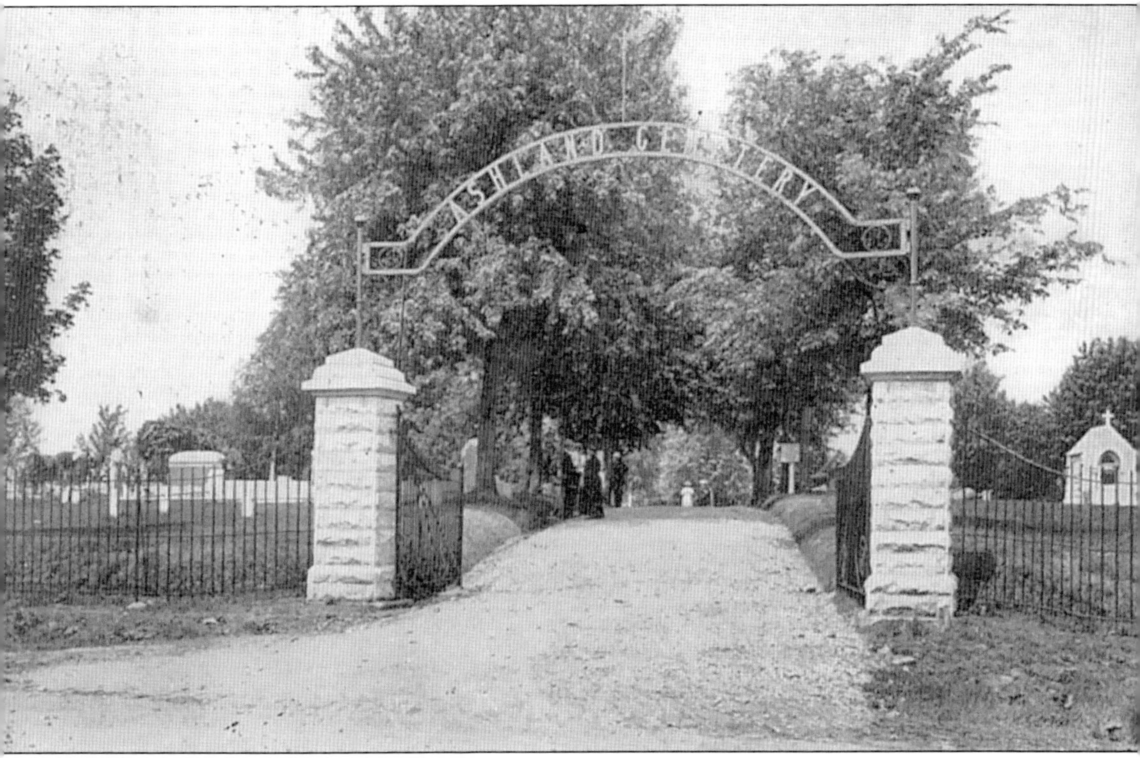

This view of Ashland Cemetery, which is located just off of Ashland Avenue, shows the entrance *c.* 1911.

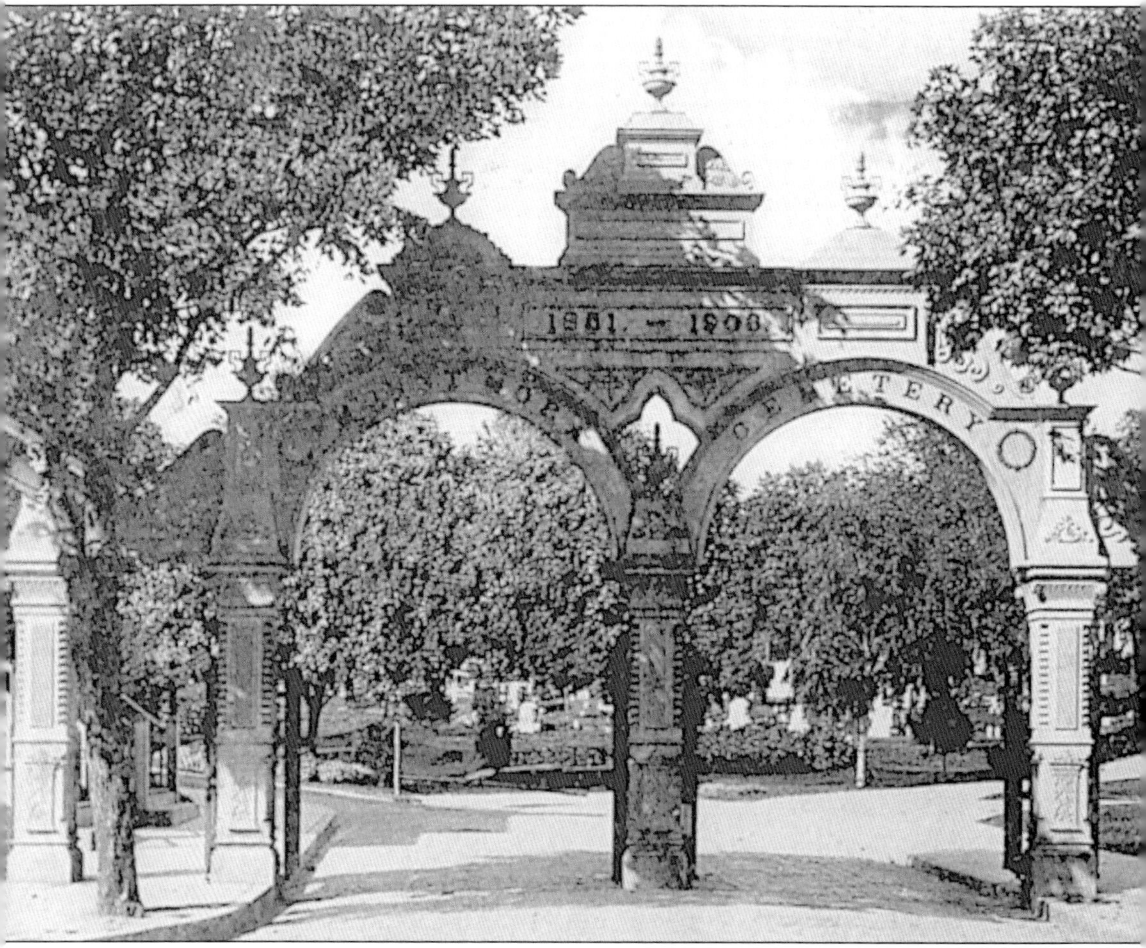

Mount Mora is the city's oldest cemetery, dating to 1851. The cemetery's elaborate entrance was later demolished. It contains the burial plots of many of the 19th century's most prominent St. Joseph residents.

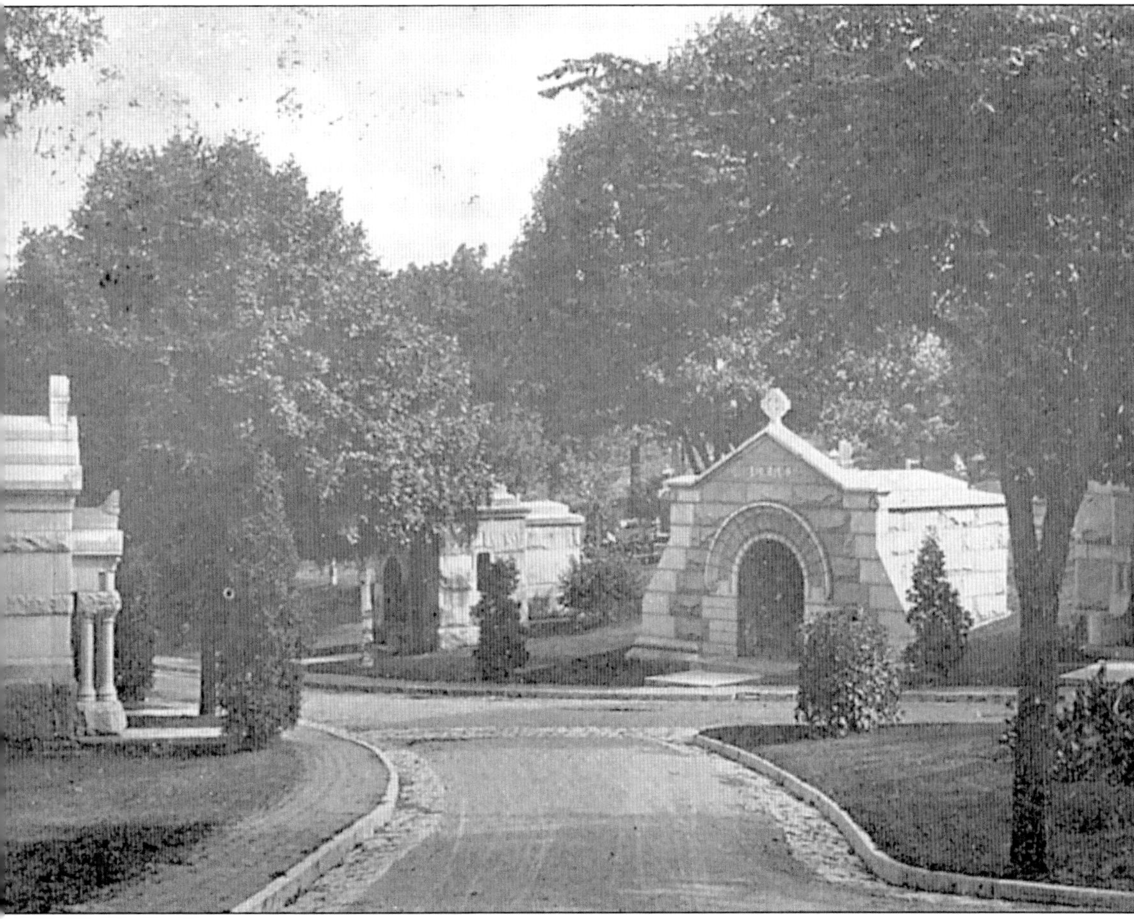

Some of the impressive monuments near the cemetery's entrance were designed by noted architects of the time, including the firm of Edmond Eckel. This view shows the road leading into the cemetery and the mausoleums, many of which were designed with Egyptian motifs.